Studies in International Relations

Edited by
Charles MacDonald
Florida International University

A ROUTLEDGE SERIES

Studies in International Relations

Charles MacDonald, *General Editor*

A GLOBAL UNION FOR GLOBAL WORKERS
Collective Bargaining and Regulatory Politics in Maritime Shipping

Nathan Lillie

Routledge
New York & London

Published in 2006 by
Routledge
Taylor & Francis Group
270 Madison Avenue
New York, NY 10016

Published in Great Britain by
Routledge
Taylor & Francis Group
2 Park Square
Milton Park, Abingdon
Oxon OX14 4RN

© 2006 by Taylor & Francis Group, LLC
Routledge is an imprint of Taylor & Francis Group

Transferred to Digital Printing 2010

International Standard Book Number-10: 0-415-97747-9 (Hardcover)
International Standard Book Number-13: 978-0-415-97747-0 (Hardcover)
Library of Congress Card Number 2005034033

Library of Congress Cataloging-in-Publication Data

Lillie, Nathan.
   A global union for global workers : collective bargaining and regulatory politics in maritime shipping / Nathan Lillie.--1st ed.
       p. cm. -- (Studies in international relations)
   Includes bibliographical references and index.
   ISBN 0-415-97747-9
   1. Collective bargaining--Merchant marine. 2. International labor activities. 3. Globalization. I. Title. II. Series: Studies in international relations (Routledge (Firm))

HD8039.S4L55 2006
331.88'11387--dc22   2005034033

ISBN10: 0-415-97747-9 (hbk)
ISBN10: 0-415-88297-4 (pbk)

ISBN13: 978-0-415-97747-0 (hbk)
ISBN13: 978-0-415-88297-2 (pbk)

Taylor & Francis Group
is the Academic Division of Informa plc.

Visit the Taylor & Francis Web site at
http://www.taylorandfrancis.com

and the Routledge Web site at
http://www.routledge-ny.com

for Riitta and Osmo

Contents

List of Tables

List of Figures

List of Acronyms and Abbreviations

AB	Able Seaman
AJSU	All-Japan Seamen's Union
AKT	*Auto- ja Kuljetusalan Työntekijäliitto* (Finnish transport workers' union)
AMOSUP	Associated Maritime Officers and Seamen's Union of the Philippines
APL	American President Lines
BIMCO	Baltic and International Maritime Council
CBA	Collective Bargaining Agreement
CGT	*Confédération Générale du Travail* (French trade union confederation)
CIIR	Catholic Institute for International Relations
CMLC	Consolidated Maritime Labour Convention
DAG	*Deutsche Angestellten-Gewerkschaft* (German white-collar union)
DIS	Danish International Ship Register
ECSA	European Community Shipowners' Association
EFBWW	European Federation of Building and Wood Workers
EFJ	European Federation of Journalists
EI	Education International
EIF	European Industry Federation (trade union body)

EMF	European Metalworkers' Federation
EPSU	European Public Service Union
ESD	European Social Dialogue
ETF	European Transport Workers' Federation
ETUC	European Trade Union Confederation
EU	European Union
EWC	European Works Council
FO	*Force Ouvrière* (French trade union confederation)
FOC	Flag of Convenience
FPC	Fair Practices Committee
GFA	Global Framework Agreement (also known as IFA)
GUF	Global Union Federation (same as ITS)
IBF	International Bargaining Forum
ICEM	International Chemical, Energy, Mine and General Workers' Union
ICFTU	International Confederation of Free Trade Unions
ICONS	International Commission on Shipping
IDC	International Dockworkers' Council
IFA	International Framework Agreement (also known as GFA)
IFBWW	International Federation of Building and Wood Workers
IFJ	International Federation of Journalists
IFWTWU	Independent Federation of Water Transport Workers Unions
IGO	Inter-Governmental Organization
ILA	International Longshore Association
ILC:	International Labour Conference
ILO	International Labour Organization
ILWU	International Longshore and Warehouse Union

IMEC	International Maritime Employers' Committee
IMF	International Metalworkers' Federation
IMMAJ	International Merchant Mariners Association of Japan
IMO	International Maritime Organization
IOMMP	International Association of Masters, Mates and Pilots
ISF	International Shipping Federation
ITF	International Transport Workers' Federation
ITF ROA	ITF Report on Activities
ITGLWF	International Textile, Garment, and Leather Workers' Federation
ITS	International Trade Secretariat (same as GUF)
IUF	International Union of Food, Agricultural, Hotel, Restaurants, Catering, and Allied Workers' Associations
JMC	Joint Maritime Commission
JNG	Joint Negotiating Group
LO	*Landsorganisationen* (Swedish Trade Union Confederation)
MDHC	Merseyside Dock and Habour Company
MOU	Memorandum of Understanding (Port State Control)
MUA	Maritime Union of Australia
NGO	Non-Governmental Organization
NIS	Norwegian International Ship Register
NMU	National Maritime Union
NOL	Neptune Orient Lines
NOPEF	*Norsk Olje- og Petrokjemisk Fagforbund* (Norwegian Oil-workers' Union)
NSU	Norwegian Seamen's Union
NUSI	National Union of Seafarers of India
OCAW	Oil, Chemical and Atomic Workers' Union

OECD	Organization for Economic Cooperation and Development
ÖTV	*Gewerkschaft Öffentliche Dienste, Transport und Verkehr* (German service employees' union)
PMA	Pacific Maritime Association
POEA	Philippine Overseas Employment Administration
PSC	Port State Control
PSI	Public Services International
PTMC	Preparatory Technical Maritime Conference
SDU	Swedish Dockworkers' Union
SIRC	Seafarers' International Research Centre
SIU	Seafarers' International Union
SMU	*Suomen Merimies Unioni* (Finnish Seamen's Union)
SSA	Stevedoring Services of America
STCW	Standards of Training, Certification and Watchkeeping
SUR	Seafarers' Union of Russia
TCC	Total Crew Cost
TGWU	Transport and General Workers' Union
TUI	Trade Union International (also called Trade Department)
UAW	United Autoworkers Union
UFCW	United Food and Commercial Workers' Union
UIS	Union of International Seamen
UNCTAD	United Nations Commission on Trade and Development
UNI	Union Network International
UNI-Europa	Union Network International, Europe
UNITE-HERE	Union of Needletrades, Industrial and Textile Employees—Hotel Employees and Restaurant Employees union
URW	United Rubberworkers' Union
USD	US Dollar
USWA	United Steelworkers of America

Ver.di	*Veriente Dienstleistungsgewerkschaft* (German service employees' union)
WCL	World Confederation of Labour
WFTU	World Federation of Trade Unions
WTO	World Trade Organization
WWC	World Works Council
WWF	Waterside Workers' Federation

Acknowledgments

I would like to thank Lowell Turner, Sidney Tarrow and Harry Katz for providing valuable advice, comments and practical assistance during the years of research for this book. Ed Heery, Tony Lane, Valeria Pulignano, Nik Winchester, Ian Greer, Marco Hauptmeier, John Kelly, Sarosh Kuruvilla, Jeremy Waddington, Harold Lewis and James Mittelman deserve thanks for comments on bits and pieces of text, which eventually became chapters. I am grateful to Elisabeth DeSombre for a very useful peek at her forthcoming book manuscript, and also to Thorsten Müller and Stefan Rüb for sending me their book, and helping me interpret some of their findings. Many of the better ideas herein arose from collaborations at various points with Ian Greer, Marco Hauptmeier, Nik Winchester, Sarah Swider, Susan Christopherson, Mark Anner and Miguel Martinez Lucio, so I am in their intellectual debt. Nik Winchester and Tony Lane helped me get access to the ILO talks, and our discussions were also very useful for developing what little understanding I have acquired of how the shipping industry works. They are, however, not to blame for any errors I've made. Thorsten Schulten and Hannu Ohvo deserve thanks for facilitating my field work. I am grateful to Timo Pankakoski for helping with editing, proofing and making tables. International Transport Workers' Federation staff were extremely friendly and helpful in providing information and access to their library. This work was not sponsored or authorized by the ITF in any way, however, so they are not culpable for my conclusions. I would like to thank all the unionists, shipowner representatives, government officials and others who generously took the time to be interviewed.

Financial support, aid and comfort came from numerous sources. This book was written with the support of the Helsinki Collegium for Advanced Studies. Financial support for field work came at various points from the United States Department of Education, Ford Foundation, Benjamin Miller

Fund, School of Industrial and Labor Relations, Mario Einaudi Institute for European Studies, Cornell Center for International Studies, Friedrich Ebert Foundation, International Labour Organization, and the People's Education Foundation of Finland. The Hans Böckler Foundation in Düsseldorf, Germany, and SASK, the Finnish Trade Union Solidarity Center, generously allowed the use of their facilities. Their support is gratefully acknowledged.

Most importantly I would like to thank Riitta Nissinen and Osmo Ronny Lillie for reminding me that there are more important things in life than labor unions and writing books.

Chapter One
Introduction

The global maritime shipping business has often been portrayed as the archetype of unbridled free-market capitalism, burst free from the constraints of government and trade union regulation. Under the Flag of Convenience (FOC) system of ship registration, shipowners[1] can flag their vessels in whichever country they choose, selecting the regulatory framework and tax structure they see most conducive to the business strategy they wish to pursue. Effectively freed from national hiring restrictions, most shipowners no longer crew their vessels with the highly unionized seafarers of the traditional maritime countries, such as Greece, Japan, Norway, or the United Kingdom, instead preferring to hire from lower wage maritime labor exporting countries, such as India, the Philippines and Russia. As a result, a global and transnational labor market for seafarers developed, with fierce global competition sending wages, union power, and respect for workers' rights in a downward spiral.

Out of this apparently very hostile environment, however, new forms of regulation are emerging, stopping the downward spiral, and bringing new stability to maritime labor markets. This global and transnational regulatory framework involves a mixture of public and private instruments, including governments, business associations and unions in its formulation, monitoring, and enforcement. The new framework arises not so much out of the interests and interactions of states, as traditional international relations paradigms would assert, as from efforts by capital to contain and to channel global class conflict in the industry. Although much of the new system is layered on top of preexisting intergovernmental regimes, and therefore bears the mark of intergovernmental practice, the emerging global regulatory system is shaped first and foremost by the interactions of capital and organized labor. This case demonstrates how the development of global class capacities can drive the development of global politics.

Global trade unionism in shipping developed under the auspices of the International Transport Workers' Federation's (ITF) Flag of Convenience Campaign. What is interesting about the Flag of Convenience campaign is not so much the actual impact on seafaring working conditions, although this has been substantial, as the unique pattern of trade union influence emerging in the industry, and the effect this has on global regulatory politics. The ITF and its national affiliate unions possess the sort of global and transnational power resources which have proven elusive to unions in other industries. The ultimate extension of this influence into global political regulation is driving the reconstitution of transnational state forms functionally similar to those which economic globalization and the FOC system have so effectively undermined at the national level.

This is not to suggest that there is now a New Order of just and equal labor practices in maritime shipping. Even given the new global unionism and strengthened transnational regulation, treatment of seafarers today is still generally less favorable than it was under the more tightly regulated national flags in the past. Pay rates under ITF union contracts are good by developing world standards, but this in itself says a lot about how pay expectations have changed very much in favor of capital. Serious labor rights violations still occur, although these appear to be less widespread than in the 1980s and 90s. Racist personnel practices run rampant, and gender discrimination is deeply embedded (Zhao *et al.* 2003). Seafarers still work long hours under difficult and dangerous conditions and spend long periods of time away from home, sometimes with little opportunity to communicate with their families. While global unionism has put a bottom on the downward spiral, in many ways it only partially compensates for ground lost due to the FOC system. Instead, we see what Elizabeth DeSombre refers to as "a race to the middle" for maritime labor standards (DeSombre forthcoming). Things are still bad for seafarers, although not quite as bad as they have been in the recent past. However, there are good reasons to think they will continue to get better.

This book combines analytical traditions in industrial relations and international relations, to show the participation of industrial relations actors (maritime unions and employers) in global political arenas, and conversely the effects of global politics on industrial relations practices (Haworth and Hughes 2002; Harrod and O'Brien 2002; Trubek *et al.* 2000). Although the relationship between international arenas and industrial relations practices is perhaps sharper and more obvious in maritime than elsewhere (Alderton and Winchester 2002), these interactions have broad and increasing importance in other sectors as well.

THE FOC SYSTEM AND HOW THE CAMPAIGN WORKS

Under the Flag of Convenience system, shipowners can register their vessels under any flag which will have them, allowing them to freely select the regulatory system under which they will operate. Not surprisingly, many shipowners opt for as little regulation as possible. Because of this, maritime shipping firms operate in an environment driven by a deregulated competitive dynamic. While the "race to the bottom" in shipping isn't always exactly a beeline straight to the bottom (DeSombre forthcoming: Ch.2), the FOC system leaves openings for what the industry has labeled "substandard shipping" to cut costs by avoiding adherence to international standards. In addition to engaging in poor labor practices, and creating environmental and safety hazards, the sub-standard element drives freight rates down, outcompeting law abiding shipowners (OECD 2001).

The ITF's FOC campaign began in 1948, when seafaring unions first took notice of attempts by some shipowners to "flag out" to developing countries with "open"[2] ship registers. Over time the campaign emphasis shifted from ending the FOC system completely to wage bargaining for FOC seafarers. During the 1950s and 60s, the ITF engaged in political and industrial efforts to stop FOC ships from operating, and/or to improve working conditions on board (Metaxas 1985). Since the 1970s, the campaign has taken on a more directly industrial focus, with unions attempting to force shipowners to sign ITF collective agreements to reduce the incentive to flag out by raising FOC labor costs (Johnsson 1996: 44–51; Koch-Baumgarten 1999: 448).

Although not all ships competing in international trade are FOCs, labor market competition in the industry is defined by the FOC institution. In the absence of nationality based hiring restrictions, a global institutional infrastructure has developed to hire ship crews from low-wage seafaring labor supply countries for work anywhere in the world (Alderton *et al.* 2004). The freedom to hire from anywhere allows maritime labor sourcing to shift geographically, mixing and matching nationalities in an effort to find adequately skilled labor at the lowest possible cost. For "unlicensed" seafarers, also referred to as ratings, this has resulted in a massive shift in labor sourcing from high-wage industrialized countries to mid- or low-wage developing or post-communist countries. For "licensed" seafarers, also known as officers, the picture is more varied, but the FOC system has caused a shift in labor sourcing, and put pressure on these groups as well.

Despite a certain amount of inter-union political struggle, often exploited by employers, the ITF has so far been able to successfully integrate into its bargaining system, or exclude from the market, each new labor supplier market entrant. ITF bargaining strategy balances the need for bargaining leverage with the requirements of the inter-union political consensus. The ITF segments the global labor market into internationally competitive shipping (including FOCs), high standard national flags (which are left to national unions), and developing country national flags. Shipowners flying flags labeled as "FOC" must sign union contracts providing for wage levels approved by the ITF's Fair Practices Committee (FPC) or risk ITF organized industrial action by port workers. This system eventually drove some employers to agree to industry level wage bargaining. Industry level bargaining takes place in the International Bargaining Forum (IBF), where FPC representatives and the Joint Negotiating Group (JNG), representing employers, bargain over wage rates and conditions on ITF contracts. The 2004 base labor cost for an Able Seaman (AB) as agreed in the IBF forum was $1400 per month, which is several times higher than what many non-ITF scale AB's receive (Lillie 2004: 49–50).

The global industry level bargaining system which has resulted from the ITF FOC campaign serves as a basis for global politics in maritime shipping, by formulating the specific strategies the actors pursue and the interests they express in other contexts. The ITF attempts to differentiate sections of the maritime labor market, to limit wage competition and make it possible to raise wages without overreaching or upsetting the delicate inter-union consensus which holds the campaign together. The labor market segmentation is strategic, reflecting the political realities of inter-union politics, and the need to build bargaining leverage. Without the ITF system, many seafaring unions, including those in low wage labor supply countries, would have no influence in the labor market at all. While individual ITF affiliate unions often look for ways to exploit their positions within the ITF labor cartel, they generally do not question the system's underlying logic (Anner *et al.* 2006).

The creation of the ITF bargaining system relied on building a consensus between capital and labor supply country unions—in essence overcoming the North-South divide in transnational inter-union politics. This consensus is based on ensuring that FOC campaign bargaining strategy benefits unions from developed and developing countries alike. The ITF excludes non-ITF affiliate unions from representing workers in the part of the FOC labor market the ITF controls. ITF strategies in political arenas bolster and protect ITF collective bargaining efforts. The system does not benefit all unions under all circumstances, and certainly does not benefit all ITF affiliates equally, but those unions who have less to gain have no better alternative.

There is no consensus among employers on which strategy to pursue to counter the FOC campaign. As a result, there is no unified coherent policy within the employers' main representative group, the International Shipping Federation (ISF). [3] There are conciliatory and hard-line employer fractions, although the groupings are fluid. The conciliatory fraction seeks accommodation with the ITF, hoping to moderate ITF demands through bargaining. The conciliatory fraction reluctantly aids the ITF in extending its political strength, seeking to extend regulation, to ensure that they are not unduly disadvantaged vis-à-vis non-union and/or less regulated competitors. The hard-line fraction seeks to avoid and/or undermine ITF strength. Some employers mount political and legal challenges to ITF influence in global, national and local arenas. Employers in the hard-line fraction avoid entanglement with the ITF, serving ports where the ITF cannot mount boycott actions, and taking their chances in ports where the ITF has a presence.

In this way, the differential impact of ITF action on different groups of employers structures the formation of maritime capital fractions. ITF policy strategically encourages the growth of the conciliatory capital fraction, and penalizes uncooperative employers. DeSombre conceptualizes this strategy as the creation of a "club" of cooperative employers. Only employers who pay to become part of the club by signing ITF agreements can service ports where the ITF is able to mount industrial action. Access to these ports becomes an "excludable good" (DeSombre forthcoming). However, in many ports, ITF actions can be mounted on some occasions, but not on others, and they are not always guaranteed to succeed. Therefore the boundaries of the "club" are subject to contest, creating friction between employers inside the club, and employers outside the club, not to mention between the ITF and employers generally.

Collective bargaining has become the centerpiece of ITF strategy in implementing social regulation on Flag of Convenience shipping, replacing the campaign's original emphasis on a political solution. The immediate purpose of ITF political strategy is to bolster and protect the ITF's collective bargaining strategy. The development of global collective bargaining, and related industrial action, drives some segments of maritime capital to seek the effectively enforced re-regulation of shipping at the global level. Potentially, this could eliminate the appeal of FOCs to shipowners, not by making FOCs illegal as the ITF originally sought to do, but by ensuring that FOCs, too, must maintain relatively decent labor standards. Employers seek re-regulation at the global level in part to undermine the ITF's position by pre-empting its issues, in part to provide a more employer friendly wage determination venue to IBF bargaining,[4] and in part to try to extend a higher cost structure to those employers able to avoid paying ITF equivalent wages. Structural interests within union and employer transnational groups shape the political alliances expressed in global regulatory forums.

OFFSHORE GOVERNANCE AND HEGEMONY

Maritime shipping is an example of an industry driven by an offshore governance system. A transnational network of banking, crewing, insurance, and other support institutions facilitate transactions and mobilize resources at a global scale, while enabling owners to avoid taxation, regulation, legal liability, and social responsibility (Metaxas 1985; Stopford 1997; Alderton and Winchester 2002). Offshore governance is by no means exclusive to maritime, but is also a highly influential factor in sectors such as banking, telecommunications, and internet commerce. Ronen Palan plausibly argues that the offshore concept of defined arenas and geographic spaces of deregulation is not an aberration, but rather is crucial to the development of global capitalism in its current form (Palan 2003). The development of social control over a global offshore industry such as maritime shipping has broad relevance to the prospects for democratizing the global political economy generally.

The ideal-type of international system as conceived by traditional international relations and comparative political science is a world of national "varieties" of capitalism (Hall and Soskice 2001) represented in international politics through the mediation of national governments (Richards 1999). Palan observes that this characterization has always been a simplification. States have never been completely insulated and parallel systems, but rather form interpenetrating regulatory networks. As Palan puts it, the "global market does not inhabit a homogenous judicial space" but is formed from a "patchwork of national system of laws joined together by a set of bilateral and multi-lateral agreements." (Palan 2003: 87) Be that as it may, for the most part, nation states, with their national myths, bureaucratic capacities, and sometimes democratic legitimacy, have had sufficient authority within their borders to provide stable environments for capitalist accumulation.

Palan observes that the offshore phenomenon results from attempts, starting in the 19th century, to reconcile the contradictions between the inter-state system for organizing global politics and the transnationalizing and globalizing imperatives of capital. Offshore, however desirable to capital from the perspective of freedom from social control, also creates an inherently unsustainable situation, undermining the national identities which lend capitalism legitimacy and sustain the accumulation process

(Palan 2003). Authority concentrates in insular transnational systems of governance which emphasize alienation and coercion over incorporation and consent (Gill 1995). Undermining the nation state system also undermines the collective goods and stability states provide, necessitating increased coercion to maintain the accumulation process.

Global governance is an effort to re-establish capitalist hegemony in a global neo-liberal environment, and to avert the systemic crisis the undermining of nation states and increased use of coercion is causing (Brand 2005). The new order of global governance has not yet clearly taken shape, but is based on elements of the old order (such as national varieties of capitalism and international regimes), patched together in new interdependent ways. While state power has always been contested, and is not necessarily disappearing as a result of global governance, it is argued here that state power is *fragmenting,* and that this creates a fundamentally different situation than one in which states are unified coherent entities. Maritime shipping regulation is less and less structured around the model of unified sovereign states enforcing standards on their own ships, and more and more around the actual existing structure of the industry. This reconstruction of state authority is not the all-encompassing sort of authority traditionally provided by states operating as parallel self-contained systems, but rather is specific and circumstantial, with the role of state power defined by interactions with private actors, and by international agreements made in intergovernmental as well as private and quasi-public contexts. Capital seeks to reestablish hegemony by reconstructing bits and pieces of the inter-state system, and making them work together coherently. International regimes provide the context, or opportunity structure, in which the transnational actors make these pieces fit together in a coherent, global and functional way.

Global governance generates new transnational political spaces in which the terms of subordination are subject to negotiation and contestation. The Gramscian concept of hegemony in this argument requires that capital engages subordinate groups, meaning those not in the "ruling coalition" (i.e. not capital), in supporting capitalist relations of production, by granting material concessions and allowing a degree of political power (Cox 1996: 113–115). Subordinate actors seek to influence the new rules as these develop, and exploit them for their own purposes—generally seeking to maximize the power and material concessions they receive in the new order. In the context of global regulatory politics, moribund international regimes receive new meaning and life, as they become arenas for politics between transnational classes and class fractions (Van der Pjil 1998). These intergovernmental regimes spill over into private and quasi-private realms through the involvement of non-state transnational actors.

In shipping, as in other industries, global and transnational governance structures blur the distinction between public and private, and generate new sources of authority not dependant on specific national states (Cutler *et al.* 1999; Overdoest 2004). There has been a shift in maritime shipping from relatively ineffective governance based on inter-state relations to one based on new transnational state forms, more adapted to the fluid global industrial environment. Global actors are constructing a transnational infrastructure of industrial relations governance on top of existing intergovernmental regimes, based around international conventions, private bargaining institutions, and private international law. Although maritime shipping is admittedly an unusual and idiosyncratic case, its governance structure can be viewed as a leading indicator of what could be a broader transformation of the world political system.

CAPITAL AND LABOR AS GLOBAL ACTORS

The term "global politics," as opposed to "international politics," implies politics driven by coherent transnational interests rather than by nation states and their interactions. For the term "global politics" to be meaningful, there must be transnational classes. This does not require that these classes are represented by unitary actors who agree on all issues. Fractionalism is inevitable for both capital and labor, particularly at the global level where there is so much diversity. Many fractions continue to bring to global political processes their own nationally defined interests, and there are non-nationally specific material bases for fractionalism as well. Nonetheless, for a transnational class to be a transnational class there must be a degree of cross-national coherence and commonality, i.e. shared structural interests and/or organization.

Shipping is perhaps an exceptional case because there are sufficiently well-articulated class based interests to justify and support the development of global and transnational state forms. As Timothy Sinclair points out, a "genuine and lasting set of trade-offs between competing interests" has yet to develop in global politics generally (Sinclair 1999: 161). The global working class is not coherent enough to be considered a viable "competing interest." In other contexts, global politics is entirely dominated by capital because the transnational capitalist class is not only structurally more powerful (as one would expect the "ruling class" to be), but is also far more class conscious, and usually better organized as well. Capital clearly perceives common global interests, and has organized in various ways to pursue these interests, while for labor the situation is more complex. In shipping, the primary difference to other industries is not the globalization of capital *per se,* nor even existence of a transnational class consciousness among sea-farers and dock workers (although an argument could be made that this exists, more than in other industries). Rather the key factor is the existence of viable transnational working class capacities, expressed through global unionism, and developed as a political project arising out of the interests and ideologies of unions and union leaders.

The Transnational Capitalist Class

Capital is perhaps inherently more prone to global and transnational orga-nizational forms than labor. Nonetheless, for capital as well, globalization has been a difficult and painful restructuring process. Corporations strug-gle with managing different kinds of global business organizations, and with overcoming ethnocentricity while retaining the advantages of national models (Ramsay 2000). Transnational firms are complex entities, and sites of social contest embedded in national practice (Amoore 2002). Nonethe-less, a common global business ideology has emerged, and is advocated by a "transnational capitalist class." This class consists of "corporate execu-tives, globalizing bureaucrats and politicians, globalizing professionals and consumerist elites," and "pursues people and resources all over the world, in its insatiable desire for private profit and eternal accumulation." (Sklair 2001: 4) In addition to a common perspective, the transnational capitalist class and the firms it controls are involved in various forms of transna-tional association. Many of the firms themselves are, of course, transna-tional in their own right. There are transnational production networks and alliances, as well as transnational business associations, which give further coherence to the common interests of otherwise competing firms (Cutler *et al.* 1999).

Given the overall structurally common interests, common ideology, and degree of transnational organization, it is quite clear that the transna-tional capitalist class not only exists, but is also conscious of its existence and of the common interests which hold it together. The transnational capitalist class has captured the agenda of key global institutions, and suc-cessfully portrayed its agenda as the common agenda, relying on market "freedoms" and consumerism to assert Gramscian hegemony. Internal con-tradictions, however, threaten to undermine this hegemony (Sklair 2001: 255–288), leading fractions of capital to seek to incorporate labor and other subordinate actors into the mechanics of global governance, in order to reestablish global hegemony on a more solid basis.

The transformation of national capitalists into a transnational capital-ist class is incomplete, and will probably never be definitively over. Nation-ality remains a salient factor in the formulation of fractions, even within supposedly global firms and industries. Within maritime shipping, the most global industry of all, national origin remains an important part of the identity of many firms and shipowners. Rifts within maritime shipping's transnational business associations sometimes occur along the lines of nationally identifiable groups—although these national groups are rarely totally cohesive. National shipowners and their associations can also be transnational actors in their own right. For example, some national shipowners' groups have engaged directly with the ITF on various occasions. Many of the larger shipping companies, such as Maersk-Sealand or P&O, are transnational firms with multinational management structures, making national identification problematic. The national structure of the International Shipping Federation might be considered in some ways outdated given the transnationalization of key firms. As will be seen in Chapter Three, some shipping companies have sought new forms of association to bargain with the ITF, perhaps partly as a result. Nonetheless, the multinational structure seems likely to continue to shape shipowners' associational politics, even as parallel transnational relations are built.

The Transnational Working Class?

When discussing the formation of a transnational working class, it makes sense to look first and foremost at the activities of the existing labor movement. Although the working class and organized labor are not the same thing, unions are the expression of the organizational capacities of the working class, and are key instruments in the generation of resistance. Even to the extent that labor unions are integrated into capitalism, and support capitalist hegemony, the reason for their incorporation is their potential to generate resistance (Hyman 2001). The assertion that unionism can stand in for the working class, or even that unions represent working class interests at all, is not universally accepted. However, if one accepts the idea of class analysis, and wishes to look at empirical evidence of class capacities, methodologically, looking at unions is really the only way to do this. Class capacities require organization, and this only rarely and intermittently occurs independently of established trade unions. Although other forms of worker representation exist, and are in certain isolated cases quite important, trade unions are overwhelmingly the organizational form of choice for workers the world over seeking to better their conditions (Harrod and O'Brien 2002).[5] This is not intended as a normative judgment that unions are the best and only true representatives of the working class, but rather a methodological judgment following on an empirical observation that unions, even with their many flaws, are by far the most consistent, and most powerful, representatives of working class interests.

The transnational working class is less conscious of itself and its interests than is the transnational capitalist class. Unlike capital, with its transnational firms, product markets and production networks, its global aspect is not an automatic reflection of its day to day activities, but rather something which it must independently construct as a political project. Workers live in (usually) localized communities, and participate in local and national politics, but these forms of inclusion tend to focus them on local or national arenas. Whatever transnational representation they have as workers is almost always intermediated through national union organizations. This continues to be the case even in maritime, although ITF strategy has resulted in transnational structures linking local unionists as a practical outgrowth of the FOC campaign. European Union centered inter-union cooperation, European Works Councils, rank and file transnational links, and even mergers between national unions in different countries, may provide more direct contacts in time, but these remain underdeveloped compared to the transnationalization of employers. Transnational working class resistance, such as it is, is mostly a construct of national labor union activity.

The formation of a global working class is inhibited by a numerous factors, not the least of which is the ideological dominance of the transnational capitalist class (Sklair 2001). Weak transnational structures (Turner 1996), embeddedness in national industrial relations frameworks (Tilly 1995), and competitive dynamics set in force by employer whipsawing strategies (Tuckman and Whittall 2002) all play a role in enforcing the division of global labor into numerous national working classes. However, the way in which global capital strips away national specificities and the protection these provide to workers also serves to build commonalities of interest, and provides a structural basis for transnational class formation (Van der Pjil 1998). As the protections formerly afforded to the relatively fortunate workers of the North are increasingly removed, structurally similar interests may emerge between workers in the global North and South (O'Brien 2004).

Beverly Silver, however, casts doubt on this possibility, arguing that capital movement will not necessarily result in the construction of working class internationalism. Rather, she observes that the movement of capital results in a decline in labor militancy in those places capital moves from, and an increase in worker militancy in those places capital moves to. Accordingly, there is no strong basis for cooperation between the "losers," whose jobs have left, and the "winners," who receive those jobs. There are windows of opportunity during which unions can exert power in local and national contexts, but these opportunities inevitably erode in time, as capital again casts its gaze toward greener pastures. Unions are most likely to respond to capital movement not by internationalism, but by erecting labor market boundaries, and by seeking to influence local and national political leaders. In the context of the current world political economy, this leads to a North-South axis of conflict between unions, which is often more important in defining transnational labor politics than is class conflict (Silver 2003: 8–25)

Silver's pessimistic conclusions assume that labor leaders will never be able to figure out the problem of capital movement, and devise counter strategies. This reasoning suggests very strong organizational and/or cognitive constraints on unions and union leaders. The recent literature on labor union strategy and revitalization, on the other hand, sees unions as actors with choices that influence their effectiveness, and even their structural development (Bronfenbrenner *et al.* 1998, Frege and Kelly *et al.* 2004). Accordingly, union leaders can deliberately construct a transnational agenda, set off a process of internal structural change, and implement new strategies appropriate to the new geography of production. There is substantial historical precedent for assuming a role for union leadership and strategic agency in the geographic expansion of union organization. The classical industrial relations work of J.R. Commons (1909), for example, establishes the link between product markets and the geographical extent of union bargaining structures. The reasoning is that union power within a capitalist framework depends on unions maintaining labor monopolies, either by organizing everywhere within a product market or establishing social mechanisms for excluding competition from cheaper producers. Unions therefore seek to expand their influence to match the geographic extent of the product market in which they compete.

The labor revitalization literature shows that unions can adapt new strategies successfully, and these influence organizational effectiveness. However, the evidence also tends to support Silver's contention, because of the localized focus of the revitalization strategies unions actually successfully implement—the FOC campaign is the only example of a successful attempt to implement J.R. Commons' organizing imperative on the global level. Unions in many countries have developed a raft of new strategies, including new organizing and recruitment (Bronfenbrenner *et al.* 1998; Heery and Adler 2004), corporate campaigning (Hickey 2004), and social partnership (Fichter and Greer 2004). Unions have merged, primarily for financial efficiencies (Behrens *et al.* 2004), and have built alliances with communities and other social movements (Frege *et al.* 2004). Traditional alliances with leftist political parties have weakened, and unions have sought new avenues for political influence (Burgess 2004; Hamann and Kelly 2004). Strategic renewal is occurring, and in many cases unions have devised more effective ways to organize and represent workers in a hostile environment. These changes, however, focus not on restructuring the labor movement to match the new geography of production, but rather on making existing national structures work more efficiently.

Transnational union alliances, on the other hand, have usually been more tactical than structural, arising from momentary convergences of interest (Lillie and Martinez Lucio 2004). Unions have not attempted mergers across national boundaries,[6] and efforts at coordinated multinational bargaining in European metalworking have stalled in the face of unions failing to fulfill international commitments (Hassel 2004). For unions, strategic possibilities other than geographical extension, though inferior in terms of developing organizational power over the long term, appear to union leaders as more immediately realistically attainable. This is not surprising, as serious and fundamental changes in internal priorities and resource allocation, of the sort which would be needed to transnationalize union structures, often result in difficult internal struggles.[7]

A pessimistic dismissal of labor transnationalism, however, does not square with the ITF experience of global unionism. The FOC campaign case suggests that despite the apparent difficulty of building transnational structures, a coherent global agenda could result from unions following a "path of least resistance." If transnational extension results from organizational changes which extend and promote the power of the existing union leadership, then union leaders will support it. This allows a strong role for agency in designing strategically ideal transnational strategies, such as Commons' labor monopolies defined by product markets—if these can be designed and implemented in ways acceptable to union leadership. Agency, however, is limited by the constraints of past structures, and the continuing parochial influence of national affiliates. The outcomes of past political struggles, embedded union interests represented in governance bodies, and strategic interactions with employers, governments and international regimes, all leave their mark on transnational union institutions and strategies as these develop.

Operationalizing Transnational Class

It makes sense to speak of capital and labor as global and transnational classes. They are not unified entities, but neither are they entirely abstract. They have at least some degree of structurally defined collective interest, and they are represented in global politics by identifiable individuals and organizations who act in their name. Cleavages between class fractions are just as important as class coherence in defining global politics, however. These cleavages influence the agendas of the "representative" organizations. They also sometimes prevent agendas from being clearly defined, in order to preserve internal consensus, as will be seen both from the development of the ITF policy of labeling FOCs (Chapter Three), as well as from shipowner negotiation strategies at the International Labour Organization (ILO) vis-à-vis the proposed Consolidated Maritime Labour Convention (Chapter Six). The organizational capacities of the transnational classes shape emerging institutions of global governance. Labor's weakness is, and will continue to be, a problem for the establishment of a stable hegemony through global governance. The FOC campaign case shows, however, that potential exists for the working class to overcome that weakness, and hold up its end of the globalization process. What might be referred to as the fulfillment of labor's global mission in maritime shipping is not exactly welcomed by capital, however, and varying reactions to increasing labor power have formed important cleavages within the transnational capitalist class. Some capital fractions seek accommodation, while others advocate more effective coercion.

The most obvious way to operationalize class is to look at the activities, statements and decision making processes of representative organizations. Representative organizations, however, include or exclude certain voices based on their institutional peculiarities, their internal balance of power, and their strategic interactions with other organizations and their environment. It must be kept in mind that organizational politics distorts the broader structural interests of classes or class fractions. Therefore, it also makes sense sometimes to shift to a more abstract level of analysis and look at classes and at class fractions as structural interests only imperfectly defined and represented by organizations. The problem is that these are only imperfectly articulated, and to deduce them from perceived material interest runs the danger of tautology. This study endeavors, therefore, to extend a bit into class analysis to show the broader significance of the findings, without straying too far from the empirical basis of those findings.

TRANSNATIONALIZATION OF ITF STRATEGY

The ITF is one of several Global Union Federations (GUFs),[8] which together with the multi-sectoral International Confederation of Free Trade Unions (ICFTU), and regional European organizations, make up the mainstream international labor movement.[9] Chapter Seven presents these other organizations and their activities. The ITF represents some five million workers in transportation and related industries. A London based professional Secretariat staff coordinates the ITF's activities. There are smaller regional offices as well. The ITF is divided into sections, including railroads, aviation, road transport and several others. Affiliates set broad strategic guidelines at ITF Congresses once every four years, under a weighted voting system, so that affiliates with greater membership have greater influence. Decisions relating to specific industrial sections occur at Congresses, and also at the more frequent section meetings. The ITF's non-maritime sections are less well resourced, have different governance methods, and follow a somewhat different dynamic. Among GUFs, the ITF is unique in the extent to which it controls its own resources and engages directly with employers in the context of the FOC campaign.

The ITF Seafarers' Section, the Dockers' Section, and the Special Seafarers' Department (SSD), are all engaged in the politics of the FOC campaign. The Seafarers' and Dockers' Sections support cooperation between various national seafaring and dockworking affiliates. Over the years, the business of these sections has become very much entangled with the FOC campaign, so that there is now coordination between the activities of the various maritime sections. Seafaring and dock union affiliates collectively govern the FOC campaign through the Fair Practices Committee (FPC), which takes decisions such as which flags to declare FOC, and what the ITF benchmark wage should be. The FPC has grown into a large and unwieldy body, but much of the detailed work is done by the FPC Steering Committee which meets frequently and consists of ITF staff and the leaders of key unions. As of 2001, there were 16 representative from capital supplier country unions, 5 from major labor supplier countries, and 6 from other developing countries in the FPC steering committee. The ITF makes an effort to ensure that all major political groupings in the FOC campaign are represented on the steering committee.

TRANSNATIONAL LINKAGES AND NATIONAL UNION AUTHORITY

The Secretariat, and in particular the SSD, has autonomy to make day-to-day decisions relating to the practical management of the campaign, within the guidelines set out by the affiliates at Congresses and committee meetings. The Secretariat's capacities and authority have grown greatly since the FOC campaign's beginning. Over time, the increasing transnationalization of the shipping industry, and its disembedding from national contexts created the conditions for growth in ITF authority and the transnationalization of union structures. Since the early 1990s, the ITF has developed truly transnational structures and independent capacities for action. Many affiliates rely on the ITF system for bargaining leverage and income flow (ITF 1998a), which gives the ITF influence over affiliates' decision making. The politics of collective bargaining, including the need to maintain discipline on the wage level, has resulted in a major shift of authority from national seafaring unions to the ITF.

However, ITF influence still depends on its constitutive unions, and these unions sometimes have a legitimacy and direct access to membership which the ITF lacks. Because of this, rather than conceiving of the ITF as an independent global union body, it is more accurate to think of it as an organization for pooling union authority, and for coordinating national activity in systematic ways. National unions use the ITF as a forum to collectively decide policies which they would be unable to implement individually. The Secretariat attained its current influence by filling a void, and assuming a needed role affiliate unions are not situated to fill. Now, as key affiliates become more transnational in their own right, it is possible that the ITF will assume less of a power broker role, and more of a facilitator role, as a provider of expertise, interpreter of rules, and an organizer of transnational politics between affiliates.

The past 15 or 20 years have seen substantial changes in ITF strategy, with new emphasis on designing procedures for effective solidarity, building flexible non-hierarchical structures, training and professionalizing ITF staff, and readjusting goals to create effective representation of seafarer interests. As a result, the FOC campaign is more powerful now than it was in the 1970s and 1980s. Part of the Secretariat's strategy has been to create transnational structures which directly tie local union officials into global strategy. Robert Cox explains that the national structure of union hierarchy presents a fundamental obstacle to transnational union cooperation. By default, unions conceptualize transnational relations as an activity for the top of the hierarchy, so that proposed transnational actions must also involve political decisions by the national leadership (Cox 1971). This inhibits transnational cooperation, since it is simply not practical to make a new policy decision every time a minor transnational action is contemplated. By creating a framework for action through the collective decisions of ITF affiliates, and implementing these decisions through autonomous structures, the ITF avoids this problem.

ITF Secretary General David Cockroft has, on numerous occasions, cited the need for "horizontal structures" and "flattening the hierarchy" to facilitate the transmission of information, and more subtly, to empower the local and global levels with independent transnational power resources. At the 1998 ITF Congress in Dehli, Cockroft related:

> Significant improvements had been made in recent years and part
> of the ITF's function was to help affiliates to communicate better.

> However, how unions were organised was sometimes a barrier to the
> effective exchange of information. Bureaucratic structure existed to
> ensure political control but these led to a communications pyramid
> which often did not allow information to travel from the top to the
> bottom quickly enough. This pyramid needed to be flattened, not as a
> substitute for, but as a complement to the democratic structures (ITF
> 1998b).

In referring to "bureaucratic structure" and "democratic structures,"
Cockroft means the affiliates themselves (which are apparently bureaucratic and democratic at the same time), and their influence on ITF policy through ITF governance institutions. While the growing power of the
ITF has not gone unnoticed by affiliates, with discomfort in some quarters,
many union officials realize that the decision they face is not really whether
to keep power at home or delegate it to the ITF. Rather, the real decision is
between exercising power collectively through the ITF, and losing power
altogether. Regardless of his assurances, Cockroft's ideas about flat pyra-
mids *do* threaten national union autonomy and political control vis-à-vis
the ITF. Flat structures circumvent and undermine national authority by
building up and connecting the local and global levels. However, as Chapter
Four shows, flattened structures are an essential part of a practical global
strategy. FOC campaign structures, though they undermine national union
autonomy, also ensure that those unions have *more* power vis-à-vis external
actors such as firms and governments, if less autonomy vis-à-vis the ITF
Secretariat and other ITF affiliates.

UNIONS, FIRMS, AND REGIMES IN GLOBAL POLITICS

International regimes constitute part of the transnational political opportunity structure for the global labor movement. The concept of international regimes developed in international relations theory to explain why
sovereign states, in an anarchic world, often organize their inter-state relations through systems of norms, expectations and institutions, which do
not always serve the immediate interests of every state involved (Krasner
1983). In recent years, growing interest in private transnational relations
has brought forth new research agendas in international regimes with an
emphasis on non-state actors in world politics. While new regimes can be
formulated by private actors for their own purposes (Cutler *et al.* 1999;
Koch-Baumgarten 1998), pre-existing regimes, both private and intergovernmental, constitute a transnational "political opportunity structure," as
sort of a weak form of institutionalization in transnational political space.

Political opportunity structures shape the strategies of actors by influencing the strategies that are likely to be successful and the goals that are likely to be achievable. Sidney Tarrow notes that intergovernmental organizations (IGOs) can provide transnational political opportunity structures, facilitating the transnationalization of social movement organizations (Tarrow 2001). International regimes also exist around and independently of intergovernmental organizations, however, although they frequently interact with and/or are dependant on IGOs. Regimes influence the transnational political strategies available to unions, both generally and within specific industries. Regimes can be more or less open to union involvement, can be constituted and implemented in public or private forums (or a mixture of the two), and can be intended to influence the behavior of states, private actors, or both. In shipping, unions are involved in the regimes regulating labor standards, shipping safety, and industrial governance more broadly.

In maritime regulatory politics, labor rights issues and industry standards have become very much mixed together, so that actors move strategically back and forth between the arguments, practices and precedents of the different arenas. In particular, maritime unions have sought to extend enforcement mechanisms from the shipping safety regime to labor rights issues, albeit with limited success so far. Defining the applicable regime for a given issue becomes part of the contest, and framing a tactical decision made at a particular moment. In this way, the transnational actors define and create the global governance system out of the sets of existing rules drawn from intergovernmental regimes. Since these sub- and trans-national actors do not have the same sets of interests and capabilities as the sovereign states who formulated the regime originally, the rules take on new meaning and application. Clearly, this process can only occur when transnational actors express coherent interests, and have autonomous capability to implement, or at least influence the implementation of, the rules. The actual practices of the labor market actors and governmental bureaucracies in concrete contexts bring the maritime labor regulatory regime to life, and create the practices and interest configurations on which future rules are formulated.

Maritime regulation essentially derives from the distinct but overlapping needs of capital to re-establish hegemony and to resolve collective action dilemmas. For labor standards, the primary focus is the containment of class conflict, while for the industrial governance regime, collective action dilemmas come to the forefront. However, the two goals cannot always be separated, since hegemony, for capital, can be regarded as a collective good, and class interests are very much a part of the superficially technical regulatory process.

The International Labor Rights Regime

The norms of the global labor rights regime are based on the international human rights regime (Swepston 1998), codified through an International Labour Organization tri-partite decision making process, in the form of conventions. These are intended to be ratified and implemented into law by national governments. Recent years have seen a general worldwide decline in union strength (ILO 1998), workers' living standards (Kapstein 1996) and respect for workers' rights (ICFTU 2004). Many see this trend as a direct result of globalization and the declining influence of national regulation in the face of mobile capital (Tilly 1995). Capital has grappled unsuccessfully with the problem of downward spiraling labor standards. Unwilling to grant power and legitimacy to unions, firms are nonetheless concerned about the threat to capitalist accumulation presented by the growing recognition that few workers have gained, or are ever likely to gain, from neo-liberal globalization. The decline in state regulatory capacity inherent in neo-liberal globalization ensures that firms can no longer fall back on the justification that their behavior is regulated through law and/or collective agreement. The failure of national systems to protect labor rights, and the inability of corporate standards to become a legitimate and effective private sector replacement, mean that corporations have increasing difficulty presenting themselves as socially responsible actors in the global economy.

Capital is attempting to re-assert hegemony while modifying its private, transnational, corporate-authoritarian model of governance as little as possible. In general, this means self-regulation within firms, or within business associations, through corporate social responsibility (CSR), codified in corporate codes of conduct (CoCs). These have become the basis for private corporate sub-systems of labor rights governance within TNCs and their supply chains. Self-regulation attempts to 'cosmeticize' labor relations problems for purposes of preserving corporate image (Arthurs 2001), or to preempt unwanted legislation (Haufler 2000). However, the cosmetic nature of private labor standards also prevents them from being very effective. In insisting on maintaining control of the process of labor rights enforcement, corporations undermine the independent voice needed to give the process legitimacy (see O'Rourke 2000, for example). Labor unions, on the other hand, seek to remove labor rights issues from the purely private realm of business standards, and place them in the context of public discussions on human rights. Labor exploits the opening presented by the CSR discourse to contest and re-define the terms of neo-liberal hegemony.

Industrial Governance

Unions are involved in global industrial governance in some industries, in both private and intergovernmental contexts, although, with the possible exception of shipping, they have not generally been very influential. This lack of influence is a crucial handicap for labor in global politics, as labor standards enforcement mechanisms tend to be extremely weak, while economic governance mechanisms sometimes contain very effective sanctions for non-compliance. The debate around using World Trade Organization sanctions to punish countries which allow labor standards violations makes this clear (O'Brien *et al.* 2000).[10] Furthermore, if labor cannot influence the fundamental rules of the game, then there is very little room for improving labor conditions through a purely rights based discourse. Any gains made through the establishment of norms will sooner or later be undermined by competition.

Political formulation of international regulatory regimes takes place in a variety of contexts. Often rules are generated in intergovernmental organizations tasked with maintaining technical, safety, or environmental standards. Businesses also produce regimes, through voluntary associations, or through the practices of dominant firms. Private transnational regimes serve much the same function for non-state actors as inter-state regimes serve for state actors—that of standardizing expectations and reducing risk (Haufler 2000)—and arise out of and reflect a particular pattern of global capitalist competition (Jessop 2002). Businesses need regimes to establish standards, which, for example, preserve the reputation of an industry or firm, ensure the technical interoperability of equipment, reduce transactions costs through standard practices, or preempt unwanted government regulation. Cutler *et al.* (1999) detail six common categories of interfirm cooperation leading to the generation of private authority and international regimes, and suggest that there are many others—and even these leave aside the various forms of public regime which dominate some issue areas. The diversity means that participants, their goals, and political dynamics can be very different from one issue area to the next, with varying possibilities for labor union involvement.

Participation in global regulatory policy formation is conditioned by technical expertise, and acceptance of the limits of the policy discourse of the decision-making community in question. The growth of epistemic authority, that is the deference to "professional, technical or other specialized knowledge," (Hewson and Sinclair 1999: 17) means that expertise can trump even free market ideology in certain policy discussions (for example, by showing that market structures reduce collective economic welfare).[11]

Epistemic authority, however, is rarely a weapon of the weak. More frequently, it is a weapon which can be bent to the will of the powerful (McKenna and Graham 2000). Nonetheless, its need for consistency to legitimate its function serves as a constraint on the powerful, a vulnerability which on occasion can be exploited by the weak. Labor unions, particularly when well resourced, often have excellent access to inside industry knowledge, allowing them to exploit existing epistemic authority, even if their subordinate status prevents them from defining the terms of the discussion in the first place.

The highly technical and industry specific nature of international governance, combined with the very conscribed boundaries of the issue areas dealt with through international regimes (Goldstein *et al.* 2000) shape politics in global arenas. Opportunities to exploit governance regimes tend to be contingent on the specific circumstances of a particular issue area. In the case in point, these include the technical requirements of specific seafaring jobs, the organization of production, and traditions of training. Industrial structures, production processes and environmental dangers inherent to segments of the industry create power resources and give political salience to issues of shipping safety. These power resources are used by unions and other shipping actors to promote a high-skill and professionalized labor market and organization of production, on the basis that it is necessary for public safety and environmental preservation, and for the long-term reproduction of the seagoing labor force. As we will see, unions have also attempted to capitalize on the emergence of an effective safety standards enforcement regime by advocating their application to shipping labor standards.

International regimes as outcomes of inter-state politics do not determine the shape of global industrial governance—the logic of production and the collective requirements of capital, as mediated by fractional politics and class conflict, do that. However, they do provide a pre-existing structure, which shapes the strategies of both states and transnational actors. International institutions provide forums in which the transnational actors debate global standards. States and private actors then apply these, or have them forced on them, or manage to avoid them, as the case may be, in a variety of ways and in a variety of settings.

PLAN OF THE BOOK

The central theme of this book is to show how the globalization of maritime unionism has pushed capital into re-regulating the maritime industry at the global level. First, Chapter Two will describe how the maritime industry has "globalized," even though it was arguably a global industry even before the contemporary period. The labor market and industrial relations conse-quences of these developments are discussed. Chapter Three deals with the development of the ITF's labor market strategy and the growth of industry level collective bargaining. Chapter Four details the functioning of the ITF ship inspector network, which monitors ITF contracts, and describes how dock workers are brought into the campaign to enforce ITF agreements through industrial action. Chapters Five and Six deal with the global poli-tics of industry regulation in the IMO and ILO, respectively. Chapter Seven discusses labor transnationalism in other industries, and the prospects for global unionism to become a more general phenomenon, in light of the ITF experience. In Chapter Eight, discuss the implications of the ITF's success-ful attempt to reassert social control over an offshore industry for industrial relations and international relations theory, and for the future of unions in global politics.

Chapter Two
The Maritime Industrial Environment

Shipping has always been global and transnational by nature, since ships move from one country to another in the normal course of their business. Historically, it has been common for ships to hire crew from various places, sometimes for convenience, sometimes for skills and/or cheap labor, and sometimes to fill vacancies appearing during the course of a voyage. Transnational ship ownership and management is also nothing new. Greek owned shipping, for example, has long (at least since the early 19th century) been defined along national-ethnic rather than national-geographic lines, with ownership and control maintained through blood ties and personal connections between ethnic Greeks in maritime centers around the world (Harlaftis 1996). The current phase of globalization has had a massive impact on the maritime shipping industry, but the exact nature of the change has in some ways been different than in other industries. Globalization has wrought specific structural changes to shipping regulation, ownership, and production organization, changing the nature of globalization an industry which has, in effect, always been global (Thanopoulou 2000). Thus, to understand changes in the political economy of shipping which have shaped union and employer strategies, one needs a more specific operationalization of the "globalization" concept.

Broadly speaking, there have been two types of changes which have occurred in the industrial structure of the shipping industry, and can be said to constitute "globalization." The first is the move to an offshore ownership structure in an effort to avoid unions, regulation and taxation—i.e. the shift to the FOC system. This change began in the 1930s, almost as soon as unions and government labor regulations began to seriously threaten to increase costs on ships flagged in advanced industrialized countries. Flagging out picked up pace steadily from the 1950s, and continued to grow in importance into the 1990s. Although often characterized as "capital movement," the ships and firms involved in flagged out do not necessarily go anywhere—or, more clearly stated, they continue to move around as they always have, to the same ports they always visited. Ship registration has shifted from countries with normal national regulations to offshore "tax havens," but the ships themselves, and the capitalists who own them did not necessarily move as part of this process. Flagging out is not capital mobility in the normal sense of the word, but rather a legal device, intended to separate certain regulatory spaces (ships) into offshore jurisdictions, allowing labor and resources to be mobilized on a global scale without regulatory interference. De-nationalization through offshoring in maritime shipping occurred more quickly and easily than in most other industries, although it is part of the same general phenomenon. Palan shows how aspects of the media, finance, banking, communications, and pornography have all moved off shore. Geographically defined deregulated areas such as Export Processing Zones also involve similar regulatory devices to FOC shipping (Palan 2003). Attempts to define deregulate work through transnational hiring in the construction industry (Hunger 2001) bear many similarities to shipping offshoring, although the legal basis is less established.

The second aspect of globalization in maritime is the expansion of corporate ship ownership, and the consolidation into ever larger capital formations. This began in the 1980s, and has continued to the present. Part of this trend is the emergence of ship management companies, which began as firms running ships repossessed from owners gone bankrupt from the shipping downturns of the 1980s. These firms have since become an established part of the industry. There is also the growth of global logistics firms, which provide sophisticated integrated global door-to-door shipping services. These firms not only own ships, but own, or have close business ties with, ports, trucking, air freight, rail, and inland water transport. Tight coordination between different links in shipping chains allows shipping firms to deliver time sensitive goods to demanding customers. This aspect of structural change in shipping partly drives and is partly driven by developments in production. In particular, trends such as global commodity chains (Gereffi and Korzeniewicz 1994), shifts in retail production and ordering (Rosen 2002) and lean production networks mean that rapid, reliable integrated logistics have become an essential part of many business models.

Both aspects of globalization are closely tied in with broader technological and management changes in the industry. Both have major labor market implications. These changes affect the kind of jobs which need to be done on ships, how seafarers are hired, which seafarers are hired, and how they are treated. For unions, these changes represent a massive shock to their organizational environment, mandating new types of transnational representation structures, and changing the strategies needed to generate power resources and pressure shipowners. While unions have an influence on economic structure, geography of production, and industrial regulation, they are subordinate actors and hence not really in control of the process. As Richard Hyman put it, "the terrain of industrial relations is above all conditioned by capital." (Hyman 1987: 27). The organizational environment is mostly an independent variable, shaping union strategy, although as unions regain a measure of control over the global labor market, industrial environment increasingly becomes a dependant variable to union strategy as well.

CAPITAL EXODUS TO NOWHERE

The modern Flag of Convenience system of ship registration has transnationalized employment relations and globalized labor markets in maritime shipping. While shipowners have always been flexible about which flag to fly, the modern FOC system has its origins in US passenger ships flying the Panamanian flag to evade Prohibition in the 1930s. Since their humble Panamanian beginnings, FOCs have grown steadily in importance to world shipping, prompting the development of a global infrastructure to attend to their needs for financing, crewing, insurance, and so on. Maritime shipping has not given over entirely to FOCs, nor is the FOC institution the only factor in how regulation has developed. However, FOCs have been a constant presence and a defining influence in the regulation of modern maritime shipping.

Seafaring industrial relations have long been noted for their transnational aspect. Sailing vessels would often hire crew from ports they visited overseas, to make up for lost crew who jumped ship or died, resulting in multinational crews, and multinational groups of expatriate seafarers available for hire in ports around the world. The mobility of the workforce, and isolation on ships at sea presented a problem for unionization. For much of their existence, national seafaring unions have faced direct wage competition with seafarers from other countries. Often this competition has been with groups willing to accept lower pay. British unions during the imperial period, for example, had to deal with competition from seafarers from the colonies, while US shipping has historically employed Chinese seafarers, as well as foreigners of other nationalities (Marsh and Ryan 1989; Pedraja 1992).

In the period immediately after World War Two, however, most ships were owned, registered and operated from the same country. That is, a

US shipowner would generally fly a US flag on his ships, and employ US nationals as seafarers. The shipowner would be subject to US law and pay US taxes, the seafarers would belong to US unions, and the ship would be run according to US safety regulations and labor law. Before the war, in the context of relatively low wages and usually looser restrictions on employing non-nationals, there was less motivation to switch flags, except under special circumstances—such as US shipowners avoiding Prohibition laws.[1] During the period immediately following the war, seafaring unions in many countries gained leverage over employers, while national regulatory regimes constrained the ability of shipowners to employ foreign labor on national flag ships. In this context, wages and conditions on ships improved commensurate with, or in some cases more quickly than, those ashore (Donn 1989). On the other hand, in the immediate post-war period, cheaply built World War Two merchant tonnage sold at fire sale prices flooded the market with ships not necessarily ideally suited to making money using high cost post war union labor (Pedraja 1992). Already, just as the new national regulatory environment began to develop, shipowners were looking for a way out of it.

Some of shipowners began to use the flags of small Latin American countries to avoid unions and regulations, and keep marginal shipping in operation. On a larger scale, American oil companies encouraged Liberia to set up an open shipping register, where they were able to avoid taxation and the increasing demands of US seafaring unions (Northup and Rowan 1983). In time, other enterprising governments seized on this opportunity and opened their registers as a source of easy revenue. Like Liberia, these governments provided a flag, but little else, so that FOC vessels operated in an essentially lawless environment.

The move from national flags to FOCs proceeded steadily from the 1940s to the present. Some shipowners continued to operate under national flags and regulations for a variety of reasons, including cabotage laws, subsidy programs and concerns about union boycotts. Although shipping subsidies and protected national markets attenuated international competition, both these protectionist laws and employers' reliance on them have declined over time.[2] Unions from traditional maritime countries had to cope with the decline of the national fleets on which they once had exclusive jurisdiction. Figure 2.1 relates the growth of the Liberian and Panamanian flags to the decline of the Western European, Japanese, and US-flag merchant fleets. Because of mechanization, increasing ship sizes,[3] and increasing use of non-domicile crew under traditional flags, the decline in European, Japanese and US tonnage understates the decline in seafaring employment in those countries. As can be seen from Figure 2.1, the decline of the US fleet began

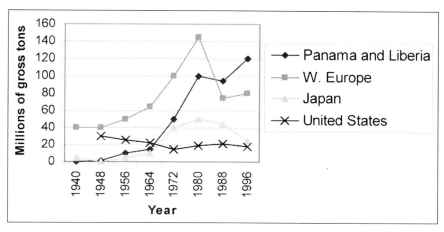

Figure 2.1: World Merchant Fleet by Flag

Source: Stopford 1997: 435 for Panama, Liberia, W. Europe and Japan. Harlaftis (1996) for United States.

almost immediately after WWII, while the Japanese and European fleets did not begin to decline until the late 1970s and early 1980s.

Since the 1980s, an increasing number of traditional maritime countries have attempted to make their flags competitive vis-à-vis FOC registers, in order to attract back their national shipping. These registers generally came in the form of "second" registers, either through formal creation of another national register, or through a dependant territory setting up a register of its own. Some second registers have tried to maintain relatively high safety and environmental standards, which some shipowners find to be a business advantage (DeSombre forthcoming), while allowing international crewing and giving tax breaks. In some cases, national unions have acquiesced to the second registers, usually in exchange for bargaining rights guarantees for the non-domiciled crew, and/or for retaining of some national hiring restrictions, generally for the higher skilled positions. Second registers include, for example, the Norwegian, German and Danish international ship registers. The German register is designated by the ITF as an FOC, because it is opposed by the German union.

Table 2.1 shows the growth of FOCs relative to the total world merchant fleet, by tonnage.

"International fleet" refers to all ships in either FOCs or second registers. The figures for 1983 and earlier refer only to FOCs, and exclude second registers. For the time period 1983 and earlier, second registers were not a significant factor, but after 1990s, it is necessary to add FOCs

Table 2.1: Growth of FOCs and the "International Fleet" as a Percentage of World Merchant Fleet

Year	"International Fleet" as a % of world shipping by tonnage	"International fleet" as a % of world shipping by number of ships
1953	6.2%*	
1973	22.8%*	
1983	25.3%*	
1990	46.4%	20.1%
1994	55%	24.8%
1999	64%	28.7%

Sources: Thanopoulou 2000 for FOCs in 1952, 1973, 1983; Alderton et al. 2001: 20 for "international fleet," 1990, 1994, 1999. * refers to only FOCs, excluding second registers.

and second registers to arrive at the amount of effectively "offshored" shipping. The percentages by tonnage and number of ships are different, because the international fleet consists disproportionately of large vessels. Owners of small vessels in coastal or regional trade are less inclined to "flag out" (Bergantino and Marlow 1998), despite the greater labor to capital ratio.[4]

CAPITAL CONCENTRATION AND THE GROWTH OF TNCS

In addition to the trend to offshoring, there has also been a consolidation and transnationalization of ownership, and integration of maritime transport into other transportation processes, particularly in the liner trade. These changes in transport are both causes of and caused by the transnationalization of production processes generally. Supply chains are becoming more integrated, and the integration of transportation links is part of that process. Not all shipping submarkets are affected equally however. The maritime shipping industry is segmented into many submarkets, each with its own structure and economic logic. These submarkets overlap partly but not completely. The most common analytical division is between the liner market, and the bulk trades. While there is overlap (some bulk goods can be containerized for liner shipment on back haul, for example, if no normal container cargo is available), these generally serve distinct markets, have different (though sometime overlapping) structures of ownership, use different types of ships, and are served by different types of cargo handling facilities in port (Stopford1997).

Liner Shipping and Containerization

Liner companies ship high value items for numerous customers according to fixed schedules. Most of this is containerized for ease of handling, although liners handle a small percentage of non-containerized general cargo as well. A given container ship might hold cargo from hundreds of different customers. In the past 20 years or so liner companies have transnationalized their corporate structures. There has been a trend for liner companies to become involved in other aspects of the shipping business, branching into logistics as well establishing links to stevedoring,[5] trucking and railroads. They have expanded vertically, into logistics, and horizontally so that the liner trade itself has become more concentrated (Notteboom 2002). As a result, it is possible for a manufacturing TNC to contract with a single logistics firm to move cargo to dispersed production facilities and customers around the world, without ever becoming involved in the details of the operation. According to Stopford, in 1997 the ten largest companies controlled 11 per cent of the dry bulk fleet, 17 percent of the tanker fleet, but 35 percent of the container ship fleet (Stopford 1997: 376–377). Since Stopford's book was published, there have been more mergers taking the process yet further, including the UK-owned P&O with the Dutch Nedlloyd, the Danish Maersk with the US-owned Sealand, and the Singapore-based Neptune Orient Line's acquisition of American President Lines.

Intermodalism and concomitant tightly timed delivery schedules characterize this industry segment. Starting in the 1960s, cargo handling has become more and more standardized by containerization; i.e. cargo is packed into uniform twenty and forty foot containers. All equipment in the transport chain is designed to handle containers, so that cargo can be smoothly moved from ship to port storage to train to truck without ever needing to be re-packed. The uniformity of containers means that the shape and characteristics of a container's contents are not relevant between the time the container is packed for shipping and the time it is unpacked at its destination. Dock workers, seafarers, and other workers in the transportation chain never need know, or care, what they are carrying. Cargo handling skills and techniques are uniform for all containerized freight facilitating management's desire to make labor cost/efficiency comparisons across ports and other transport links. Containerization, more than any other factor, has shaped the liner industry, defining the types of ships used, the organization of work in ports, and facilitating a vast expansion of world trade by making geographically dispersed production networks technically feasible (Pedraja 1992; Stopford 1997: 337–379; Turnbull 2000).

Bulk Shipping

Bulk shipping involves moving items which usually have a low value to weight ratio, are uniform in character, and are generally moved in entire ship-loads. Bulk shipping uses specialized loading and unloading facilities. In many cases, ship designs are quite specialized as well. Raw materials are commonly shipped bulk: iron ore, oil, grain and wood chips are examples of common bulk cargos. Examples of highly specialized bulk carriers include liquid natural gas tankers, chemical tankers, and reefers (refrigerated ships). Vehicles are also considered bulk cargo (although they are high value, low weight), because they are shipped on dedicated vehicle carriers. Unlike the liner trade with its mostly containerized, and therefore uniform, cargo, the bulk trade is much more diverse, even to the point where some of it operates similarly to the liner trade (Thanopoulou 2000: 5)

Some of the larger shipowners in the bulk trades are not shipping companies at all, but subsidiaries of large TNCs. Oil companies, for example, frequently own enough oil tankers to carry a large fraction of their shipping needs. This allows them to ensure that enough ships will be available at a predictable cost for their basic transportation needs. Generally, oil companies do not own enough tankers to carry all the oil they may wish to transport. Part of the remainder they contract from independent shipowners on time charter, which can be fairly long term (from 12 months to several years). The rest they hire on the spot market, for a particular journey. This structure allows companies to adapt quickly to changes in their own need for transport, while retaining a core transport capacity (Stopford 1997: 26–28).

Bulk carrier ship ownership is divided between shipping divisions of large TNCs, which are not interested in shipping per se, and dedicated shipping companies who service the time charter and spot markets. Some of these dedicated shipping companies are bulk divisions of shipping lines (such as P&O Nedlloyd, or Maersk/Sealand, which are primarily liner companies, but have bulk cargo divisions), while others are relatively smaller independent bulk shipping companies. Many of these latter are entrepreneurial "tramp" shipping operations, which rely more on ship speculation on the second-hand market for profits than on income from shipping freight (Stopford 1997: 32–33). These companies often have complex offshore structures divided into anonymously held "one-ship companies" to avoid taxation, regulatory oversight and legal liability (Metaxas 1985; Stopford 1997: 438–439).

Implications of Industry Structure

Although changing industry structure clearly shapes class conflict in the industry, there is no simple deterministic link between shipping market segments and union organization. As Ulman shows in his study of the growth of national unions in the USA, capital concentration both helps and hinders unionization. While larger firms and cartels may generate greater rents which unions can capture, they also have more political and industrial resources with which to resist unions and strikes (Ulman 1955). Idiosyncratic factors can be determinative; for example, large oil transnationals are often very anti-union, and resist the ITF very effectively. However, they are not at all understanding with subcontractors caught by ITF boycotts, and sometimes require that these take out ITF agreements (Metaxas 1985). Depending on local union structure, certain kinds of cargo handling facilities may be unionized, and others not, or they may be organized by different unions, which may or may not be ITF affiliates. Thus, which industry segments are vulnerable to ITF pressure can depend on the interaction between industry structure and local inter-union politics. The trend toward integration in liner shipping may sometimes make container vessels more vulnerable to boycotts than bulk vessels because there can be hundreds of customers waiting for time sensitive goods to arrive. Many industrial processes can be shut down by a single container ship boycott. Increasing capital intensiveness in the industry should in general increase union leverage, because a small strike can idle expensive equipment, but if this results in lower employment levels and greater competition for jobs, it will decrease union leverage instead.

MARITIME LABOR MARKETS

One result of the move to FOCs has been the opening up of the labor market, and the construction of a global infrastructure for supplying seafarers to FOC shipowners around the world. Seafarers working on FOC vessels find themselves traveling between different national jurisdictions, working daily with multinational colleagues, for denationalized employers, under an internationally determined set of rules and regulations. Labor sourcing has shifted its geographic emphasis over time according to price, availability of needed skills, and employer prejudice. Just after World War Two, FOC crews were drawn from diverse countries including northern Europe. By the 1970s, northern Europeans had become too expensive, and sourcing shifted to southern Europe, Korea, and Africa. Through the 1970s and 80s, Filipinos began to displace other groups, in part as a result of the Filipino government's policy of encouraging the export of cheap labor for foreign exchange (CIIR 1987). With the opening of the eastern Bloc, Russia and other post-communist countries challenged the primacy of the Philippines and India by flooding the market with highly trained seafarers (Johnsson

1996). Currently, new entrants such as China and the Ukraine threaten the wage norms Filipino seafarers have come to expect. In traditional maritime countries such as the United States, Norway, Japan and the United Kingdom only small numbers of ratings remain, usually on trade routes sheltered from global competition. The situation for officers is somewhat different, as pay for officers is generally reasonably high, but with the declining stock of maritime skills in industrialized countries most retiring senior European officers will be replaced by Asians in the coming decades (BIMCO/ISF 2000). Andrew Guest of *Lloyd's List* succinctly sums up the labor sourcing situation:

> From China to the Baltic Sea shipowners, managers and manning agents, like prospectors, continue to pan for human gold—seafarers with the right qualifications, suitable skills and, of course, the right price. Relentless competition drives these latter-day prospectors on as they sieve the local material through the fine mesh of costs and quality . . . can they speak decent English? Can they pass muster when the ship is vetted by keen eyed and strict port-state control inspectors, especially those from the US Coast Guard. Are their certificates White-Listed?[6] China, for long the El Dorado of [recruiters], continually hints at its potential, [while in Eastern Europe training colleges], starved of funds . . . are operating below capacity . . . [There is] the gathering perception, false or real, that Filipinos are becoming too expensive (*Lloyd's List* 9 Nov 2000).

Shifts in labor sourcing mean that the nationality of ship ownership is no longer necessarily connected to the nationality of the crew or flag, as Table 2.2 shows.

Five of the top ten flags in the world are Flags of Convenience, including the four largest flags. None of these FOC countries are in the top ten countries of beneficial ownership, or in the top ten suppliers of seafaring labor. Germany is the only major ship owning country also designated as a flag of convenience; this is because the German international ship register does not have the approval of the German unions, because it allows the employment of non-Germans at lower wages than Germans (ÖTV 1998). While many of the top ship owning countries are also major flags, the largest (Japan) is not even in the top ten flags, and the others are fairly far down the list. Except for Greece, none of the major ship-owning countries are among the top ten among seafaring labor suppliers.

Figure 2.2 shows the decline of seafaring employment in selected western European countries between 1965 and 1992.

Table 2.2: Comparison of Major Countries of Ship Registration, Ownership and Crewing

Top Flags of Ship Registration by Tonnage	Top Countries of Ship Ownership by Tonnage	Top Seafaring Labor Suppliers
1. Panama*	1. Japan	1. Philippines
2. Liberia*	2. Greece	2. Indonesia
3. Malta*	3. United States	3. China (PRC)
4. Bahamas*	4. Norway	4. Turkey
5. Greece	5. Singapore	5. Russia
6. Cyprus*	6. China	6. India
7. Singapore	7. United Kingdom	7. Ukraine
8. Norway	8. Germany*	8. Greece
9. China	9. Korea (South)	9. Italy
10. United States	10. Hong Kong	10. Korea (South)

* Denotes Flag of Convenience (as determined by the ITF)

Source: Lloyd's Register of Shipping for flag and beneficial ownership information (2000), BIMCO/ISF 2000 Manpower Report for labor supplier information.

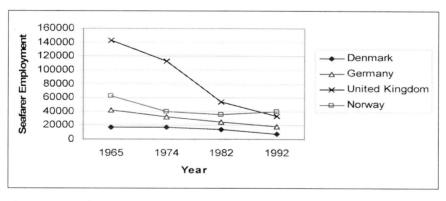

Figure 2.2: Seafarer Employment in Selected Countries, 1965 to 1992

Source: Alderton et al. (2001): 32.

Substandard Shipowners and Seafaring Labor Markets

As we have seen, the tendency of capital to move in search of newer and cheaper sources of exploitable labor is very visible in maritime shipping, and occurs more rapidly than in land based industries. This dynamic structures the interests of capital fractions, as some employers seek to preserve their "low-road" options, while others seek to cartelize the shipping market by exploiting the push for higher shipping standards. The availability of cheap labor from developing countries and peripheral areas, and the ability to further lowering costs through extremely exploitive labor practices not only gives to shipowners a "low-road" option, but, through competitive mechanisms, tends to push them down that road whether they like it or not.

While the labor market for maritime shipping is not a completely free and open market as some observers (Johnsson 1996, for example) make it out to be, a lack of certainty in the enforcement of minimum standards regulations tends to undermine the stability of existing labor market structures. The maritime shipping labor market is not formally regulated, but nonetheless shaped by the mechanics of global labor sourcing. Generally, shipowners prefer to work through known manning agents or hire ship management companies with stable labor sourcing arrangements. Ship management companies tend to specialize in certain nationalities. Acromarit, a Swiss ship management company, for example, hires many Russians (*Lloyd's List* 6 Feb 1999), while Barbar ship management is known for hiring Poles and Filipinos (*Lloyd's List* 24 Aug 1999). Norwegian shipowners pay into a collective training fund for Filipino recruits (*Lloyd's List* 25 Nov 1991), and have invested in training schools in the Philippines since the 1980s (CIIR 1987). Labor source countries change over time, but only gradually, because opening each new labor supplier requires an initial investment in developing networks of contacts and familiarity with a new local labor market situation. There are therefore geographic patterns to maritime labor supply, which do not strictly follow the price of labor, or at least not without a substantial lag.

The substandard segment of the maritime shipping market has always been innovative in its labor sourcing. This substandard market segment uncovers new sources of cheap labor, and, through cost competition, forces other firms to follow as well. Not as concerned about qualifications, substandard companies can hire from countries without recognized training establishments or maritime traditions. Substandard shipowners are less constrained by the existing institutional framework of the labor supply system, and are freer to hire from less well established sources of labor.

Successfully opening a cheap new labor market can set off a downward spiral in wages, conditions, and professional standards, as happened in the 1980s when the Filipino labor market opened up to FOC shipowners (Johnsson 1996). This makes it more difficult for the ITF to balance the interests involved in its labor market strategy, and more tempting for shipowners to seek to employ labor at less than ITF rates. The mere fact that seafarers, albeit perhaps employed under abusive conditions and lacking in professional qualifications, can be hired for a very low price, encourages shipowners to attempt a low-wage low-standards strategy. As long as labor standards are not enforced, and new low wage labor markets remain to be exploited somewhere in the world, the specter of a sudden labor market crisis always looms.

Industrial Relations on FOCs

The shift to FOCs has not only affected where seafarers come from but also how well they are treated. Global labor sourcing reduces the capacity of seafarers to organize and resist, by isolating them from their actual employer, and placing them in a legal vacuum, where no effective state authority applies. Deregulation of the work environment makes it possible for unscrupulous employers to commit serious violations of human rights. FOC countries often have neither the ability nor the will to enforce their legal systems on the vessels they flag (Chapman 1992), and most seafarers do not have means to pursue legal claims in courts in far away FOC countries they have probably never visited. Furthermore, the multinational nature of ship crews creates social and cultural divisions among seafarers (Sampson and Wu 2003). Where unions represent FOC crew, quite often there are different unions representing crew from different countries, not to mention different crafts.

The trend to flagging out has had many negative consequences for the work environment of modern shipping, from the perspective of unions and seafarers. Seafaring is a difficult and dangerous occupation involving long periods away from home, and FOC seafarers are very vulnerable to exploitation and abuse. Many severely abusive situations have come to light, particularly in the so-called "substandard" portion of the shipping market. Chapman of the International Center for Seafarers Rights cites numerous examples of seafarers being cheated of wages, abandoned in ports around the world, forced to work excessive hours, living in unsanitary conditions, and fed inadequate and unhealthy food (Chapman 1992). Couper *et al.* find many of the same problems, and furthermore show how the transnationalized structure of shipping allows substandard shipowners to escape the consequences abusing and cheating seafarers (Couper *et al.* 1999).

Even seafarers working in relatively decent employment situations have had to cope with mechanization, declining crew sizes, longer tours of duty, and generally less favorable terms of employment. These factors have taken their toll in terms of increased stress and fatigue, fewer opportunities for shore leave in ports of call, and fewer trips home to see the family (ICONS 2000; Alderton *et al.* 2004). Seafarers from industrialized countries working on ships flagged in their home country generally have more opportunities to spend time at home, and often have long paid leaves built into their contracts. However, FOC seafarers, particularly those from developing countries, often return home only once a year, taking a severe toll on family relationships (Kahveci and Sampson 2001). As a result, many developing country seafarers see seafaring not as a long term profession, but rather as a way to build up a stake, perhaps to finance a marriage or buy a house, after leaving the seafaring profession for good (Couper *et al.* 1999).

Seafaring has always presented unique difficulties for union organizing. For example, seafarers can only participate in union activities while in port (Chapman 1992; Marsh and Ryan 1989). Seafaring unions tend to be centralized, staff driven, and service oriented (Beasley 1996; Marsh and Ryan 1989). This is an issue for the ITF; even in a theoretical sense effective channels for FOC seafarer input into ITF decision-making are diffuse. In a practical sense seafarers have no effective democratic control (Amante 2004), and ITF representation of seafarers is driven by ITF staff, and the demands of sometimes undemocratic seafaring affiliates, rather than by seafarer demands. This is recognized as a problem by the ITF, although proposed solutions seem more oriented toward improving servicing and ensuring accountability in the use FOC campaign funds than on making structures more democratic (ITF 1998a)

Chapman notes that while many FOC seafarers immediately see the advantages of unionism and collective bargaining, they do not feel they are in a position to organize themselves, because of intimidation from employers, or because of their isolation while at sea. Furthermore, they only plan to go to sea for a short time, and lack the incentive to take the risk of organizing (Chapman 1992: 80–81). Blacklisting of seafarers who contact unions is obviously a major disincentive, and many seafarers report threats of violence or other reprisals against themselves or their families if they contact trade unions (Chapman1992; Couper *et al.* 1999; ICONS 2000).

CONCLUSION

Changes in the industries governance and structure shape opportunities for union leverage, and influence the conditions under which seafarers work.

Increasing speed and turnover in ports resulting from logistics linkages increase union leverage, but also increase pressure on and isolation of seafarers. The legal vacuum created by the FOC system allows employers to abuse and cheat seafarers, but it also opens a political space for global unionism. In these ways, industry structures shape opportunities for global unionism. The move of shipowners to FOCs has also set off a process of competitive deregulation among non-FOC registers, highlighting the relationship between offshore and deregulation. Both are functionally similar, and show the subordination of state sovereignty to the needs of transnational capital. Transnationalization of corporate structures, and the development of logistics chains, link structural change in maritime to the transnationalization of production in other industries. As Chapter Three will show, this complicates the ITF's strategy of labeling certain flags as FOC, because capital mobility is no longer always simply a result of fictional offshoring.

Chapter Three
Global Collective Bargaining[1]

Despite the often observed phenomena of globalization of production networks and product markets, organized labor's bargaining strategies have remained mostly national in scope. Although recent efforts at cross-border union collaboration have attracted attention, particularly in the European Union (EU) (Ramsay 1997; Sisson and Marginson 2002; Hassel 2004) the only well developed example of union-driven transnational wage bargaining coordination covering large numbers of workers is in the maritime shipping Flag of Convenience sector. Maritime shipping is an interesting example because, unlike other many transnational bargaining initiatives,[2] bargaining outcomes in maritime have immediate, direct and significant real world impact in terms of worker welfare and labor costs. This case affords the unique possibility to observe a functioning industry level bargaining system, with all the attendant employer-union and inter-union conflicts played out in a transnational environment.

The International Transport Workers' Federation and global employers' federations, the International Maritime Employers' Committee (IMEC), and the International Mariners Management Association of Japan (IMMAJ), now negotiate in the International Bargaining Forum (IBF) over pay scales for seafarers on Flag of Convenience (FOC) ships. The 2003 IBF agreement created a pattern agreement for pay and working conditions for approximately 50,000 seafarers on about 2000 ships (*Lloyd's List* 25 Sep 2003). In 2003, about 6,500 ships total carried ITF approved contracts (*Lloyd's List* 9 Oct 2003), including the IBF agreement ships. The process by which global wage bargaining developed in the FOC sector sheds light on the mechanics of transnational class construction and fractionalization.

Global bargaining in maritime shipping is predicated on a bargaining coalition between seafaring unions from high wage capital supplier countries,[3] and seafaring unions from mid-to-low wage labor supplier countries.[4]

Global bargaining developed in face of resistance from maritime employers who sought to undermine the union bargaining consensus by exploiting disagreements between capital and labor supplier country unions. The ITF balances the strategic need for labor market influence with the politics of maintaining inter-union consensus by dividing the labor market into three distinct segments: high-standard national fleets, the international, or "offshored" fleet, and developing country fleets. The FOC campaign system reduces competition between these three segments using targeted industrial action by port workers to identify and separate out FOCs, in order to impose a global uniform labor cost scale on them. The centralized wage determination system, in which ITF affiliates collectively participate in deciding the wage rate, but are then obliged to maintain the agreed rate, significantly undermines national union autonomy. Affiliates acquiesce to the growth of ITF authority because they receive financial benefits and power resources from the campaign.

THE IMPORTANCE OF THE ITF IN MARITIME WAGE DETERMINATION

To say the ITF has created a wage cartel implies that the ITF is able to raise wages above what they would be in the absence of union intervention. It is not as straightforward as it sounds to determine whether this is occurring, since there are many factors influencing seafaring wages, and statistics for the industry are not very good. Furthermore, the existence of high union wages can pull non-union wages up, as non-union employers compete with unionized employers for qualified staff, reducing the observable union differential. However, despite the relatively poor statistics, there is evidence of a differential between ITF and non-ITF wages. An employer study published in 2001 indicates that a typical qualified Able Seaman (AB) sailing without an ITF contract might earn around $800 total compensation. The same seafarer under ITF contract at that time would have earned a total compensation worth $1200 per month.[5] Wages of alternative shore side employment are lower than market rate seafaring wages (see Table 3.1). ITF wages, in turn, are substantially higher than the non-ITF rate for seafarers from developing countries. Table 3.1 compares the median wages of an AB with wages ashore, by country. Although the AB figures are quite close to ITF standards for many countries, more specific data from the same survey reveal that wages from major labor-supply countries form two clusters: USD 1000–1200 per month (close to the ITF figures), and USD 700 to 900, the "market" rate (ISF 2001: 11).

Table 3.1: Comparison of Shore-side vs. Seafaring Income, in US Dollars, 1999

	Monthly Wages for Industrial Worker Ashore	Median Able Seaman Monthly Wages	Differential*
India	48	1050	21.9
China	113	600	5.3
Indonesia	50	750	15
Philippines	140	1025	7.3
Latvia	189	1100	5.8
Ukraine	149	1100	7.3
Poland	233	1100	4.7

*Median AB/Average Wage Ashore
Monthly wages for industrial workers are from the ILO LABORSTA database, from male industrial workers in occupations comparable to seafaring, to the extent such figures are available. Able Seaman wages are International Shipping Federation (ISF) Year (2000) figures. These are derived from a survey of employment contracts of ISF members, and do not represent the entire population of shipping industry work arrangements. These statistics should be considered with caution, as they are not uniformly reliable.

In 2001, ITF contracts covered approximately 85,000 seafarers on around 6,000 out of between 13,000 and 21,000 FOC ships (giving at least 27% union density by number of ships covered, depending on which ships are included in the denominator).[67] Many shipowners also voluntarily pay close to ITF wages to avoid problems with the ITF, but do not have ITF contracts. It is difficult to assess the extent of this practice, although wages of non-union seafarers in general appear to be converging upward to ITF norms. This upward convergence may also in part be due to more effective industry regulation, which constrains the degree to which shipowners can use unqualified labor (ITF 1998a). Also, officers have been generally less affected by ITF wage scales, because a global skill shortage in the context of more effective skill standards enforcement (see Chapter Five) is forcing employers requiring specialized workers to pay above the union scale to attract qualified workers (ICS/ISF 2005: 25). While upward convergence of non-union pay makes the influence of the ITF less obvious, it is actually a sign of increasing ITF influence. Furthermore, it bolsters the ITF position by reducing employer incentives to avoid or undermine ITF agreements.

GLOBAL LABOR MARKETS AND UNION LABOR MARKET CONTROL

ITF influence has grown over the past three decades as a result of successful strategies to cope with the transnationalization of maritime labor markets. In particular, contract enforcement has improved, and the campaign has changed focus from protecting the jobs of seafarers in capital supplier countries, to bargaining for seafarers from labor supplier countries. By shifting the campaign focus, the ITF has engendered a broader inter-union consensus on strategy. This consensus enabled the ITF effectively to impose a global uniform wage level, which eventually led to the development of formal global industry level collective bargaining in the year 2000.

The growth of a global labor market for FOC seafarers has driven the development of the FOC campaign strategy. Arriving at a global inter-union consensus was a long and difficult process, however. Despite the economic imperative, the ITF did not build a sufficiently cohesive consensus among maritime unions to compel employers to negotiate at the industry level until the 1990s. During the 1970s and 1980s, the campaign remained handicapped by internal strife, particularly between unions from capital and labor supplier countries. Resolution of this conflict, coupled with associated improvements in the ITF's capacity for industrial action and contract enforcement, eventually brought reluctant employers to the bargaining table.

Prior to the 1960s, FOCs did not compose a major portion of the world fleet. Although many maritime unions recognized the FOC threat and undertook significant cooperative transnational political and industrial action to reverse the trend to "flagging out," action was not consistent or coordinated, and did not result in the development of functioning transnational institutions (see Metaxas 1985). In the 1970s, as European wages rose, flagging out began to pose a significant problem for European seafaring unions. With rising concern about FOCs some ITF affiliates at a 1972 ITF Congress demanded intensification of the campaign. The ITF sanctioned the appointment of inspectors, who would organize actions against FOC vessels without ITF-approved collective agreements. A standard ITF agreement was formulated, and ships with such contracts were to be issued with ITF "Blue Certificates." Other agreements, with non-ITF affiliate unions for example, were not to be recognized on FOC vessels, and risked industrial action. Through the 1970s, unions in Australia, Finland, Sweden, and the UK strongly backed the campaign, and conducted ship boycotts on a regular basis. Boycotts also seem to have occurred from time to time in Italy, Spain, France, Israel and Canada (Northup and Rowan

1983: Appendix B). The number of ships with crews working under ITF agreements grew steadily.

Employers were less than enthusiastic about these developments, and as ITF actions became pervasive, they devised counter-strategies. These included purchasing substandard agreements from compliant ITF affiliates. Employers kept two sets of books, one showing ITF wages, and the other the actual wages paid to the seafarers. Complicity with the double-book-keeping system was a condition of employment for seafarers sailing under these contracts. Although the ITF signed large numbers of contracts relative to the size of then much smaller FOC fleet, it is not clear that all of these employers actually paid ITF wages (Northup and Rowan 1983).

Fissures developed within the ITF, and were exploited by employers. In particular, some Asian unions opposed what they saw as a western-dominated protectionist union agenda. The National Union of Seafarers' of India (NUSI) politically opposed the ITF wage within the ITF, and under-mined ITF efforts within the Indian context (Arora 1997: 22–25). NUSI cooperated with attempts by employers to recover "excess" wages paid to Indian seafarers due to ITF action, resulting in NUSI's expulsion from the ITF in 1978. Western unions threatened to boycott Indian-manned ships if NUSI did not comply with ITF policy. NUSI responded that Indian dockers would back it up by boycotting Western-manned ships. Many Asian unions voiced sympathy for NUSI's position (Arora 1997: 25).

The ITF resolved the issue by watering down its stance on a uniform wage level. First, the ITF agreed to a lower wage level for seafarers sailing exclusively within the Asian region, which was phased out over the next several years. Second and more importantly, the ITF established the Total Crew Cost (TCC) concept. Instead of having a single, uniform "Standard Agreement" for all FOC seafarers, with all wages and benefits specified precisely, shipowners could negotiate agreements with ITF affiliates which need only add up to an ITF-determined labor cost level. The TCC rate was intended to allow more flexibility to unions and employers in adapting to local conditions, while still preventing inter-union wage competition. NUSI rejoined the ITF, although it remained relatively inactive in the campaign until the 1990s (Arora 1997).

Although the compromise with NUSI saved the ITF from being ripped apart by political disagreements, it also made the seafaring labor market more difficult to control. The complexity of administering a large num-ber of different agreements provided opportunities for unions to undercut one another on price, and resulted in many TCC agreements not adding up to the agreed cost level (Johnsson 1996). This, in addition to the overall decline in ITF agreements during the 1980s (probably in part because of new anti-union legislation in the UK) meant that ITF strength looked to be on the wane. Many predicted an eventual demise for the FOC campaign (*Lloyd's List* 4 Oct 1994).

On the other hand, the ITF Secretariat continued to lay the ground-work for future expansion. In 1983, the inspector network expanded to include Japan, and in 1986 the USA. Eastern European and other countries followed. Inspector training and cooperation improved, and the ITF standardized its policy implementation. The ITF also improved enforcement of uniform labor costs in TCC agreements. In 1989, the ITF undertook a review of agreements, and began standardizing them, to ensure that no agreement offered wage costs below the agreed minimum (Johnsson 1996: 85–86). Unions, particularly in the USA, found they could successfully use the courts to enforce ITF contracts and collect back-pay for crew underpaid due to double-bookkeeping, resulting in expensive back-pay judgments against shipowners (Northup and Scrase 1996). During the 1990s, the number and geographic spread of ITF inspectors increased considerably. In particular, the ITF gained a presence in Russia, Eastern Europe, South Africa, India, and South Korea. Inspectors became more active, inciting ship boycotts in places where they had not occurred previously, such as Denmark, Germany, Poland, Russia, South Korea, and India (see Chapter Four). Figure 3.1 shows the growth in the number of ships operating under ITF contract.

Better contract enforcement and the expanded inspector network put employers under pressure to pay ITF wages. Some large employers attempted to maintain dual wage structures, paying only part of their workforces at ITF rates. For example, Mobil Transport paid seafarers on ships sailing to ports with a strong union presence TCC rates (at the time around $900 per month for an AB), while paying seafarers on ships sailing to non-ITF ports at Indian levels (around $250 per month for an AB). Seafarers paid Indian rates were aware that others working the same job for the same employer earned much higher pay. Mobil decided to move to a uniform ITF-level wage structure, and as a result began to look for ways to moderate ITF demands.

In 1993, a number of maritime employers, including Mobil, formed IMEC, to coordinate the employers' side of collective negotiations in India and the Philippines. They attempted to exploit old divisions in the ITF by supporting the Indian and Filipino unions against the ITF Secretariat. IMEC did not succeed in inciting the unions to break ranks. On the contrary, in 1994, both the Indians and the Filipinos negotiated contracts valued at exactly the TCC wage rate. Although these unions had certainly been reluctant supporters at best in the past, the entry of Russian and

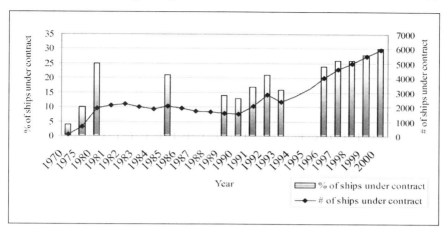

Figure 3.1: Ships with ITF Agreements, Absolute Numbers and Percentage of FOC Fleet

Source: ITF FOC Campaign Annual Reports 1996, 1997, 1998, 1999, 2000, Northup and Scrase (1996) (for the year 1993), Koch-Baumgarten 1999 (for the years before 1993), ITF Reports on Activities 1974, 1978, 1986, 1990, 1994. 1975 total FOC figures are actually from 1974; 1970 total FOC figures are from 1967. For 1981 through 1984, and for 1986-88, the number of FOC ships is not available (and the percentage under FOC contract could not be calculated). For 1994 and 1995, the number of ships under contract is not available.

Eastern European seafarers onto the labor market helped them recognize the desirability of ITF controls.

Russian and Eastern European seafarers could have undermined the ITF wage consensus instead of bolstering it, had Indian and Filipino unions felt it necessary to compete on wage costs. One source estimated that from Russia alone, up to 900,000 seafarers were available for hire, willing to work for around half of the wages of Filipino seafarers (*Journal of Commerce* 26 Oct 1992). Unions from established maritime countries watched with alarm as shipowners started "kicking off Filipinos and rushing to hire Russians and Ukrainians," while "they scour[ed] the world for the cheapest labor" (Cockroft interview in *Lloyd's List* 3 Mar 1993). The ITF rushed to fill in the gaps in its wage policies, by establishing more uniform principles for its old members in order to prevent the new entrants from setting off a downward spiral in wages. In a 1994 ITF Congress, for example, a Polish unionist mooted a suggestion about "regional wage standards," which was quickly squashed by ITF officials before it could be discussed or voted on (*Lloyd's List* 8 Aug 1994). As Lloyd's List, puts it, "With the international labor market under increasing threat from the newly-independent states of eastern European and the former Soviet Union, the last thing the ITF needed was job-chasing competition among its members." (*Lloyd's List* 13 Sep 1994) The inexperience of unionists from those countries and their reliance on ITF technical support also made them less effective advocates for lower wage standards.

Other international union organizations, such as the International Metalworkers' Federation, were too concerned about internal stability to move quickly into Eastern Europe and the former Soviet Union (Herod 1998). For the ITF to continue to build its bargaining coalition, however, it was essential to either integrate the maritime unions in post-communist countries into FOC campaign structures, or find ways to exclude them from competing with seafarers currently under ITF contract. Although the ITF quickly signed a favorable contract with Sovcomflot, dealing with the new unions had its risks. In 1991, the ITF was embarrassed by its association with a scandal involving the Soviet Independent Federation of Water Transport Workers Unions (IFWTWU), which misused USD 12 million of its members' welfare funds paid through the Sovcomflot contracts. As the Soviet Union collapsed, the Russian unions broke up too, and a number of different seafaring unions emerged in the successor states. The ITF sought to prevent these new unions from competing with one another. Among the Russian seafaring unions, the ITF favored the Seafarers' Union of Russia (SUR), by providing material, training and technical assistance. It also delegitimated competing unions as "company unions" signing "substandard" contracts, advising them to merge with the SUR. Unions that did not cooperate did not have the credibility of being authorized to sign ITF-approved contracts (*Lloyd's List* 22 July 1997).

Interest conflicts between unions from developed capital supplier country unions and developing labor supplier country unions have defined the fault lines of inter-union conflict within the FOC campaign system. However, during the 1990s the ITF successfully reframed its objectives, so that unions in major labor supplier countries could also benefit from the FOC campaign. As new labor supplier unions emerged in the post-Communist countries, the ITF had to decide which ones to integrate into the bargaining system and which ones to exclude.

EMPLOYER INITIATED MOVES TO TRANSNATIONAL BARGAINING

The growth of ITF internal consensus supporting a unified bargaining agenda in the 1990s eventually brought maritime employers to the bargaining table in an effort to contain labor costs. Some authors on labor transnationalism, such as Dølvik (1997: 361), have noted that employer resistance inhibits the development of transnational bargaining. Employer opposition, however, is to be expected as long as unions cannot coordinate bargaining objectives and industrial action amongst themselves. In maritime shipping, employers opposed global industry level bargaining on principle, but were eventually obliged to reconsider their position when the ITF gained more effective control of the labor market. Many national employers' associations and individual employers felt that the ITF should bargain with them directly, asserting that seafarer wages should be based on cost of living and wage expectations in the seafarers' country of origin rather than on global norms (ISF 2001). The German Shipowners' Association, for example, held discussions with the ITF, but always came away disappointed when the ITF proved unwilling to budge on basic labor cost issues.[8] Because the ITF set wage rates unilaterally, many employers began to see the benefit in moving to institutionalized collective bargaining arrangements.

Employers created IMEC specifically to deal with ITF attempts to coordinate national bargaining in 1994 in India and the Philippines, and phase out national distinctions between TCC agreements. A *Lloyd's List* commentator writes:

> The local employers, such as the Filipino Association for Mariners' Employment, are merely fronting for their international clients, represented at last month's talks by IMEC. In addition, any collective bargaining agreements reached at these talks have to be approved by the ITF. So local pay levels in shipping covered by ITF-acceptable deals do not yet exist, as long as the ITF continues to check agreements reached by its affiliates with sufficient rigor (*Lloyd's List* 13 Mar 1994).

At its inception, IMEC was primarily interested in undermining bargaining coordination rather than in creating global bargaining structures. Employers criticized the TCC benchmark as unilaterally imposed through union "coercion." The ITF responded by declaring its willingness to bargain, but in fact only committed itself to negotiate in earnest when bargaining held out the prospect for expanding ITF coverage and legitimating its role.

IMEC kept a low profile in negotiations, presumably to avoid acknowledging that ITF rates were reached through negotiation. In order to bring IMEC to the table, the ITF needed to demonstrate it had the internal consensus to increase the TCC rate. In 1997, the ITF increased the AB rate to USD 1100 (as negotiated in the 1994 talks), and this rose to USD 1200 in 1998. Before the 1998 rate took effect, the ITF announced the TCC rate would rise again to USD 1400 in 2001, unless decided otherwise in negotiations with employers. During this period IMEC and ITF "behind the scenes" bargaining coordination expanded from India and the Philippines in 1994, to Poland in 1997, and then Sri Lanka in 2001.

At first, employers merely denounced the planned increase, but as the date of implementation drew closer, the ITF and IMEC agreed to bargain directly, starting what came to be known as the International Bargaining Forum (IBF). Talks started in December 1999, and in July 2000, both sides signed a contract agreeing that the TCC rate would increase from USD 1200 by USD 50 per year until 2004 to a total of USD 1400, instead the rise taking place all at once. The agreement served as a pattern contract for TCC agreements with the ITF's national affiliates. National agreements could be slightly different providing the total labor costs remained the same.

Despite evident support among ITF affiliates for the idea of a global wage, the exact level of wage to push for remains contentious, and IMEC was able to exploit these differences during bargaining in late 2001. The emergence of China as a potential labor supplier to FOC shipping worried labor supplier unions, particularly those in Asian countries.[9] Tensions over the wage rate came to a head during negotiations in late 2001, when the Filipino union, the Associated Marine Officers' and Seamen's Union of the Philippines (AMOSUP), dissented from the ITF consensus. Although AMOSUP officials had agreed to the wage increase schedule in the year 2000 agreement, they now argued that the proposed rate increase placed Filipino seafarers at a competitive disadvantage relative to other labor supplying states, especially China (*Lloyd's List* 21 Dec 2001). As a result the FPC acceded to employer demands to defer the planned wage increase for a year, ensuring the continued support of labor supplier unions. Although some affiliates, such as the Danish ratings union, criticized the decision (*Lloyd's List* 14 Mar 2002), the ITF upheld the fragile consensus underpinning global wage bargaining (Anner *et al.* 2006).

Multi-employer negotiations continued to expand in 2003, when the Japanese shipowners,' represented by the International Mariners Management Association of Japan (IMMAJ) joined the talks as well, forming, together with IMEC, the Joint Negotiating Group (JNG). Additionally, IMEC membership doubled in 2003 from 40 firms to 80 (*Lloyd's List* 25 Feb 2005). While the new IMMAJ participants questioned the basis of the talks prior to beginning 2003 bargaining round, reiterating their belief that seafarers' pay should relate to the standard of living in a seafarers' country of origin (*Lloyd's List* 9 Sep 2003), in the end this appears to have been posturing. Out of the talks came a clear differentiation between the old "Blue Certificate" still issued by the ITF to non-IBF participants, and new "Green Certificate" now offered only to IBF participant companies.

While employers not involved in the talks continued to pay according to the 2000 and 2001 agreements (i.e. USD 1300 in 2003, and USD 1400 in 2004), IBF companies have more flexible agreements. "Green Certificate" agreements set the minimum total pay packages for "model" crews, allowing the shipowner some flexibility in negotiating pay categories with national unions, as long as the total labor cost adds up to the ITF rate.[10] They allow shipowners to allocate a part of the pay package to crew training costs, and target a portion of the shipowners' contractual union contributions toward improving conditions for those particular shipowners' seafarers. The parties also agreed to a conflict resolution procedure to be used before undertaking industrial action against a ship owned by a JNG company.

The FPC has announced a benchmark increase from USD 1400 to USD 1550 for January 1, 2006, perhaps with the intention of driving yet more employers to the JNG for the next bargaining round (ITF Press Release 19 Apr 2005). In showing flexibility to its negotiating partners, the ITF has essentially shored up the position of the conciliatory employer fraction, presumably with the objective of encouraging more employers to join the JNG. Having employers in the association reduces the amount of effort involved in obtaining and monitoring contracts, allowing the ITF to concentrate its inspection efforts on uncooperative employers. The ITF also has more confidence that the terms of the contracts will be maintained over time (DeSombre forthcoming: 142).

Some employers have maintained that greater observance of ITF contract terms and convergence between ITF wage rates and market wages is because of more reasonable ITF demands. However, it is clear from the continued existence of extremely high shipboard/shore-side wage differentials (ISF 2001) that other forces are at work. Rather than becoming more moderate, the ITF has brought employers to the table by putting them under increasing labor cost pressure. The ITF standardized its TCC rate upward from the various lower rates negotiated by national affiliates in the late 1980s to USD 1000 in the early 1990s, and then increased it steadily prior to the advent multi-employer bargaining. On the other hand, it is clear that the ITF is now mainly interested in wage bargaining for FOC seafarers rather than putting FOC shipowners out of business, or finding a political way to end the FOC system. In this respect, ITF demands have become more "moderate" from the employers' perspective.

Wage Bargaining at the ILO

Parallel to the IBF bargaining system, the ILO also provides a context for global wage negotiations for seafarers in a sub-committee of the Joint

Maritime Commission (JMC). The formal basis for these negotiations is the ILO Seafarers' Wages, Hours of Work and the Manning of Ships Recommendation, 1996 (R187), updated from a 1946 recommendation of the same name. This wage determination machinery has been in operation since 1946, periodically revising upward the global minimum wage for seafarers. The ISF and various national shipowner groups, rather than IMEC and IMMAJ, represent the shipowners in these talks, while the union side is represented by the some of the same figures involved in the IBF discussions. JMC discussions, including the minimum wage mechanism, are bi-partite, between unions and employers, rather than tri-partite.

The ILO minimum wage is intended to be applicable to all seafarers within the scope of the recommendation, including those under national flags, although it is (perhaps deliberately) unclear as to its application on fishing vessels. Unlike with the ITF wage scale, where the Able Seaman wage is a reference point from which other job categories are scaled, the ILO negotiations only put a figure on the AB wage. In 1995, this was USD 385 per month base pay. This was raise to USD 435 in 1996, USD 465 in 2003, and USD 500 in 2005. To the "base pay" figure is added overtime pay, leave, and holidays, which, by JMC agreement, brings the 2005 total labor cost to USD 871 per month. This figure, rather than the USD 500 figure, is comparable to the ITF agreement labor cost figures.[11]

The wage determination machinery is based on an ILO recommendation rather than a convention, so its legal status is weak and ambiguous, and ILO member countries are not asked to ratify it. It serves mainly as a referent point for unions, employers and governments as to what constitutes a "fair" minimum wage. The Filipino government uses the ILO benchmark as a minimum wage for Philippines Overseas Employment Administration (POEA)[12] employment contracts, although it has not been updated since the year 2000 from the USD 385 figure. Both unions and shipowners find the ILO wage useful on some occasions, but have misgivings about its application by the other side. Prior to 2003, both the ITF and ISF had their own interpretations of what it meant in terms of actual pay packages with overtime and benefits included. Predictably, the ITF arrived at a higher figure than the ISF, and the lack of agreement made it even more difficult to apply the wage in practice. Since 2003, the ITF and ISF have both agreed on the total labor cost application of the figure.

The ISF puts forward the ILO wage as an alternative to the ITF contract rates, presenting it as more legitimate since it has a least *some* legal basis. The ILO rate is regularly referred to by shipowners who feel under pressure to pay ITF rates, but have not yet come to terms with the idea of negotiating with the ITF. For example, both the Danish and the Japanese shipowners' groups, immediately prior to joining the JNG, extolled the virtues of ILO wage rates, in statements explaining why they had no intention to join the JNG (*Lloyd's List* 15 May 2003; 19 Sep 2003). Of course, the ISF rejects uniform global pay scales on principle in any case, asserting that pay should depend on the cost of living in the seafarer's home country. Shifts and inconsistencies in the employer position on the ILO minimum wage reflect different capital strategies for dealing with ITF pressure.

The ITF views the ILO rate as an appropriate minimum only for national flag shipping, and presumably only on shipping flying the flags of developing countries. As a rule there is little point for the ITF to enforce it on FOC shipping through industrial action, since if it is possible for the ITF to obtain a contract, the ITF might as well apply its own higher pay rate. However, there has been some discussion of enforcing ILO rates on national flag shipping under certain circumstances. This has not yet become ITF policy, however, probably because of the difficulty of achieving internal consensus (ITF 1998a). Although not systematically enforced by the ITF or anyone else, the ITF has fallen back on ILO minimums in special cases.

GLOBAL EMPLOYERS' ASSOCIATIONS

Peak associations now represent capital and labor in wage bargaining at the global level. The most important international employers' associations dealing with employment issues are the International Shipping Federation (ISF), the International Maritime Employers' Committee (IMEC), and the International Mariners Management Association of Japan (IMMAJ). The ISF is part of the International Chamber of Shipping, which represents shipping politically at the global level. IMEC and the ISF are closely associated, to the point of sharing office space and staff. Although the ISF "bargains" with the ITF in the tripartite ILO context over ILO minimum wage rates and other maritime employment standards, it is careful to make the distinction between this, and actual wage bargaining. Despite interest by some affiliates, there is no consensus within the ISF that it should have a bargaining mandate. IMEC's and IMMAJ's members are shipowners and ship management companies. IMEC's and IMMAJ's members represent a small (though growing) subset of the membership of ISF member organizations. IMEC and IMMAJ's structures differ from the ISF's in that companies join directly, while the ISF is a federation of national employer federations. IMEC, IMMAJ and some national shipowners' associations coordinate their bargaining vis-à-vis the ITF in the Joint Negotiating Group (JNG).

THE NORTH-SOUTH DIVIDE AND THE ITF

The ITF is governed by its affiliates and shifts in the interests of ITF affiliates have implications for ITF strategy (Koch-Baumgarten 1998; 1999). Collective bargaining coordination at the global level is complicated by large differences in wage expectations between unions from capital and labor supplier countries. Employers and some unions use the discourse of North-South conflict over jobs to undermine efforts at global standards and union labor market control. Underlying this discourse is the assumption that developed country unions have superior power resources, and are using these to impose high wages and labor rights standards on developing country workers and unions. According to this way of thinking, high wages and labor rights standards are not to be in the interest of the developing country unions and workers (Hensman 2001). In the FOC campaign, the North-South conflict over jobs is reflected in the division between capital and labor supplier country unions. Koch-Baumgarten (1998), for example, portrays the FOC campaign as a vehicle by which unions in industrialized capital supplier countries impose high wage norms on unions and seafarers from developing labor supplier countries. These later, she presumes, would prefer lower wage norms, in order to better exploit their comparative advantage.

However, the FOC campaign is by no means simply a device by capital supplier country unions to protect their jobs from low wage competition. Labor supplier country unions have also come to see union control of the global labor market as important for reducing competition between developing labor supplier countries. Labor supplier country ITF affiliates have an interest in excluding new market entrants, and the FOC campaign allows them the possibility to do this. Furthermore, most of the campaign's industrial leverage is generated by countries in the "Global North," without which, labor supply country unions would have no way to impose ITF agreements on employers. The ITF is very restrained in the extent to which it protects the jobs of capital supplier country union members. Instead, significant financial side-payments through the FOC campaign financial system ensure a political consensus in support of the campaign even among unions losing jobs and members as a result of FOCs. Labor supply country unions also benefit from these side payments, as they frequently end up administering ITF contracts as well.

Unions from capital supplier countries tend to be relatively influential within the ITF, but with dwindling membership rolls threatening their influence. These countries continue to supply significant numbers of seafarers, both domestically and internationally, but do not present the ITF with a bargaining problem because of high wage expectations. In the FPC, they tend to push for a higher benchmark wage.

The most important suppliers of maritime labor to the international labor market are India, Latvia, the Philippines, Poland, Russia, Sri Lanka and the Ukraine. The bargaining freedom of ITF affiliates from these countries is severely circumscribed by ITF policy. There is a well-developed market for labor working under ITF-acceptable contracts, and to supply seafarers to that market, these unions must comply with ITF policy. Although labor supply unions tend to argue for moderation in ITF wage demands, they also depend on the FOC campaign system more than unions from capital supplier countries. New labor market entrants such as China and Indonesia threaten the position of established labor supply countries, moving the interests of unions from these countries closer to those of the capital supplier country unions.

Table 3.2 shows the major countries supplying labor to the international seafaring labor market. [13] Unions from capital supplier countries and from established labor supplier countries are invested in maintaining FOC campaign structures and wage norms. Emerging labor suppliers, on the other hand, present a problem for FOC campaign strategy. The ITF seeks, if possible, to integrate these seafarers into the bargaining structures, or, if not, to exclude them from competing with seafarers under ITF contract.

Port unions have always been the backbone of the Flag of Convenience campaign. Without their active participation, the ITF would have no leverage, few resources, and there would probably be no ITF agreements on FOC ships. The campaign's strategies and goals have been influenced by the demands of dockworkers and the frames needed to mobilize them. Port unions have come under increasingly intense attack from employers and governments starting in the late 1980s and early 1990s. As Chapter Four shows, port unions have found FOC campaign structures useful in their own fight against privatization, deregulation, and de-unionization in ports. However, port unions have no consistent structural interest in the politics of FOC campaign bargaining.

THE FINANCIAL SYSTEM

The ITF financial system ensures that maritime unions have a steady incentive to support the campaign, by funneling money to unions who hold the representation rights to seafarers on FOC ships. Employers with ITF agreements pay their seafarers' dues to the ITF affiliate concerned, and pay a fee to the ITF Seafarers' International Assistance, Welfare and Protection Fund. Employer contributions to the ITF essentially pay for the Flag

Table 3.2: Labor Supply of Seafarers by Country

	2000 ratings	2000 officers	%world total ratings	% world total officers
Established Labor Suppliers				
Philippines	241129	52089	27.98	12.54
India	30375	12930	3.53	3.11
Russia	27588	19898	3.20	4.79
Poland	6500	5445	0.75	1.31
Latvia	8136	6108	0.94	1.47
Ukraine	13859	24000	1.61	5.78
Sub-Total			38.01	29
New Entrants				
Indonesia	83934	16334	9.74	3.93
China	58597	30570	6.80	7.36
Sri Lanka	7384	500	0.86	0.12
Sub-Total			17.4	11.41
Established Capital Suppliers				
USA	24525	20524	2.85	4.94
Greece	15335	22000	1.78	5.30
Norway	7540	8850	0.88	2.13
Japan	15164	23778	1.76	5.72
United Kingdom	10649	11000	1.24	2.65
Sub-Total			8.51	20.74
World Totals	861666	415397		

Source: BIMCO/ISF (2000).

of Convenience campaign, and are also used to finance the ITF Seafarers Trust, which gives grants to seafarers' welfare groups, and to researchers working on issues related to seafarer welfare. The ITF assigns the right to represent seafarers based on the beneficial ownership of the ship, the national origin of the crew, or on which union took industrial action to obtain the contract. Unions from the country of beneficial ownership have first priority. If a union from this country does not obtain a contract, the union crewing the ship has the right. Finally, if a contract is obtained through industrial action, the union conducting the industrial action has the right for one year, if it wants to claim it. Employer contributions to ITF affiliates are supposed to be used to finance benefit schemes for FOC seafarers. Some affiliates have become extremely dependant on FOC campaign related revenues. Unions in the global North have used them to preserve their organizations in the face of declining members. Some, but not all, of these also use campaign funds to provide representation and benefit services for their FOC members. The Norwegian Seamen's Union (NSU) and the All-Japan Seamen's Union (AJSU), for example, provide service to non-domiciled seafarers under NSU and AJSU contracts, although these seafarers do not have full voting rights in these unions (JSU website; NSU video).

There have been allegations that officials of certain unions in both the global North and the global South have diverted funds for personal financial benefit. Some North American ITF affiliates administer ITF contracts through an offshore "union" called the Union of International Seafarers (UIS), based in the Cayman Islands (Northup and Scrase 1996). This in itself is not evidence of malfeasance, as there are good legal reasons for keeping FOC campaign activities outside the jurisdiction of the often anti-labor United States legal system. In any case, US law does not allow US unions to administer ITF agreements. While it is not clear whether or not the funds in the UIS go to legitimate union purposes, the past associations of some participating unions with gangsterism do not inspire confidence.[14] Furthermore, the UIS's predecessor, the IMU (International Maritime Union), was referred to as a for-profit undertaking by its founder, former National Maritime Union president Shannon Wall. Wall unsuccessfully advertised the IMU as a "large and lucrative" venture to attract the participation of other seafaring unions (*Journal of Commerce* 31 May 1990). While there is no direct evidence of criminality, the unions involved also do not widely advertise the UIS system.

Similarly, many in maritime circles express doubts about certain labor supplier unions. Although it is not clear how, seafaring ITF affiliate union leaders in the Philippines and India are alleged to have become very wealthy as a result of the FOC campaign. The ITF has pressured these unions to show that benefit programs exist. In recent years, these unions have created or expanded their seafarer benefit programs, including hospitals, pension funds, and career development.

Occasional battles over who is entitled to "bargain" over which ship underline the importance to seafaring unions of being allocated "bargaining rights" for FOC crews. For example, when the Cypriot ITF affiliate attempted to claim bargaining rights for certain Cyprus-flagged FOC vessels, other affiliates objected. Because genuine national tonnage operates under national flag rules, some shipowners tried to claim Cypriot nationality, in order to be allowed to pay the lower Cypriot wages.[15] In this, they were abetted by the Cypriot affiliate, which signed national agreements with these shipowners.[16] The issue resulted in a meeting of seafarer unions from Russia, Greece, Sweden, Latvia, Estonia, Germany, Israel, and Cyprus, i.e. for the most part those unions with claims to the bargaining rights, and dues, from Cypriot FOC contracts (*Lloyd's List* 9 May 1998).[17] The dispute highlights the nature of seafaring unions' interest in the FOC campaign: although the ITF Secretariat certainly focuses on improving the wages and conditions of seafarers, many affiliates are primarily interested in how contracts are allocated.

THE FLAG GAME AND THE DELINEATION OF LABOR MARKET BOUNDARIES

ITF bargaining strategy seeks to limit wage-base competition between three distinct, though interrelated, maritime labor submarkets, using targeted industrial action and other means to support these distinctions. The FOC campaign is focused around bargaining for FOC seafarers, and leaves seafarers under flags which the ITF has labeled as "national flags" to affiliate unions to apply national standards. This means that seafarers on ships which have not been declared FOC can earn much more or much less than FOC seafarers depending on which flag they are sailing under. It allows the ITF to bargain significantly higher than "market" based wages for the "offshored" internationally competitive market segments, while not directly impinging on the jurisdictional authority of national affiliates. It also means that the declaration of a flag as FOC by the FPC has important economic (as well as sometimes political) implications for unions, employers and governments. The three labor submarkets are:

1) **Industrialized country flags:** This labor market consists of seafarers working on vessels under the flags of traditional maritime nations. These ships are well regulated. Seafarers on these ships have traditionally been

well trained, well paid, and covered by national union collective agreements. Because of high costs, these fleets are under intense competitive pressure, and have declined in size. Where high wage conditions still apply, it is usually because of government policies to maintain a national flag fleet, or because of unusually effective trade union activity.[18]

2) **International flags:** This labor market consists of seafarers working on ships under FOC and international second register flags, such as the NIS (Norwegian International Ship Register). Employers in this market have few or no nationality based hiring restrictions, and commonly hire from low- or mid-wage maritime labor supplier countries. ITF strategy for the FOC and international register submarket is to ensure that employers pay seafarers at rates equivalent to or exceeding the Total Crew Cost (TCC) standard (USD 1400 as of 2004 for an AB, due to rise to USD 1550 in 2006, but slightly less for IBF employers).

3) **Developing country flags:** When the shipowner, ship, and seafarer share the same nationality, wages are determined by national rather than international standards. The ILO minimum wage for seafarers (USD 500 per month in 2005) sets down an international standard, but is not strictly enforced. Depending on seafarer wage expectations and the strength of national unions, national employers can sometimes pay lower wages than FOC shipowners. Competition with the FOC sector, however, is limited by the lack of capital in these countries.

The ostensible goal of the ITF campaign is to prevent ships from moving from markets (1) and (3), i.e. national flags, to market (2), i.e. FOCs. In reality, most campaign activity focuses on supporting bargaining in the FOC labor market, and very little on preventing ships from changing flags. However, the ITF does sometimes use the threat of declaring a national flag or company fleet as FOC as leverage to gain union recognition, or to motivate a government to ratify ILO conventions. National unions seek to influence whether their own flag (or sometimes someone else's flag) is declared FOC. Depending on the situation and the affiliate's strategy, a national union may lobby within the ITF for or against having its own register declared FOC.

The Athens Policy and the High-Standard Labor Market

As a concession to the formally declared campaign objectives, and to unions capable of maintaining regional standards, ITF policy sanctions the enforcement of geographically distinct labor markets by affiliates. The ITF's

Athens Policy maintains that vessels engaged in international ferry service should provide employment standards equivalent to one or the other of the countries they service. If a ferry sails between Germany and Sweden, for example, workers on that ferry should be paid according to either German or Swedish standards, regardless of the seafarers' national origin. Unions in Finland, Sweden, and to a lesser extent Denmark, have used the Athens policy to justify boycotts of vessels paying international wage levels. These include vessels flagged in the NIS, the Baltic States, or FOC vessels with or without ITF agreements. The unions also interpret the definition of "ferry" expansively, to mean, "any vessel engaged in regular trade." Through enforcement of the Athens policy, Baltic Sea shipping continues to have a relatively high proportion of nationally flagged ships from high wage countries.

With or without the Athens Policy, national trade unions maintain the distinctiveness of market #1. Depending on the situation, they may use industrial action or political lobbying to protect their employment. This has not been very successful overall, but there are exceptions. The potential for jurisdictional conflict among affiliates limits what the ITF can do in this regard. For example, the Finnish Seamen's Union (SMU) has consistently pushed low-cost competitors out of the Finnish market by asking Finnish dockworkers to refuse to unload their ships. As a result, Finland is one of the few countries to have retained a relatively high proportion of its seafaring employment to the present without drastic labor cost concessions (Finnish Maritime Administration 1993; 1999).[19]

Over the past years, the Finnish unions' secondary boycott tactics have brought them into conflict with ESCO, an Estonian based company using Estonian labor to undercut other Baltic short-sea shipping companies. Although the SMU was reasonably successful at driving ESCO from certain routes on its own, it followed up in the ITF Fair Practices Committee by trying to have Estonia declared an FOC register, on the basis of a substantial Norwegian stake in ESCO. The previously independent Estonian seafaring unions joined the ITF, preventing the Finnish unions from using ITF organized sanctions to further damage ESCO, and their prospects for providing jobs to their members (*Baltic New Service* various issues).

In another example, from 1995 to 1997 US unions attempted to prevent American President Lines (APL) from flagging out some US-flagged vessels. Initially, negotiations occurred between APL and several US seafaring unions. Only when APL announced that the flagged out ships would not have ITF collective agreements did the ITF intervene, threatening APL with boycotts by ITF docker affiliates. APL and the US unions resolved the issue by agreeing that some APL ships would remain under US flag in a subsidy program. The ITF limited its assistance to ensuring that ITF standards were maintained, but not preventing the reflagging per se (*Journal of Commerce* 21 July 1995). In 1997, APL was acquired by the Singaporean Neptune Orient Lines (NOL), casting doubt as to what the beneficial ownership of APL should be considered under the ITF jurisdictional boundaries (ITF 1998a). Despite its foreign ownership as of 2005, APL continues to keep some of its vessels under US flag with US collective agreements on protected cabotage routes.

International Flags

ITF strategy for the FOC and international register submarket is to ensure that seafarer pay equals or exceeds the Total Crew Cost (TCC) standard (USD 1400 in 2005 for an AB). Maintaining this wage standard depends on delineating the FOC market from the developing country labor market. Ideally, the ITF treats a vessel as FOC when its beneficial ownership and control "lie elsewhere than in the country of the flag the vessel is flying." As can be seen from the ESCO and APL cases, in the era of transnational corporations, beneficial ownership does not always provide clear guidance. Beneficial ownership and control are not always the same thing, and many shipping companies have operations and assets all over the world.

In most cases, however, the identification of FOC shipping is straightforward. The ITF identifies FOC ships by declaring entire flags as FOC when they meet certain criteria. All ships in that register are then treated as FOCs by default. The FPC labels registers as FOC if it finds they are used primarily to register ships of shipowners not resident in the country in question. The views of the ITF affiliates concerned are taken into consideration. The ITF also looks at the ability and willingness of the flag state to implement international standards, the ratification and enforcement of ILO conventions, and the safety and environmental record as revealed by Port State Control inspections (ITF 1998a: 54). There is often a large gray area in the application of the rules, leaving opportunities for political considerations play a role, as the declaration of a register or vessel as a FOC can have a significant effect on inter-union job politics. Employers and FOC countries will often disagree with the ITF's assessment. For reasons of national image, and because it can make their shipping register less attractive to shipowners, some countries do not wish to be labeled as FOCs. Employers also attempt to exploit ambiguities and inconsistencies in the FOC campaign system to gain national flag status for their ships, so as to be allowed to pay lower national flag rates. See Appendix A for a list of registers labeled as FOCs by the ITF in 2005.

Whether or not a particular company or ship ends up designated as FOC and paying ITF wages depends in part on the strength of ITF port affiliates in the ship's area of operations. In October, 1998, for example, dockers in Naantali, Finland boycotted a Russian flag ship with a Russian crew, owned by White Sea and Onega Shipping Co., a Russian firm, claiming that it was an FOC. The company owned about 110 general cargo vessels, about 30 of which were registered through Cyprus, an FOC registry. Cyprus registry made it possible for the company to raise money by issuing bonds from German banks, but the ships were then leased back to Russia, flew the Russian flag, and paid their seafarers Russian wages. In other words, the ship had two flags: one to show the banks, and another to show the ITF. At the time of the boycott, White Sea was in the process of shifting the ship in question from the eastern Mediterranean, where the ITF is relatively weak, to the Baltic, where it is very strong, giving the ITF the leverage to declare the vessel FOC and force the owner to pay the higher rate despite the ambiguity (*Journal of Commerce* 16 October 1998)

International Second Registers

Traditional maritime nations which have changed their regulations to make them more similar to Flag of Convenience registers, and attract back flagged-out vessels also present a thorny problem for FOC campaign strategy. These do not fit under the beneficial ownership conditions of FOCs, yet their cost structures allow them to compete on similar terms to FOC shipping. The FPC decides on a case-by-case basis which second registers to declare FOC, based in large part on the opinion of the national affiliate or affiliates, but also taking into consideration the details of the legislation under which the second register is created, and the conditions on the second register ships. The German and French second registers have been labeled FOC, as have some UK overseas territories (which actually function more like FOCs than second registers anyway). Many Danish ships have been labeled FOC, although the register itself has not been, while the Norwegian and Japanese second registers are not considered FOCs.

Second registers generally involve tax concessions, and, most importantly, have looser employment restrictions, often allowing the employment of foreign workers at international wages for some or all job categories. They combine loose employment regulation with the stricter safety and environmental regulation characteristic of traditional maritime countries. In essences, second registers allow employers to select a regulatory regime which saves on labor costs and taxation, but does not attract higher insurance costs and unwanted attention from Port State Control, as under-regulated registers tend to do (DeSombre forthcoming). Second registers present opportunities for shipowners and governments to cut deals with some or all of their national unions, and possibly drive a wedge in the ITF wage coalition. In particular, where ship officers have separate representation, they have sometimes been more supportive of the second register concept than ratings unions. This is because they are less likely to lose jobs as a result, and often receive explicit employment protection in the second register legislation. Since one of the main purposes behind second registers is to allow employment of cheaper ratings on national flag vessels, ratings unions have taken a more skeptical view.

In the case of the Norwegian International Ship Register, Norwegian unions work together with unions from the seafarers' country of origin to represent seafarers on Norwegian shipping. There are separate collective agreements under Norwegian law applying to Indian and Filipino seafarers, for example, with different (i.e. lower) wages and conditions than Norwegian seafarers. The Norwegian Seaman's Union's has an incentive to maximize employment under the NIS flag because it can collect dues from non-domiciled seafarers. This fuels a tendency to accept slightly lower wage rates than ITF norms for NIS shipping.[20]

On the other hand, in the legislation behind the Danish International Shipping Register (DIS), established in 1988, does not allow Danish unions to represent seafarers who are not resident in Denmark. Only unions from the home countries of the seafarers in question are allowed to negotiate and provide representation on their behalf. The Danish unions and the ITF maintain that in practical terms this violates ILO Convention 87: Freedom of Association and Protection of the Right to Organize, and ILO Convention 98: Right to Organize and Collective Bargaining, since the right to representation is entirely theoretical. The Danish ratings union, is which is a department of SiD, the Danish General Workers Union, has opposed the DIS vociferously. The Danish officers unions agree with SiD in principle. However, they have not been seriously engaged in the political campaign to change the law. In particular, within the ITF context, they argued against the ITF's proposed solution of declaring Denmark a Flag of Convenience. The fact that SiD's membership has been much more affected by flagging out and the DIS than have the officers' unions perhaps explains the difference in positions. Matters came to a head when in 2003, when after many years of negotiating with the Danish government, an effort to change the DIS law failed in Parliament. The FPC threatened to declare Denmark an FOC unless a way could be found to allow Danish unions to represent workers on Danish ships. After talks in early 2004 failed to bring a satisfactory result, the ITF declared that while the DIS would not be made into an FOC registry, certain Danish ships would be declared FOC.

Unions in some countries, including Sweden, Germany, and France, have unambiguously opposed the introduction of second registers. Swedish unions cite the examples of Norway and Denmark, where, they claim domestic seafaring employment continued to decline despite the return of some ships to those flags. No second register has been introduced in Sweden. The German union (the ÖTV, now merged with other unions into ver.di) fought the introduction of a second register in the courts on the basis that it allows non-domiciled seafarers to be paid less than German seafarers. The union claims this violates the principle of equality under law, but eventually lost this case in the Federal Constitutional Court (ÖTV 1998). With the blessing of the ÖTV the FPC declared the German international register a FOC. In comparison to the Norwegian and Danish second registers, the German second register has failed to attract back much German owned FOC shipping, perhaps because of its FOC status. When France introduced a second register in 2005, the French unions opposed it vociferously. The FPC wasted little time in declaring it FOC shortly after its introduction. In the German and French cases, the ITF affiliates concerned were united in their opposition of the second register. In Germany, ver.di represents in principle all German seafarers, although at the time of the political battle, ratings were represented by the ÖTV, while some officers were represented by the white collar DAG (*Deutsche Angestellten-Gewerkschaft*).

LOW STANDARD NATIONAL FLAGS

The ITF strategy of segmenting the labor market satisfies the political requirements of ITF affiliates, in that affiliates are allowed to pursue national job protection where feasible (to defend market #1). In drawing on ITF resources, however, affiliates are limited to defending the standards in market #2. Market #3 was not widely regarded as a major competitive threat in the original design of ITF strategy. The FOC campaign has not systematically targeted Market #3, although the potential for developing country fleets to grow at the expense of higher standard competitors, and even potentially ITF-agreement carrying vessels, is recognized (ITF 1998a). The ease with which anonymous capital can be shifted around and the difficulty of pin-pointing the national origin of the increasingly important transport TNCs complicate the issue further.

There is a potentially serious conflict between the ITF's politically necessary strategy of leaving national flag shipping alone, and bargaining higher wages for FOC seafarers. Among its affiliates, however, the ITF does not have a clear policy mandate to launch a systematic campaign for enforcing a global minimum wage on non-FOC shipping, where there is a clear connection between the beneficial owner, flag state, and crew. Furthermore, it is not clear that the ITF has the industrial strength to do this in the face of political opposition from the rest of the global shipping industry (ITF 1998a: 22–23). On FOCs, there is generally no ITF affiliate from the country of registration with a realistic claim to represent crews on FOC shipping. For national flag shipping, there often is an ITF affiliate union, which may in some cases be complicit in agreeing to concessionary rates of pay to obtain or retain jobs. So far, the solution for the ITF has been to continue its ambiguous commitment to the ILO wage rate, and pursue other political avenues for tightening maritime labor markets, such as improved skill standard enforcement.

CONCLUSION

FOC campaign bargaining strategy reflects both the political realities of global inter-union relations, as well as the economic and industrial logic of union bargaining leverage in the maritime labor market. Outside maritime shipping, with a few rare and relatively insignificant exceptions, employers have not conceded to engage in serious transnational bargaining. As is shown in Chapter Seven, global framework agreements, European Social Dialogue and the European "coordination rule" represent limited advances in this direction, but each approach has weaknesses related to the inability of unions to coordinate their demands, and the lack of union power resources to wrest substantive concessions from employers.

Hyman (2001: 174–175) suggests that unions should focus their transnational objectives on developing internal capacities, rather than on bringing employers to the table for negotiations that are unlikely to produce concrete results. This is exactly what the ITF has done. ITF strategy encouraged centralized bargaining, but not through concessions or emphasizing integrative bargaining; instead of offering carrots, the ITF concentrated on developing its stick. This has had negative consequences for integrative bargaining, but these appear not to have been serious or long lasting. The ISF, for example, called off integrative negotiations (on piracy and skill certification, among other issues) in 1997 because of ITF industrial action. The ITF did not, however, forswear industrial action to gain an ISF presence at the bargaining table. Watering down ITF strategy to bring employers to the table would have been counterproductive because it would have reduced ITF leverage, which in the long term would have reduced rather than increased employer incentives to bargain.

Despite the setback of the 1980s, by the end of the 1990s, the ITF emerged as a substantial player in the global labor market for seafarers.

The reasons for this have already been alluded to: the growth of the inspector network, increased commitment of affiliates to campaign activities, and the standardization of TCC contracts. All these point to a transnationalization of union structure and strategy. In particular, the ITF Secretariat has assumed more resources and authority, either through specific delegation by affiliates or through the independent growth of transnational structures because of the increasing requirements put on them. This has allowed for the development of a more globally inclusive bargaining strategy, incorporating the interests of established labor supplier countries, further strengthening and globalizing the campaign.

Many ITF seafaring affiliates have little or no independent bargaining strength, or if they do, they do not have the reach to affect FOC shipping. Only through global collective action can they organize this sector, allowing the ITF, *de facto,* to wield considerable policy influence. Key to the bargaining coalition is a consensus by affiliates on the TCC wage. This required the reframing of the FOC issue from one of protection of union jobs in rich countries to one of establishing global collective bargaining structures for the benefit of all working seafarers. It also helps considerably that the FOC campaign's financial arrangements funnel money to participating seafaring unions, in part compensating for dues shortfalls from job losses suffered by some affiliates.

Sisson and Marginson's analysis (2002: 213–214) suggests that the speed with which bargaining trans-nationalization takes place can vary by industrial sectors. Evidence from FOC campaign bargaining supports this contention. ITF strategy was clearly important to the development of global bargaining, but this strategy depended on conditions present in maritime shipping, namely the declining ability of national unions to influence labor markets independently, and the nature of ITF industrial leverage. Nonetheless, regardless of industry, it is becoming more difficult for unions adequately to represent workers producing for global product markets using nationally bounded bargaining strategies. Typically, unionists accept employer arguments that wage disparities are inviolably linked to national norms, so that it is counterproductive or even impossible to equalize wages cross-nationally. The FOC campaign shows, however, that given the right conditions transnational bargaining can overcome the forces causing cross-national wage disparity and avoid a global "race to the bottom."

Chapter Four
Transnational Union Networks and Enforcement[1]

Enforcement is a thorny problem for any global labor rights implementation system. The strength of labor as a global actor, and the labor movement's ability to play an important role in global governance, depend on the construction of transnational class capacities. In practice, the construction of transnational class capacities means the construction of global and transnational union structures capable exerting pressure on transnational capital. An essential component of FOC campaign success is the enforcement of union contracts through transnational structures for worker mobilization, contract monitoring and seafarer representation.

Under the auspices of the Flag of Convenience campaign, maritime unions have developed transnational global structures which exploit interdependencies in transportation production chains by leveraging union strength in one part of the chain, ports, to further the interest workers in another part of the chain, on board ships at sea. The basic tactic is the ship boycott by port workers,[2] performed at the point when a ship attempts to load, unload, or exit a port. Because time spent in port is expensive for ship owners, this is effective. The ITF's enforcement strategy highlights the power-resource building nature of seemingly altruistic solidarity, and the ways in which solidarity can be reframed to counter new transnational capitalist strategies of worker alienation as these develop. Port unions, tied together by the ITF's inspector network, provide the main power resource on which the ITF's global bargaining and political strategies are based.

Maritime cargo transport on ships and cargo handling in ports are interdependent aspects of the same production process. Seafarers work on seagoing ships, which, due to the FOC system of ship registration and transnational recruitment, are to a large extent disembedded from any unified national regulatory or social context. As described in Chapter Two, national seafaring unions in the developed world have been in decline since the 1950s due to the growth of FOCs. In contrast, dock workers are generally thoroughly embedded in local social and political contexts, and have a high degree of industrial leverage because of their position in the production process. However, the increasing vertical concentration of maritime capital has fuelled an impetus for greater managerial control over all links in the transport production chain, including ports. The assault on dock workers' working conditions manifests itself somewhat differently than that on seafarers—instead of shifting labor sources to circumvent nationally based labor organization, employers have attacked labor organizations and mobilizing capacities directly. The ITF connects the struggles of seafarers and port workers through union networks and coordinated industrial action. Seafaring unions draw on the industrial leverage of port workers to negotiate minimum standard pay agreements, while dock unions leverage the growing influence of the ITF to thwart union busting in ports.

This chapter will show how capital has strategically exploited globalization by transnationalizing the work process in ways which alienate workers and undermine their organizations, and how class conflict on the shop floor is shaped by this within the transport industry. It will then show how the different manifestations of globalization in different maritime industry segments have produced different challenges for transnational union structures. The ITF's development of a transnational union network of ship inspectors will be described. Finally the ways in which seafaring unions and dock unions use these ITF structures to regain control of labor markets and work processes will be analyzed.

GLOBALIZATION AS AN EMPLOYER STRATEGY OF ALIENATION

Globalization restructures industrial processes, and thereby creates new and differently formed political spaces of contestation (Amoore 2002). These new spaces, at least initially, are less amenable to worker resistance—if nothing else because one motivating factor in capital's restructuring along transnational lines is to reduce the capacity of workers to resist. As Wennerlind (2001) shows in his analysis of alienation, capital strategically adopts social and technological innovations to protect its ability to extract surplus value. A variety of devices, including restructuring manufacturing processes (Braverman 1974), new technology (Marglin 1974), and so on are deployed to regulate the level and means of alienation of workers from their product, depending on the circumstances, and the specific manifestations of worker resistance. Geographical strategies, such as moving investment, dividing production chains spatially to optimize the characteristics of workforces involved in specific production tasks (Herod 1992), or "off-shoring" to deregulated political spaces, can be regarded as components of capital's repertoire of alienation strategies.

Nationally organized labor unions evolved to suite the geography of production and political economy of the international nation state system (Cox 1987). Globalization is in part a capitalist strategy specifically designed to reduce labor's capacity for resistance by undermining and circumventing this national basis of organization. The outcome has been the fragmentation of national industrial relations systems, bargaining structures, and trade union organizations. The shift to a global stage ensures that current union structures are unsuited to effectively organizing and channeling worker resistance. While union structures are not static, substantial barriers exist to union restructuring along transnational lines (Ramsay 1997), so that current configurations are not necessarily suited to building industrial strength through solidarity (Lillie and Martinez Lucio 2004). Translation of capital's new vulnerabilities into actual leverage for worker representation requires the restructuring of union organizations and the adoption of new strategies along lines dictated by the new logic of production. The specific nature of these structures and strategies therefore depends on the logic of production and the opportunities for contestation within each industry (Anner *et al.* 2006).

The specific ways in which transport has restructured along global lines, in part driving and in part driven by the globalization of production in other sectors, impact the strategies of transport workers and unions. Cargo transport is a key sector for organized labor because it links other sectors. Militant labor organizations in transport allow the strategic exertion of leverage in dependant and connected processes (James and James 1963). Transport workers, and especially dock workers, often find themselves in a position to undertake direct solidarity actions in support of other workers, and not infrequently actually do so. In particular dock workers are well known for their ability to organize effective shop floor action (Turnbull, Morris and Sapsford 1996), although other transport sectors have above-average levels of industrial militancy as well (Silver 2003: 97–102).

Maritime capital works at various levels to undermine, circumvent, or outright challenge the control of transport workers over their production processes, and limit their capacity to act in solidarity with other workers. The movement of ships to FOC registers, and increasing direct attacks on port unions can be seen as aspects of capital's counter strategy. Geographic movements and organizational restructuring to undermine labor's capacity to resist are long established strategies (Cowie 1999), and not inherently connected to the current phase of globalization. However, globalization extends the contest to a wider stage, providing both capital and organized labor with new sets of opportunities and constraints, as well as new organizational imperatives in terms of structure and strategy.

GLOBAL LABOR MARKETS AND THE DISPLACEMENT OF NATIONAL SEAFARING UNION STRUCTURE

The move to global labor sourcing reduces the capacity of seafarers to organize and resist. The global institutional infrastructure which has developed to hire ship crews from low wage seafaring labor supply countries for work anywhere in the world, has a strong coercive aspect—as ship crews can be quickly replaced. Globalization of labor sourcing, and the disconnection of shipping from legal spaces to which unions have regularized institutional access, dictate the structure of the new transnational union networks. Structures for industrial action must extend to those areas where industrial leverage is high, and these should be combined with and connected to representational structures which are effective in the places where seafarers work. Ideally, these structures should also be present in the places where they live when they are between jobs and when they are being trained and recruited. Union representatives must be able to act locally in the rapid time scales prevalent in the shipping industry—there is little point in union representation which is unable to get to a ship which may only be in port several hours[3]—and local action must be consistent with and embedded in a global strategy. As a result of the need for new transnational structures and forms of action, nationally based seafaring unions have been sidelined by the transnational network based around the ITF.

PORTS RESTRUCTURING AND GLOBALIZATION

Capital in ports is in a very different situation, being to a large extent fixed and within the territories of nation states. Ports cannot shift themselves away from national labor regulation, unions and shore-based communities so easily. Rather, port based capital has been obliged to fight it out in spaces where labor is capable of mounting effective resistance. Despite the difficulties, the concentration of capital in fewer and larger global firms, often vertically integrated into multiple transportation chain links, has provided both the motive and opportunity to reduce the influence of port unions. Before the 1980s, the structure of relations between ports, shipping lines, and shippers interfered with initiatives to break dock unions and change the highly unionized labor relations systems in ports. Port unions could rely on divisions between the interests of relatively smaller and fragmented shipping lines, shippers, stevedoring companies and governments to pressure ports to come to a quick settlement. Fragmented shipping interests found it too difficult and expensive for port workers to remain on strike, and too easy to settle and pass the increased labor costs on to port customers.

Changes in the structure of the shipping industry over the past two decades mean the larger transnational shipping companies of today have a vested interest in shifting the balance of power in ports, because passing on the costs has become more difficult. Some giant shipping liner firms such as P&O Nedlloyd have transformed into vertically integrated logistics companies, through the acquisition of cargo handling facilities. Alternately, cargo handling firms such as the Seattle-based Stevedoring Services of America (SSA) or the Singaporean PSA have expanded globally but horizontally, remaining specialized in the operation of port facilities (*Containerisation International* Mar 1999: 99–101). Furthermore, the new emphasis on logistics, including "door-to-door" delivery in some firms, has created an imperative for greater managerial control in all production nodes (Robinson 2002), and a lower tolerance for the effects of industrial action in ports. For labor, the news is not all bad, however. To the extent that labor can act transnationally, the new globally integrated companies are in some ways *more* vulnerable than they were in the past, because any local dispute can quickly become a liability to tightly integrated operations around the globe.

The rapid and total workforce replacement by presumably compliant workers from developing countries seen on many FOC ships has not been possible in ports. Instead, maritime capital has had to take advantage of the resources available in each particular national and local context to challenge dock union power. For example in Santos, Brazil, the port users and the port authority, Cosdep, have long wanted to reduce the size of the workforce, and introduce new work rules (*Containerisation International* Jun 1995: 95–97). In 2001, a combination of competition from smaller newly expanded Brazilian container ports, self-loading by some liner companies, and a greater collective spirit among port employers and port users enabled the port to take on the unions and win a two week strike (*Lloyd's List* 5 Apr 2001). Similar stories can be told about New Zealand (Green 1996) and the Bangladeshi port of Chittagong (*Lloyd's List* 19 Mar 1997; 10 July 2001), where Stevedoring Services of America helped provide the backing needed to take on the power of the dock unions. SSA is also thought to be the most influential actor within the Pacific Maritime Association (PMA), behind the 2002 drive to break the coast-wide contract with the union on the US West Coast (*Pacific Business Journal* 18 Sep 2002). In Marseilles, port employers endured long strikes to win concessions, with the explicit backing of the port users' association (*Lloyd's List* 18 July 1994). In the Indian ports of Mumbai and Chennai as well as in Colombo in Sri Lanka, P&O Ports took on local unions to push through unpopular (with the workers) privatization plans (*Lloyd's List* 2 July 2002; 29 Feb 1997). Global maritime capital is now more ready to get behind port employers who take on dock unions creating "local" problems for them. Dock unions, however, have responded by building up their international linkages. Although dock unions' international linkages have an existence and logic of their own, they are also closely linked to FOC campaign strategy. Production processes and increasingly common threats from common employers make construction of solidarity along the production chain an important strategy.

THE ITF'S ROLE: THE INSPECTORATE

As has been shown, maritime unions, both on ships and in ports, have come under attack, and successful resistance has required globally coordinated union action. Because of this, the role of the ITF, as a coordinator and mediator between national unions, as a distributor of strategic information, as a center of a global union network, and as a union actor in its own right, has increased over time. The ITF's presence on the ground is ensured by the FOC campaign's own power resource—the ITF ship inspector network. The network provides the power basis for imposing collective negotiations on shipowners. Although conceived as an FOC campaign resource, the inspectorate directly, as well as indirectly through ITF influence with shipowners, also provides port unions with leverage.

The purpose of the ITF inspector network is to obtain and enforce collective bargaining agreements (CBAs) on FOC ships. There are 105 ITF inspectors and coordinators listed as "full time,"[4] who monitor compliance with ITF contracts, coordinate industrial action against ships without contracts, and assist seafarers in distress. Though formally employed by their local or national unions, inspectors are in fact answerable to the Secretariat.[5] When an FOC ship visits a port, it may receive a visit from an inspector. If the ship has an approved ITF CBA, the inspector will talk to the crew and check the payroll to ensure standards are being maintained. If it does not have a CBA, the inspector will attempt to obtain one, using persuasion and the threat of industrial action by port workers (Northup and Rowan 1983; Northup and Scrase 1996). The ITF "Actions Unit" in London provides advice and support for industrial action, including information on ships and ship owners, such as past movements, disputes with the ITF, and agreements signed (ITF FCR various years).

Today's inspectorate is the result of a 30-year development process, during which it has changed to reflect the global and transnational structure of the industry. The inspectorate has developed along three distinct, though related, dimensions. First, the inspectorate has expanded geographically, from its core in countries with very strong labor movements, to include most of Europe, North America, Japan, and more recently many developing and formerly state socialist countries (ITF FCR various years; ITF ROA various years Northup and Rowan 1983; Northup and Scrase 1996). Second, it has become more transnational, so that policies are uniform and centrally coordinated. Information about agreements, actions, and vessels is now instantly available to individual inspectors (Lee 1997). Third, the inspectorate has become more professional, so that inspectors are skilled in mobilizing port workers, in negotiating with ship owners, and in implementing uniform procedures. There is accountability to the ITF for job performance, measured, among other things, in terms of contracts obtained relative to the difficulty in obtaining contracts in that inspector's port.

When the FOC campaign began in 1948, it was conducted without any formal transnational structures. Industrial and political action took place, but entirely through national unions. Throughout the 50s and 60s, unions agreed from time to time on global FOC boycott actions, none of which had permanent impact (Northup and Rowan 1983; Metaxas 1985). In a 1971 meeting of the FPC, some unions asserted the campaign, as it had been conducted, had failed utterly. Only an insignificant number of FOC vessels operated under ITF contracts, and the FOC fleet continued to grow. ITF affiliates committed to appointing inspectors responsible for enforcing the ITF minimum wage level for seafarers on FOC vessels (Johnsson 1996: 44–51; Koch-Baumgarten 1999: 448).[6] With this renewal, unions in Australia, Finland, Israel, Sweden, and the United Kingdom began conducting boycotts of FOC vessels regularly. Employers reported occasional boycotts and ship inspections in Belgium, Canada, Denmark, France, Germany, Italy, the Netherlands, New Zealand, Norway, and Spain (Northup and Rowan 1983: Appendix B). Throughout the 1970s, Australia, Finland, Sweden, and the UK formed the backbone of the campaign's industrial strength (Northup and Rowan 1983: Appendix B; Johnsson 1996).

ITF industrial action during the 1970s remained uncoordinated and unsystematic. ITF affiliates in Australia, Finland and Sweden used the most effective methods, monitoring the maritime press to discover ships not covered by ITF contracts. In Finland and Sweden, most ship boycott activity was (and still is) legal, and nearly 100% successful. In Australia, the legal situation has never been clear, but effective boycott activity occurred consistently nonetheless. In the UK, despite the cooperation of the dockworkers in observing boycotts, lack of systematic methods meant that ships without ITF agreements could sneak in and out of port, though they certainly risked a boycott if caught. As in Australia, ship boycotts were not always clearly legal (or illegal), but ship owners were generally compelled by circumstances to seek a negotiated settlement before the legality of the boycott could be tested (Northup and Rowan 1983: Appendix B).

FOC campaign structure during the 1970s, however, remained substantially national rather than transnational in character. Although ITF records indicate a large number of inspectors in various countries, it is not clear that all these inspectors really undertook substantial FOC campaign work (ITF ROA various years). Accounts of ITF boycotts and inspector activities indicate inconsistency in what ITF affiliates and inspectors tried to accomplish. On the one hand, the number of vessels under ITF contract rose consistently throughout the period, both as an absolute number and as a percentage of the rapidly growing FOC fleet (see Chapter Three). On the other hand, not all FOC campaign actions had the objective of obtaining ITF contracts at consistent wage levels. On some occasions, ITF actions only backed up industrial action by the seafarers themselves, settling for whatever the seafarers were willing to accept (usually less than ITF rates).[7] On occasion, boycott activity aimed at replacing the FOC crew with a national one of seafarers from the boycotting country (Harrigan 1984).

There was also a lack of follow up to ensure that ITF wages continued to be paid after the boycott was finished. Problems occurred in remitting back pay obtained through boycott action to seafarers. Once seafarers returned home, they were frequently blacklisted. Employers sometimes attempted to recover ITF pay through legal (or illegal) means, and there was no way to protect seafarers from this.[8] An ITF inspector relates:

> In the early 1980s, ship inspections started taking place [in the United States], but the inspections were not well managed, or coordinated. Everybody just did what they could, and didn't understand the consequences. Action against ships did not always work out well for the seafarers because there was no way to follow up. It wasn't organized.

Despite its geographical limitations and lack of coordination, the FOC industrial campaign grew in strength and effectiveness through the 1970s. By the 1980s, ship owners clearly considered the ITF a threat to their operations, even if not resigned to complying with ITF demands. In 1982, the International Shipping Federation began coordinating employer responses (Northup and Rowan 1983; Johnsson 1996). The ISF noted that most of the campaign's leverage derived from secondary action in relatively few countries. The ISF attempted to weaken this leverage by challenging the legality of boycotts in test cases where the ITF was "set up" to take action on the borderline of legality. In the UK, in the early 1980s, changes introduced by Thatcher altered the industrial relations landscape to make secondary action unfeasible. In Australia, Finland and Sweden, however, ship owners' efforts failed to change the situation, except briefly in Sweden in the early 1990s (Northup and Rowan 1983; Northup and Scrase 1996). By the end of the 1980s, however, in terms of the number of ITF approved CBAs on FOC vessels, the FOC campaign looked to be in a state of serious decline (Lillie 2004: 53; Chapter Three).

This decline, however, turned around during the 1990s, as a result of improvements in geographical coverage and coordination in the inspector network, which began in the early 80s, and continued in the 1990s. In 1983, the ITF appointed inspectors in Japan. In 1986, the ITF appointed several inspectors from US unions on the East Coast. With the affiliation of the International Longshore and Warehouse Union (ILWU) in 1988, the inspector network expanded to the West Coast as well (*Journal of Commerce* 26 Dec 1995). Through the 1990s, the ITF also expanded the number of ITF inspectors in previously underrepresented regions, including Poland, Russia, India, South Africa, and South America. In Europe, the traditional bastion of ITF support, industrial action now occurs in many more countries than before.

Appendix B shows the deployment of ITF inspectors. Broadly, major changes to the ITF inspector system since the 1970s reveal that: 1) The campaign is less geographically Europe-centered, although Europe is still overrepresented. 2) More labor supply countries now have inspectors. 3) More developing countries, including countries with only a small maritime labor market presence, now have inspectors. 4) Major trade routes are now all covered, with the notable exception being the Middle Eastern end of oil tanker routes to the Middle East. 5) Aside from the Middle East, and large parts of Africa, there are no longer any major world regions completely free of ITF action.

The geographical growth in support, and, in particular the increase in support from unions in developing and labor supplier countries indicates a major strategic effort on the part of the ITF Secretariat to include unions from those countries actively in the campaign. Continuing geographic imbalances in inspector deployment and campaign participation are a weakness. In many ports, however, the political and industrial situation is such that an inspector would not be able to accomplish much anyway. The deployment of an ITF inspector in a particular port is therefore an indication of at least a minimal level of commitment to the campaign. There are apparently some exceptions, where inspectors exist purely for political reasons. However, the most important changes (such as the appointment of inspectors in India) represent legitimate and real expansions of FOC campaign activity. The significance of these changes (aside for the obvious increase in organizational effectiveness) is that they show a transnationalization and globalization of campaign goals. In the 1970s, the campaign was largely driven by North-South competition for employment. Nowadays, however, labor-supplier countries have demonstrated a significant commitment to monitoring global wage norms. Also, the expansion into strategically important areas (such as trans-Pacific routes) suggests an autonomous strategy at the global level.

The inspector network exists in continued tension between the need for global systems and procedures, and local requirements for flexibility. Every port has a different legal, industrial and political situation, meaning that each inspector faces a different set of opportunities and constraints on his or her ability to mobilize support. If ship inspections and boycotts are legally and institutionally supported the inspector's job is easier. In Finland, for example, an inspector can successfully rely on institutional channels for mobilizing boycotts, because permissive industrial legislation protects workers in their action. A Finnish dock union official states: "It [the FOC campaign] is not controversial, and the stevedoring companies have accepted the boycott practice. Finnish boycott actions are always successful." On the other hand, if secondary industrial action is legally constrained the inspector needs a more subtle approach. In the USA, an inspector cannot always legally order a boycott, and has to find other ways to pressure ship owners. One US inspector relates that, "in some countries, like Norway and Finland, they can stop a ship just because it has no labor agreement. We need more reason here; we have to look for discrepancies between conditions and existing employment contracts."

ITF inspectors are officially employed by their affiliate union, but are supervised by and answerable to the ITF Secretariat. They maintain contacts with local port and seafaring unions, and, to work effectively, must rise as much as possible above these unions' rivalries and disagreements. They also cooperate with unions not affiliated to the ITF, such as independent unions, or unions belonging to other Global Union Federations. Although there are often disputes between maritime unions, in some cases the ITF inspector is able to smooth these over for FOC campaign purposes. The differences in ITF effectiveness from port to port are not just legal, but also relate to the attitudes of dockworkers and their local unions. A German ship inspector notes:

> In Germany, the port workers are conservative. It is easier to stop a ship in Scandinavia. This is because the dockworkers are more eager to boycott, not because of any legal differences. . . . In Rostock [in the east of Germany], it is less easy [than in the other German ports] to get a ship boycott together, because the port does not get as many ships, and the dockworkers are reluctant to lose business.

Industrial factors, such as which sort of goods are being transported, how easily the transportation can be disrupted, and tightness of the transportation timetable, also play a role. Just-in-time production and integrated logistics mean that employers can ill-afford disruptions. It can be a problem for the ITF if a particular facility is not unionized, or even if it is just inaccessible. Tankers, for example, can be difficult to access because they do not generally use conventional port quays. Small, geographically isolated port facilities also provide opportunities for ship owners to sneak in and out without an inspection, even in areas where the ITF is otherwise strong.

The ITF inspector network is crucial to making the FOC industrial campaign work, by providing the infrastructure with which the ITF connects global strategy with local tactics. Prior to the growth of the inspectorate, transnational union cooperation in maritime was more similar to that in other industries where, whenever a transnational action of any substance is contemplated, unions generally start from a position of little knowledge about their counterparts in other countries. New contacts need to be made, repertoires devised, and conflicts of interest negotiated. The legal situation for secondary action may be unclear, and the unions will most likely have to conduct research, or just use trial and error, to discover a company's vulnerabilities (Greven and Russo 2003). The ITF resolves these issues by having inspectors who are simultaneously local union officials and global activists. ITF policies and methods can be decided collectively by the affiliates in London and implemented by the Secretariat through its own channels without revisiting political disagreements between affiliates each time a transnational action is contemplated.

INSPECTORS AND ITF BARGAINING STRENGTH

For seafaring unions, the main purpose of the inspector network has been to obtain and to monitor ITF agreements on FOC ships. The inspector network's increasing effectiveness is evidenced in the steady growth in the number of ships under contract throughout the 1990s, as well as the increasing degree to which shipowners have felt the need to engage the ITF in global level bargaining. As described in Chapter Three, under pressure from the ITF's expanded inspector network, some shipowners began to the see the benefits of a negotiated relationship with the ITF. Organizing to bargain collectively has been and continues to be a contentious issue among shipowner associations, so the continuing effectiveness of the ITF inspectorate is important in keeping up union pressure on shipowners. Furthermore, as with the employers, the ITF has its own internal disagreements. Given the diversity of ITF affiliates around the world, central policy implementation by the inspector network is critical for consistency in implementing the ITF's labor market segmentation policy, because the ITF must be sure that the same categories of vessels are labeled FOC by all the ITF's affiliates, and that vessels with ITF agreements are not boycotted by national unions applying inconsistent standards.

PORT UNIONS IN THE FOC CAMPAIGN

Port unions have found FOC campaign structures useful in their own struggle against deregulation and de-unionization. Unlike seafaring unions, dock unions did not decide to create an inspector network and empower the ITF to more effectively defend against deregulation. Rather, because of their participation, the inspector network and the growing influence of the ITF in the industry have redefined their possibilities for transnational action. Specifically, the FOC campaign provides dock unions with 1) resources for combating the world-wide push by shipping companies to introduce self-handling, 2) opportunities for direct solidarity assistance during strikes and contract negotiations. Although, in principle, dock unions could create transnational networks and global capabilities independently of the FOC campaign (and some have), there is no point (except for those unions seeking to act outside the ITF for one reason or another), because the FOC campaign provides a functional global network for them to access.

In comparison with shipboard industrial relations, in ports the impact of globalization is varied. There is a locally and temporally specific aspect to port union industrial strength which allows them to exert significant leverage through purely localized action, if the appropriate repertoires of contention are in place (Turnbull, Morris and Sapsford 1996). Competition between union locals exists, and is significant under some circumstances (Bertzbach and Mujkanociv 1997), but in many cases transnational union relations are not affected by it—in particular when industrial factors do not place unions in competition, but instead provide opportunities for complementary solidarity (Lillie and Martinez Lucio 2004).

Northup and Rowan (1979; 1983), and Northup and Scrase (1996), in their largely descriptive accounts, see dock union FOC campaign participation as dependant on industrial legislation. Where it is legal, as in Scandinavia, dock unions will engage in secondary industrial action, and where it is (usually) illegal, as in the United States, they will not. Northup and Scrase (1996), however, note that on the US West Coast, longshoremen appear to conduct FOC campaign actions on a regular basis, and seem to get away with it. The authors, however, have no explanation except that ship owners are not aggressive enough in seeking injunctions (Northup and Scrase 1996). Koch-Baumgarten, in her international relations based regime-theory analysis of the FOC campaign, does not differentiate between the dock unions and seafaring unions from a given country. Koch-Baumgarten's analysis implicitly assumes that union interests are nationally rather than organizationally structured. Dock unions in industrialized countries participate to keep seafaring jobs at home. Furthermore, dock and seafaring unions from the global North conspire together to protect their jobs against seafarers from the global South (Koch-Baumgarten 1998).

Neither Northup, Rowan and Scrase's accounts, nor Koch-Baumgarten's explanation provide a realistic analysis of union behavior. Unions do not necessarily indulge in solidarity actions just because they are legal (or refuse solidarity actions just because they are illegal). Dock unions do not automatically support seafaring unions just because they are from the same country. Dock unions have interests of their own, which cannot be aggregated by country, or automatically lumped together with the interests of seafaring unions. Sometimes unions from the same country have bitter conflicts, raid each others' jurisdictions, and even cross each other's picket lines. On the other hand, many dock unions have close partnerships with foreign unions: the long association between the North American International Longshore and Warehouse Union (ILWU), the Maritime Union of Australia (MUA) and the Japanese Zenkoku is one example (ILWU 1996). To understand why some dock unions participate enthusiastically in the campaign, while others do not, or why participation in general has increased over time, requires a more complex understanding of multi-level inter-union cooperation between dockers and seafarers.

The most important way in which dock unions support each other and seafarers is via secondary industrial action, or the threat of secondary industrial action. Concerning domestic inter-union cooperation, David Walsh notes that despite occasional competition, unions tend to cooperate with one another because they are part of the same broad social movement, share structurally common interests, and a common set of norms. Unions depend on one another for resources, but resource dependence tends to be episodic. During periods of conflict with an employer, a union will suddenly have a greatly increased need for financial resources, solidarity actions, and information from other unions. At these times, the union involved in the conflict will not necessarily be able to provide resources in exchange. Unions build networks and develop norms for mutual support so that assistance will be available when needed, even when it is not possible to reciprocate (Walsh 1994: 13).

Maintaining such mutual support relationships on the international level is more difficult than on the national level, and many unions do not find it worthwhile. Historically, international ties between unions have not usually been strong enough to mobilize useful solidarity on short notice. Harvie Ramsay notes that one of the major problems unions encounter when asking for international solidarity is that by the time the need for such solidarity is evident, it is too late to develop the long term relationships solidarity implies (Ramsay 1997). The FOC campaign provides dock unions with just this sort of well-functioning global network, and thereby ensures the maintenance of strong ties between times of crisis. In this sense, dock union participation in the FOC campaign is a result of an organizational interest in maintaining the resources to resist globalization, liberalization and de-unionization in the port industry.

DOCK WORKER SOLIDARITY AS AN EXOGENOUS VARIABLE

Dock union interests explain why FOC campaign participation has increased, but do not explain why a base of support existed in the first place. Workers and unions are not generally willing to engage in solidaristic secondary industrial action at the drop of a hat. Many dock unions are different from the norm in this respect, and this provides the basis of solidarity on which the ITF has expanded. Seafaring and dock union solidarity predates the FOC campaign and the inspector network. However, ITF strategy and framing turned this sporadic and often localized solidarity into a useful tool supporting global bargaining for seafarers and opposing the degradation of work on the docks. Reconstruction of inter-union solidarity along transnational lines resulted from a labor union political project, although building on existing resources.

Dockers usually have a strong sense of union history and continuity, and are imbedded in complex inter-connected industrial processes. Historical and sociological works on dock unions point to an amalgam of workplace and community structure based explanations for this. Turnbull, Woolfson and Kelly look at dock unions in the UK before the Thatcher administration broke their power in the mid-1980s. They show that the

tactical repertoire of contention of UK dock unions derived from a collective self-defense adaptation to the industrial logic of dock work: strong
solidaristic norms produced material gains, and shored up dock union
organizational strength. For Turnbull, Woolfson and Kelly, dock union militancy arises out of a strategic worker response to the industrial conditions
peculiar to dock work (Turnbull, Woolfson and Kelly 1992: 7).

Wellman arrives at a similar explanation for militancy on the US
West Coast docks, showing that the militant culture of the ILWU dockers
is a source of shop floor strength. The ILWU dock workers form a tight-
knit union community, with their own vocabulary, norms and mythology
(Wellman 1995). Both Turnbull, Woolfson and Kelly and Wellman note
that the ability of dockers to organize quick, informal work stoppages
on the slightest provocation is a very flexible power resource. Turnbull,
Woolfson and Kelly note that in many ports, the rumor that dockers had
walked off the job on one job site could quickly cause the whole port
to shut down (Turnbull, Woolfson and Kelly 1992). Wellman relates
that ILWU dockers would often use spurious safety complaints to justify
quick, informal job actions to resolve shop-floor disputes with management (Wellman 1995). Turnbull and Sapsford show that the quick resort
to industrial action is characteristic of dock workers in many ports worldwide (Turnbull and Sapsford 2001). However, industrial conditions alone
do not always produce militancy. As Turnbull, Morris and Sapsford show,
even within the UK, strike propensity varies greatly from port to port,
suggesting that the characteristics of local workplaces or perhaps local
communities influence the militancy level at a given worksite (Turnbull,
Morris and Sapsford 1996).

The collectivism of the dockers is not based on disinterested altruism,
but rather on enlightened self-interest. Because of their strong solidaristic
norms, their organizations are powerful. Because their organizations are
powerful, their material interests are well represented. Militancy serves the
economic interests of dock workers, which undoubtedly serves to shore up
the organizational stability of dock unions. Kimeldorf observes "It is with
the promise of delivering these [economic] goods that unions are born.
Whether they endure, however, depends not only on how well they deliver
on their economic promise, but also on the socially constructed meanings
that in the course of history come to be attached to the union, its mission, and its leadership." (Kimeldorf 1988: 166) Although the collectivism
of dock workers serves economic purposes, it fits logically into a broader
non-economic normative system. The power of the dock workers' militant
value system lies in its moral integrity as much as in its utility. If its integrity is violated, the utility disappears as well. The normative framework of

militant syndicalism has implications for dock worker solidarity vis-à-vis other groups of workers. It cannot simply be turned on and off according to the dictates of the collective egoistic self-interest of the dock workers.

In many ways, the recent reinvigoration of the FOC campaign can be considered a revival of a historical tradition of mutual support between dockers and seafarers. The ITF itself was created in 1896 out of international efforts to coordinate organizing activities by dock workers and seafarers in northern Europe. ITF led efforts at international organizing of dockers and seafarers in the North Sea prior to World War I proved effective enough to force employers to respond by forming the International Shipping Federation (which was then fairly successful at putting an end to effective international union cooperation) (Marsh and Ryan 1989; Snedden 1957). The Flag of Convenience campaign began in the 1940s and 50s, a time when many dockers had once been seafarers, who had come ashore when they decided to settle down. According to Kimeldorf, the militant traditions of dock workers on the US West Coast came from seafarers and loggers, who were selectively recruited to work on the docks (Kimeldorf 1988: 24). Union histories are replete with examples of solidarity between dock workers and seafarers from this period (see, for example, Beasley 1996; ILWU 1996; Marsh and Ryan 1989; Schwartz, 1986).

In many countries, seafarers and dockers are organized in the same union, or share other organizational linkages. The Maritime Union of Australia (MUA) includes seafarers and dockers, the German ver.di[9] covers transport workers including both dockers and seafarers, and the American International Longshore Association (ILA) has an autonomous section for Masters, Mates and Pilots (the IOMMP), to name some examples. Local and national linkages are sometime a source of solidarity. Finnish dock workers, under the AKT (Transport Workers' Union), for example, generally give the SMU (Finnish Seaman's Union) whatever support it asks for, without asking for anything specific in return. On the other hand, the German ÖTV (now merged into ver.di) has had difficulty in mobilizing its dockers to support ÖTV seafarers, even though they are members of the same union.[10] Inter-union conflicts sometimes interfere with FOC campaign boycotts or other solidarity actions; in particular the exclusion of the *French Confédération Générale du Travail* (CGT) dockers from the ITF creates problems. Non-membership in the ITF does not rule out FOC campaign participation. The Swedish Dockworkers' Union (SDU) is not an ITF member, and there is considerable animosity between it and the minority *Landsorganisationen-* affiliated Swedish dock workers' union. However, the SDU supports FOC campaign boycotts and other solidarity activities when asked by Swedish ITF inspectors or by the LO-affiliated Swedish Seafarers' Union.

The usefulness of dock union militancy in producing industrial leverage for seafaring and port unions in the current context is the result of ITF strategy and framing. The FOC campaign, while no doubt benefiting from close local and national docker-seafarer relations at times, has systematized and regularized cooperation at the global level. Whether or not localized solidarity develops "organically" out of the conditions of work, the advent of FOCs, and now port restructuring has required the redefinition of solidarity along new lines, in order to maintain, or regain, union strength under a new industrial structure. ITF strategy has de-nationalized the docker-seafarer relationship by creating an active global forum for inter-union relations. Since the ITF is global in scope, FOC campaign structures conform better to unions' contemporary needs to project influence on a larger scale in the face of global shipping and port companies.

PORT UNIONS STRUGGLE WITH DEREGULATION

With exceptions such as the UK and New Zealand, where port reform started in the 1980s, most efforts at deregulation and de-unionization of ports started in the 1990s. According to the Dockers' Section Report on Activities, despite continuing technologically motivated reductions in dock employment through the 1980s, "the industry has escaped the current trend towards privatization which affects many of the ITF's industrial sections." (ITF ROA 1986: 75) However, at the 1990 ITF Congress, the ITF Dockers' Section noted "a number of massive attacks by port employers on dockers' established working conditions and employment security systems." (ITF 1990: 67) By 1994, it was clear that a systematic, global process was at work, including outright attacks on union rights in many places, unfavorable deregulation, and potentially problematic (from the unions' perspective) privatizations (ITF 1994: 69)

In the late 1980s, with proposals for port liberalization being floated in many countries, dock unions sensed the threat, and began the lengthy processes of building stronger linkages with the seafarers and with each other. In 1986, the Dockers' Section voted to hold its annual meeting in conjunction with the FPC to facilitate communication of solidarity requests. In 1987, at the request of the dockers the FPC passed a resolution stating that seafarers should not cooperate when non-union labor was used to handle their ships, and that seafarer affiliates should assist dockers in the event of a labor dispute. In 1989, again on request from the dockers the FPC passed a policy statement restricting the use of self-unloading vessels so that seafarers would not "carry out cargo handling work normally performed by dock workers." (ITF 1990: 68) Although the Dockers' Section and FPC passed resolutions, they were not broadly implemented by seafaring affiliates,[11] and the inspectorate was not sufficiently developed at that point to implement them independently.

CARGO HANDLING BY SEAFARERS

Cargo handling by seafarers is part of an attempt by employers to expand the offshore deregulated space in which maritime work can take place. Generally, the work of seafarers relates to the navigation and maintenance of ships, while dock workers are charged with their loading and unloading. There is, however a 'gray area' of tasks in the loading and unloading of ships that might be charged either to seafarers or dockers. This gray area is partly defined functionally, but since it is also a matter of union jurisdiction, safety regulation, and immigration policy, the issue has become politicized. Employers seek as much flexibility as possible in who might perform a given task—ideally defining a wide number of tasks as potentially performed by labor employed under FOC conditions. Unions, in general, have sought to preserve their jurisdictions by preventing seafarers from performing work traditionally assigned to dockers. During the 1990s, cargo handling by seafarers became a major dock union issue, as some shipowners began systematically to use seafarers for this work. Although large scale replacement of dockers is probably not practical, substitution can occur at strategic moments, such as during strikes.

The ITF role in self-loading has been defined by the natural links to FOC campaign issues. At the 1994 Congress, the Dockers' Section reported that, based on an ITF survey, incidents of seafarers performing work traditionally assigned to dockers had increased significantly. Because this was more a problem of FOCs than anything else, the FPC approved a clause for inclusion in all ITF CBAs on FOC ships stating that seafarers should not be penalized for refusing to perform dock work (ITF 1994: 73). On the global and regional political level, the ITF seeks to engender a consensus against self-loading in international law, because international law shapes and influences the legitimacy of national laws on cargo handling. One example has been the fight over the EU Ports Directive on Market Access, which, among other things, would have permitted self handling in EU ports. The Directive was defeated in an historic battle in the European Parliament after heavy union lobbying against it (*Lloyd's List* 20 Nov 2003). The European Commission has now resurrected it, although no doubt it will become contentious again if no compromise is found on crucial cargo handling language. National and international legislation can support or undermine union jurisdictional definitions and safety rules on self-handling in collective agreements with port employers and shipping lines. In this way, port workers are directly involved in the struggle to define the borders of the offshore institution.

The ITF inspectorate attends to actual implementation of self-handling restrictions, because the monitoring system relies on educating rank and file dock workers to monitor port operators and shipping lines to ensure that port union jurisdiction is not violated, and to take steps to stop self-loading when needed. Consistent violation of the ITF position on cargo-handling by certain companies becomes a matter of concern for the ITF Secretariat. The Secretariat pressures these firms at the global level to change their policies, and coordinates global action against them if they do not (*Lloyd's List* 21 July 2000; 15 Aug 2000).

DIRECT SECRETARIAT INVOLVEMENT IN STRIKES AND CONTRACT NEGOTIATIONS

Dock unions have sometimes leveraged ITF resources during difficult contract negotiations and for support during industrial disputes. This chapter will focus on two examples: the 1998 Australian dock workers' lockout, and the 2002 ILWU contract negotiations and lockout on the US Pacific coast.

In 1998, the Australian Howard government attempted to break the Maritime Union of Australia. The ITF helped define the terms of the conflict by ensuring that it was Patrick Stevedores, an Australian firm, and not the much more powerful P&O Ports which secretly partnered with the Howard government in a conspiracy to break the union. P&O Ports also had an interest in breaking the MUA, and deeper pockets to take the inevitable losses from a strike. However, P&O Ports had its parent company, P&O Nedlloyd, to consider. P&O Nedlloyd, with its global fleet of ships, was vulnerable to ITF boycotts, and consequently, eager to avoid a confrontation (Trinca and Davis 2000: 35). After a long struggle which took on national importance, the MUA forced the Howard government and Patrick to come to terms, although they made some concessions in their renegotiated contracts (*Containerisation International* Jun 2000: 68–69).

In a similar conflict, in the United States in 2002, the International Longshore and Warehouse Union (ILWU) came under attack from the US West Coast port employers' association, the Pacific Maritime Association (PMA). During contract negotiations the ILWU leadership suspected the PMA intended to incite the ILWU into industrial action, in order to provide a cover for government intervention in favor of the employers. In an unusual step, ITF general secretary David Cockroft sat in on part of the negotiations, to demonstrate ITF backing for the ILWU. ITF affiliates pressured representatives of PMA shipping lines in their own countries (*Lloyd's List* 19 Sept 2002; 7 Oct 2002). After the failure of some bizarre political and legal maneuvering, and several months of negotiation, the PMA signed a contract which kept the coast-wide bargaining system intact (*Logistics Management* 1 Nov 2002; 1 Jan 2003). How much leverage the ILWU gained from support by ITF affiliates is not clear, although it was probably a factor in closing out extreme options to break the ILWU, such as militarizing the docks.[12]

LEFT-WING ALTERNATIVES TO THE ITF

An account of the role of dock workers in the FOC campaign would not be complete without some discussion of divisions within the international dockworkers' movement. Although the ITF is clearly the strongest and most representative organization for seafarers and dock workers, the continuing legacy of Cold War anti-communist politics and a recent surge of transnational syndicalism have caused divisions within and among transport unions which are reflected in international union politics. These developments have justifiably attracted a good deal of academic attention. Some academics have portrayed the rank and file activism on the docks as a model for the "new internationalism" of the global labor movement (see Waterman 1998, for example). This overstates the case greatly. While there are lessons to be learned from rank and file internationalism on the docks, this activism occurs in the context of a global union network dominated by professional union staff, focused around the ITF Dockers' Section and the Flag of Convenience campaign. Nonetheless, transnational rank and file networks have had a role in shaping ITF politics, and influencing the conduct of the FOC campaign.

The ITF, despite its use of militant shop floor tactics and its strong internationalism, remains solidly grounded in a conservative Anglo-American model of bread and butter unionism. ITF internationalism arose at the beginning of the 20th century out of the strategically motivated desire to control the entire seafaring and dock union labor market to bring international wages up to British standards (Marsh and Ryan 1989). In the period after WWII, the ITF aggressively pursued an anti-Communist political agenda (Rumpel 1998; Koch-Baumgarten 1999; Lewis 2004). As might be expected, many left-leaning unions found the strident anti-Communism of the ITF unacceptable. The global split between the anti-Communist International Confederation of Free Trade Unions, and the pro-Communist World Federation of Trade Unions (WFTU) coincided with a split between unions in the

ITF as well, with communist-sympathizing unions leaving, sometimes to find a home in the WFTU's Trade Departments. The ITF promoted anti-communist unions over more representative and popular unions, creating problems for ITF credibility in certain countries, which would last for decades. For example, when the French CGT left the ITF for the WFTU, the ITF promoted the much less representative *Force Ouvrière* in its stead (Lewis 2004: 48), fueling continuing conflict with the CGT, and interfering with efforts to build docker support for the FOC campaign in French ports.

In the Pacific, the most important dock unions, the US-Canadian ILWU, the Japanese Zenkoku, and the Australian Waterfront Workers Federation (WWF, now merged into the Maritime Union of Australia (MUA)) had substantial communist sympathies. Instead of associating with the ITF, they pursued their own brand of internationalism through their own network, loosely aligned with the communist WFTU. The WWF joined the ITF in 1973 (Beasley 1996). The ILWU followed in 1988, and Zenkoku in 1996. These unions retain their strongly syndicalist ideologies, bringing militant new voices to ITF forums. By their participation, they help shift FOC campaign goals and tactics to the left, and place dock union issues higher on agenda.[13] Independent left-wing syndicalist unions such as the Swedish Dockworkers Union (SDU), and the Spanish Coordinadora emerged in the 1970s. Many of these unions co-operate with the ITF in particular instances (by participating in ship boycotts, for example), but for a variety of reasons have been unable or unwilling to formally join the ITF.

Post-Cold War Syndicalism Emerges

International rank and file solidarity around two local dock disputes, the first at the Mersey docks in Liverpool, UK, and the second in Charleston, South Carolina, provided the catalysts to formalize a relationship between independent dockers' unions. The Liverpool dispute began when the Merseyside Docks and Harbour Company (MDHC) summarily dismissed its entire workforce and derecognized its union in November 1995, after a minor shop floor walk-out. Frustrated by tepid support from their national organization, the Transport and General Workers' Union (TGWU), the dockers turned to unions and dock workers in other countries for support in their campaign against MDHC. Apparent, the TGWU did not see the dispute as a winner, and rather than take the risks and spend the resources to fight it out, the union sought to bring it to a quick conclusion. The ITF felt constrained by the authority of the TGWU in matters dealing with TGWU members, and also kept a low profile. The Liverpool dockers saw themselves as betrayed by their union, a feeling which then extended to the ITF when it interfered with attempts to build direct rank and file transnational contacts with ITF affiliate unions in Europe (Lavalette and Kennedy 1996).

Without the sanction or support of the TGWU, rank and file workers from Liverpool traveled to the United States, Canada, Sweden, Belgium, France and Spain, among other places, to organize international support. Many of the unions they contacted undertook industrial action, causing substantial financial damage to shipping lines using Liverpool. Despite some notable successes, industrial action proved fairly sporadic, and the Liverpool dockers were not able to bring MDHC to terms. After two and a half years, the Liverpool dockers gave up the campaign and accepted a government subsidized severance package. The dispute left as a legacy a global transnational network of union officials and rank and file activists which would eventually be formalized as the International Dockworkers' Council (IDC) in July 2000. The membership of the IDC is listed in Appendix.

The Charleston dispute began in January 2000, when Nordana, a Danish-owned shipping line, tried to undermine International Longshore Association (ILA) jurisdiction by employing non-union dockers to unload its ships in Charleston harbor. ILA Local 1422 set up pickets. This prompted Charleston police to attack the pickets, and arrest eight dockers on minor charges. Although normally the dock workers would have been fined and released, the attorney general of South Carolina, Charlie Condon, intervened personally to charge five of the arrestee's with "rioting." According to the union, Condon took on the predominately black and politically left-wing ILA Local 1422 in hopes of bolstering his popularity in a bid for the governorship (*People's World Weekly* interview with ILA Local 1422 President Ken Riley, 24 Mar 2001).[14] As had happened in Liverpool, support from the ILA and ITF proved slow in coming.[15]

The IDC, on the other hand stepped in quickly, with financial and political support coming from the ILWU, and industrial action from the Spanish Coordinadora. Strong ILWU support for the so-called "Charleston 5," followed by a direct request by the ILWU to the ITF for help, embarrassed the ILA into establishing a legal defense fund (which never really got off the ground before the dispute was resolved). Although the ITF instructed the ILWU that all requests for ITF intervention should come through the ILA, the ILA leadership was now on the defensive for its inaction and could no longer refuse ITF help. The ITF quickly pressured Nordana into accepting a collective agreement with Local 1422 in April 2000, resolving the industrial issue. In November 2001, under increasing national and international political pressure from labor and human rights groups, the attorney general's office dropped all the major charges against the Charleston 5. Despite the surface antagonism and competition between the ITF and the

IDC, rank and file networks served to mobilize power resources for dock union interests in ways the ITF itself was politically incapable of doing, ultimately drawing the ITF into the conflict.

Although the ITF initially regarded the IDC as a threat to the unity of the international dockworker movement, and potentially to the FOC campaign, the organizations appear to have reached an understanding, at least in regards to practical work. The Charleston case shows that the ITF and the IDC exist both in tension and cooperation with one another. IDC networks were able to organize solidaristic support, despite the ITF's political constraints, and in the end were able to bring the ITF into the dispute despite the ILA's position. Clearly, it was in the ITF's interest to demonstrate its industrial muscle by pressuring Nordana, and, because of IDC pressure, it was able to overcome egotistical opposition by the ILA leadership. The IDC grew out of deficiencies in the ITF governance structure and the inability or unwillingness of some ITF affiliates to represent their members adequately. Its existence is a critique of the policies of certain ITF member unions, but not of the FOC campaign or the ITF Secretariat.

CONCLUSION

Over the years, the FOC campaign structure has changed from one driven by self-directed national unions forming a global coalition around loosely agreed political goals, to one of a tightly organized autonomous transnational network. The bellwether for its development has been the ITF inspector network, through which the ITF ties local unions and rank and file dock workers into global strategies designed around the industrial logic of bargaining in the maritime sector. Global unionism in maritime shipping functions differently from national unionism, in that it is organized on a looser, network basis, and reflects the need for rapid, consistent action under a wide variety of circumstances. By exploiting interdependencies inherent in the production process through the ship inspector network, unions have regained a measure of control over the maritime labor market. They have generated the power resources to raise wages, bring employers to the bargaining table, and to prompt efforts to re-regulate maritime industrial relations at the global level. The development of these capacities has not been automatic—rather it has required the restructuring of seafaring unionism on the global level, and the strategic reframing of seafaring and dock union interests in such as way as to promote practical solidarity between workers in different parts of the transportation chain. Globalization of seafaring labor markets and threats to port union integrity have enhanced the ability of the ITF to obtain the consensus of its affiliates around a transnational agenda because the Secretariat has constructed the campaign infrastructure in such a way that seafaring and dock unions depend on FOC campaign resources, and therefore lend it their support. This construction flows naturally from the logic of the production process, which ensures that transnational structures are needed to exert pressure on employers pursuing global strategies, and builds upon existing sources of leverage and traditions of solidarity.

Seen as simply a strategic element of capital's use of worker alienation to reduce worker control and extract surplus value, globalization in its varying manifestations is no different than any other social and technical restructuring of production. Deregulation through FOCs is not fundamentally different from deregulation through union busting within countries, or from capital mobility, when these are used as capital strategies to create spaces free of social regulation. New spaces of contestation exist even within the very fluid production processes globalization creates. However, as the FOC campaign demonstrates, radically new forms of worker organization are needed to take advantage of these new opportunities. For unions this is both an imaginative and technical challenge, in understanding what the appropriate new structures are, and an ideological and organizational one, in redefining who is worthy of solidarity and under what circumstances.

Chapter Five
Global Regulatory Politics and Skill Certification

The ITF's labor market strategy shapes union and shipowner political interests in industrial governance arenas. The varying impact of ITF strategy on shipowners fragments maritime capital into conciliatory and hard-line fractions, each with a different view on how to best respond. The conciliatory fraction seeks to contain the impact of the ITF through negotiation, extend regulation to those shipowners which have so far escaped it. The hard-line fraction seeks to undermine the ITF's power resources, and to oppose in political arenas the extension of effective regulation. Global labor standards and skill regulation serve to stabilize the labor market, and limit access to cheap under-qualified seafarers by shipowners pursuing cost-minimization based competitive strategies.[1] From the ITF's perspective, more effective regulation narrows the difference between the cost structures of unionized and non-union maritime employers, taking competitive pressure off the ITF's bargaining partners.

The ITF and ISF have pushed for enforceable regulation in the contexts of two UN-associated intergovernmental organizations, the International Labour Organization (ILO), which sets global labor standards, and the International Maritime Organization (IMO), which sets shipping safety and environmental protection standards. In the IMO, the labor market actors lobbied for updating the 1978 Standards of Training, Certification, and Watchkeeping (STCW) convention, which sets minimum qualification standards for seafarers, to include a chain of responsibility for monitoring skill standards, backstopped by port state enforcement. Known as STCW 95, the amendment came into full effect in 2002. In the ILO, the main effort has come in the form of a Consolidated Maritime Labour Convention (referred to hereinafter as CMLC) under negotiation since 2001 and scheduled to come up for a vote in 2006. If it passes, the CMLC will update and consolidate many current maritime labor conventions and recommendations applicable to seafarers, and add enforcement provisions backstopped by government inspections in ports. Chapter Five and 6 make a case that the global politics of shipping regulation is essentially the politics of global class conflict, intermediated through class based transnational representative institutions. Debates and outcomes in global political arenas reflect the labor market strategies of unions and shipowners, rather than the autonomous interests of sovereign states. International regimes and autonomous state interests influence and structure this class conflict to some extent, but the regulatory system is ultimately moving in the direction of conformity to the regulatory requirements of the transnational shipping industry.

BREAKDOWN OF NATIONAL INDUSTRIAL RELATIONS REGULATION

Industrial relations, both as a discipline and as an empirical practice, has been defined by coherent, parallel national systems. These neat and useful units of comparative analysis, however, are fragmenting as the transnationalization of production drives a transnationalization of industrial relations institutions and practices (Lillie and Martinez Lucio 2004). Collective bargaining and industrial relations are cohering at the global level, prompting the transnational labor market actors to exploit, and in doing so to shape, the shipping industry's global regulatory institutions and regimes.

Skill standards and certification in most industries have been a purely national affair, bound up in national industrial relations practice and education policy. Maritime shipping's skill certification system is exceptional in that the 1978 STCW convention ensured a degree of mutual recognition and harmonization of educational standards and certificates. Until the advent of STCW 95, however, mutual recognition meant *de-facto* deregulation of skill standards, rather than legitimate harmonization. In the context of the FOC system, mutual recognition without international monitoring of training institutions and certification processes created openings for unqualified seafarers to enter the industry. Despite the existence of uniform global skill standards, mutual recognition served simply to inhibit and undermine *any* kind of effective enforcement or monitoring by national governments interested in doing this. It is not clear yet to what extent STCW 95 has really changed this picture, but there is no doubt the intent of the agreement is to raise standards and reduce the number of unqualified seafarers on ships.

The growth of global standard setting occurs in reaction to threats to the accumulation process arising out of the weakness of global structures providing public goods. Examples of such threats to the accumulation process include undesired pre-emptive unilateral government regulation (such as US laws mandating double-hulled oil tankers), the threat of consumer boycott campaigns over sweatshop labor conditions (such as the Nike boycotts of the 1990s), or the depletion of needed natural resources. To gain allies in efforts to re-establish legitimacy, and to create barriers to market entry for low-standard shipowners, certain shipowners partnered with unions in supporting the CMLC and STCW 95.

Unions, of course, also stand to gain, perhaps more than shipowners, from global re-regulation. Through the CMLC, the ITF and some shipowners hope to create a uniform minimum labor cost structure (a "level playing field"), by ensuring that all shipowners must adhere to certain ILO standards. Likewise, maritime unions promoted STCW 95 in hope of setting boundaries to the labor market, and preventing competition from under-trained workers. In this way, labor standards and skill certification help buttress the ITF's global bargaining strategy by making it less likely for employers to seek new non-union sources of labor. For the maritime industry labor market actors, global regulatory policy is collective bargaining by other means.

THE GLOBAL MARITIME REGULATORY REGIME

The institutional infrastructure of the IMO, ILO, and the labor right/human rights regime, combined with the industry specific governance structure in maritime provide the terrain on which the conflict between labor and capital to shape the global governance system takes place. Flag states are expected to regulate the ships they flag, and to implement in legislation and enforce all relevant international conventions on their ships. A bevy of other institutions and actors participate in the formulation of maritime governance rules, and the implementation of governance into practice. The multiplicity of actors allows shipowners to play "corporate shell games," exploiting gaps in the system to avoid effective regulation (Alderton and Winchester 2002). The gaps mean that there is constant cost pressure to evade regulatory oversight, and maintain the lowest possible standards. Since the early 1980s, maritime accidents and other problems created by flag state negligence have prompted port states to inspect vessels for adherence to international conventions. This practice, known as port state control (PSC), though arguably a violation of flag state sovereignty, is now accepted in international law.

A coalition of maritime interests seeks to link the various parts of this fragmented regulatory system together in a comprehensive "responsibility chain," with port state control serving as the regulator of last resort (Salvarani 1998). There are four major categories of interests involved in shipping regulation: 1) national governments 2) intergovernmental organizations 3) private and semi-private organizations 4) non-governmental organizations:

Table 5.1: Actors Involved in the Maritime Shipping Regulatory Process

National Governments	Flag State authorities (FS), Port State authorities (PSC), Labor Supplier State authorities (LSS)
Global Intergovernmental Organizations (IGOs)	International Labour Organization, International Maritime Organization
Private Interests	Classification societies, banks, insurance companies, ship owners, ship management companies, manning agencies, shippers, ports, ISF, IMEC
NGOs	ITF and other unions, Seafarer's Missions (church), environmental groups

Of these organizations, only national states and the ITF can be said to exercise regulatory enforcement. The IGOs do not have enforcement capacities of their own, but rather serve as rule making bodies. In the IGOs, treaties are negotiated which establish the regulatory obligations of states, and the legal basis on which they may intervene to regulate shipping operated by other sovereign states. Non-state actors, aside from the ITF, do not have the means to enforce standards, but can exert pressure on a shipowner (by refusing to do business, for example), or pass along information to other actors with enforcement capability. They are, however, often responsible for applying the systems which regulate shipboard practices, or are delegated by governments to inspect shipping safety. However, their role is, in a sense, intermediary—i.e. industry self-regulation occurs to standards set in the IGOs in order to preempt and avoid the application of state authority. The ITF, of course, does not have any actual legal authority, but is often in a position to compel shipowners through industrial action, giving it a *de facto* regulatory enforcement capability.

IGOs

On the global level, a body of international regulatory law agreed upon in the framework of the International Maritime Organization (IMO), and International Labour Organization (ILO), influences conditions in the maritime industry. The IMO is concerned with maritime safety and pollution, and is sometimes involved in industrial relations issues related to training, certification and safe operating procedures (Dirks 2001). As a result, it has a close relationship with the ILO. The ITF, ISF and their affiliates influence global maritime regulation by participating in the ILO process as social partners, and in the IMO process as expert observers and advisors. To give an idea of these agencies' briefs, the Table 5.2 shows some of the conventions relating to seafaring employment negotiated in the context of these organizations.

Table 5.2: Selected IMO and ILO Instruments Related to Employment at Sea

IGO	Instrument	Date of entry into force
IMO	SOLAS: International Convention for the Safety of Life at Sea 1974 as amended, and its Protocols (1978, 1988)	25 May 1980
IMO	SAR: International Convention on Maritime Search and Rescue, 1979	22 June 1985
IMO	MARPOL: International Convention for the Prevention of Pollution from Ships, and its Protocol (1978) Annex I (2 Oct 1983) Annex II (6 April 1987) Annex III (July 1992); IV; Annex V (31 Dec 1988)	2 October 1983
IMO	STCW: International Convention on Standards of Training, Certification, and Watchkeeping for Seafarer, 1978, as amended	28 April 1984
IMO	SUA: Convention for the Suppression of Unlawful Acts against Safety of Maritime Navigation, 1988, and its Protocol (1988)	1 March 1992
ILO	Minimum Age Convention 138	1976
ILO	Recruitment and Placing of Seamen Convention 179	2000
ILO	Food and Catering (Ships' Crew) Convention 68	1957
ILO	Wages, Hours of Work, and Manning (Sea) Recommendation 187	1996
ILO	Seafarers' Welfare at Sea and in Port Convention 163	1990

Source: Stopford 1997: 444: 449.

Flag States

Flag states, in theory, have sovereign authority over all vessels in their register, and are nominally the most important regulators in maritime shipping. Flag states are expected to implement in legislation relevant ILO and IMO conventions. They are also expected to maintain inspection apparatus to ensure the ships they register comply, and apply legal sanctions to the shipowner if they do not. For example, they should have legislation mandating that there are a sufficient number of crew, and that these be trained to a level meeting internationally agreed standards (as set forth in IMO conventions). They should provide a system of testing, or of monitoring and recognition of test results from other countries, to ensure that seafarers actually have the skills they are supposed to have. They should provide official certificates showing that these skills have been tested. Flag States, when they are actually regulating as Flag States, have the most consistent and comprehensive authority of any shipping industry actor.

In a world without FOCs, a regulatory regime based on flag state enforcement would probably be adequate. However, shipowners may elect to flag their ships in any country that will have them. Since choice of flag is influenced by the enforcement of standards under that flag, there is a constant temptation for countries to change their regulations specifically to attract shipowners. Shipowners operating at a high standard may choose to continue to fly high standard flags, but those seeking to reduce costs will move to flags where enforcement is weaker. Therefore, under current conditions, flag state authority does not comprise a comprehensive regulatory enforcement regime for global shipping.

STCW 95 and the CMLC draft instrument include a strong element of flag state enforcement of labor standards. However, other elements such as port state control are also included. PSC provides a backup, and encourages negligent flag state administrations to enforce international standards, because ships flying flags with poor enforcement regimes are more likely to attract the attention of PSC inspectors.[2]

Port State Control

Since the early 1980s, maritime accidents and other problems created by flag state negligence have prompted many countries to inspect vessels that call in their ports. States justify port state control in their legal right to protect their own citizens and shore lines, even when this hinders freedom of navigation and violates flag state sovereignty. PSC rights allow countries to enforce accepted international agreements on ships visiting their ports, but fall short of allowing the enforcement of national laws, as this would be too great a restriction on the principle of free navigation (Keslelj 1999).

Port state control works through spot inspections of a certain percentage of ships calling in port. Inspectors detain those in violation of safety standards until repairs are made. PSC inspections enforce rules collectively decided in the IMO and ILO, although until recently PSC officials have not usually been trained to check for labor code violations. Port state control has seen some success in improving standards in the industry, but has serious limitations. Penalties are corrective rather than punitive, so that many shipowners wait until they are caught to make repairs. There are also many possibilities for evasion, and it is impossible to carry out a thorough safety inspection in the time available to PSC inspectors (Bloor 2003). Nonetheless, tightening PSC enforcement appears to have had a positive impact on the quality of world shipping (Salvarini 1998: 21–24).

Generally, PSC has only been applied to safety and environmental issues under International Maritime Organization (IMO) conventions. Use of PSC powers is currently sanctioned by the widely ratified but not widely enforced ILO C147, Merchant Shipping (Minimum Standards), but only in regards to protection of the safety of the crew, and not for general enforcement of labor standards. If the CMLC passes it will greatly expand PSC enforcement of labor standards.

Labor Supplier States

Labor supplier state obligations have now been included in international conventions relating to skill certification, identity documents, and recruitment (Dirks 2001). STCW 95 introduced an element of LSS enforcement in the form of the "White List." The IMO monitors labor supplier states' implementation of STCW requirements in their national education and credentialing systems, and includes them on the "White List" if these are adequate. The draft CMLC proposes to include LSS responsibilities in monitoring recruitment and social security for seafarers, among other things. Compared to flag and port state control, however, the labor supplier state role is relatively weakly developed. In the context of STCW 95, states supplying seafarers to the international merchant fleet as a strategy for earning foreign exchange need to take international skill standards seriously.

SKILL, CONTROL AND REPRODUCTION

Seafaring is a skilled occupation, with both officers and ratings requiring proof of qualifications. Ratings are generally required to pass tests for certain competencies.[3] Officers must undertake many years of schooling and an apprenticeship before being "licensed." Deskilling through Taylorization, common in manufacturing industries, is limited by the conflicting desire to reduce the number of crew needed to man a ship. As with nationally embedded industries, maritime has relied on national educational systems for most of its training requirements. Capital mobility makes it difficult for the geographically and socially embedded infrastructure of labor market reproduction to keep up with the demands of the industry. Extensive systems of training academies and academic programs exist to train mariners throughout the developed world. The maritime education systems of labor supply countries, however, are less extensive, and not all of the institutions are considered of good quality. As a result of the shift in labor sourcing from northern Europe to Asia the number of properly trained and certified seafarers graduating in recent years has fallen. A Seafarers International Research Centre report to the ILO states:

> The number and range of training establishments in the traditional maritime nations has decreased substantially over the last 20 years, while there has been considerable growth in South and Southeast Asia; in Eastern Europe, there has been modest decline. The shift of training and education from the relatively prosperous northern hemisphere to the less prosperous southern hemisphere has inevitably led to an overall decline in standards of training since investment has not matched demand or output (Alderton *et al.* 2001: 53).

As labor sources have shifted, the old infrastructure based on the training schools and union hiring halls of traditional maritime nations (i.e. industrialized countries) has disappeared. The new infrastructure to train workers from the developing world, however, is still only partly complete, and is yet inadequate to provide for the growing skill requirements of the world fleet. Even as the new infrastructure is being built, it is already under threat, as old sources of labor become more expensive and capital roots out new and cheaper sources.

Labor requires certain state functions and/or social arrangements to reproduce. Lack of social structures encouraging public investment in skill formation results in less provision of training and promotes a low-skill, low-value added, "low road," organization of work. The fundamental problem with maintaining a high-skill paradigm in the global shipping industry, where escape is as easy as changing flags, is that there are few incentives for anyone to invest in training. The labor market's extreme disembedding from national contexts means there is no universal, coherent labor reproduction regime. In the absence of this, the labor market has difficulty reproducing the skills needed to run a highly complex modern industry.

Skill, and how it is used and defined, is closely involved with work organization and the struggle between labor and capital for control over the production process (Braverman 1974). Because of the opposing interests at play, skills can be regarded, at least in part, as created and defined through political and workplace class struggle. As Green puts it, "Human capital—or skills—cannot properly be defined except in social context. The same abilities can have different uses, and be acquired in different ways, in different economic contexts." (Green 1992: 417) This means that "the expansion and transformation of education . . . is as much an arena for conflict as the struggle over wages or industrial policy." (Green 1992: 431)

Employers have a schizophrenic attitude toward skill. While they often need it, and frequently state the value they place on highly skilled employees, skill also allows workers greater control over the production process. It is not clear that capital as a whole is favorably inclined toward a high-skill, high-value added model of production—there are good reasons to believe a high skill outcome in a workplace or in society as a whole is the result of class compromise. Fractions of capital are likely to contest efforts to implement a high-skill, high-value added solution, if for their market strategies or product markets, a low-skill, low-cost outcome is preferable (Amoore 2002).

Therefore, we see divisions within the capitalist camp between those groups desiring access to high skill labor, either as a high-quality market strategy, or as support for cartelization, or both, and groups seeking to pursue a low-skill, low-cost option. For unions and workers, the high skill paradigm offers high wages, greater control over the production process, and, in the case of shipping, a significantly safer working environment.

THE POLITICS OF STCW 95

STCW 95 was specifically designed to be enforced through the developing system of industry regulation involving interlocking state sovereignties and regulatory capacities. National states played a larger role in the formulation of STCW 95 than with the CMLC, due to the intergovernmental structure of IMO decision making. Nonetheless, STCW 95 was a political initiative of the ISF and ITF. In the early 1990s, a widespread consensus emerged among maritime industry actors, including shipowner associations, unions and governments,[4] that maritime shipping is experiencing a global skilled labor shortage, and that this shortage will worsen for the foreseeable future. An influential manpower survey showed the labor shortage worsening as

senior European officers retire and are not replaced (BIMCO/ISF 1995;
BIMCO/ISF 2000). Coupled with the quantitative shortfall came concerns
about declining standards. David Dearsley, then ISF General Secretary,
expressed "we have grave doubts whether training standards in some countries in the world are, even at best, adequate." (*Lloyd's List* 9 Apr 1991) At
an ISF-sponsored training conference later that year, Åke Selander, then ITF
Seafarers' Section Secretary, proposed an audit of training institutes, under
the auspices of the IMO and ILO. David Underwood of Denholms shipping
added that industry actors should set targets, and in the words of *Lloyd's
List*, "not wait around for governments or the IMO to move at the speed of
their slowest voters." (*Lloyd's List* 25 Nov 1991)

The ITF and ISF set about pressuring the IMO to take action (Dirks
2001). The IMO responded in 1995 by amending the original 1978 STCW
treaty, updating standards, and, most importantly, adding the enforcement
mechanism sought by the ISF and ITF in the form of the "White List."
STCW 95 (which came into full effect in 2002), reflects the interests of the
ISF, the ITF, and their affiliates, in stabilizing and professionalizing the maritime labor market. These actors intermediated between the positions of
their national affiliates, and the intergovernmental decision-making process
of the IMO (Dirks 2001). More importantly, to ensure that the convention
would be a success, they mobilized their members and created an international industry consensus to influence reluctant national governments into
complying with STCW 95 requirements. The interests of labor supplier
countries, some of whom would have preferred to continue to ignore training standards and supply international shipping with highly exploitable
if improperly certified labor, were subordinated to the functional requirements of global maritime capital.

Many labor supply countries regard employment of their nationals
on foreign flag shipping as a significant earner of foreign exchange. The
prospect of exclusion from the "White List" was a major threat to those
countries' market position (*Lloyd's List* 25 Feb 1999). Also, ships of certain developing countries and open registers are significantly more likely
to be arrested by PSC, and therefore, one might assume, would be likely to
oppose the convention's implementation. One might have expected these
countries to offer opposition in the IMO to the updating of STCW. Effective
opposition to the convention itself did not occur within the context of the
IMO, however, but rather in the form of "passive" resistance to its effective
application after the fact. This could be because the high value placed on
technical competence in the IMO process effectively excluded some countries from influence over the convention (Dirks 2001: 299). Very likely it is
also because some countries assumed that supporting the convention would

be cost-free, because they could simply neglect to enforce the new regulations. It was not clear in the early and mid-1990s (i.e. after the enforcement mechanism had been set in motion) that STCW 95 would actually be enforced through transnational mechanisms.

The "White List" proved to be fairly inclusive in the end, and all the major labor suppliers made it on to it. While some accused the IMO of being too lenient, the wide inclusion is probably more indicative of a major effort by shipowners to force reluctant labor supply countries to demonstrate compliance. The most important labor supplier country, the Philippines, did not initially make the White List, resulting in a major effort by shipowners to compel the Filipino government to take the STCW 95 convention seriously. There was widespread concern that the country would become off limits to hiring, potentially resulting in serious manning shortages for the world fleet (*Lloyd's List* 30 Mar 2000). The Filipino government initially did not even designate a responsible authority for communicating with the IMO, and ensuring that STCW 95 requirements would be met.

At an Asian Shipowners' Forum (ASF) meeting in Shanghai in 1996, shipowners favorably compared Chinese efforts to meet STCW 95 standards with those of the Philippines, in communiqués to both governments (*Lloyd's List* 16 Nov 1996). This was an explicit threat: the Philippines has long been concerned about China's emergence in the labor supply market (*Journal Of Commerce* 29 Mar 1995), and failure by the Philippines to make it on the White List could very well have been the impetus shipowners needed to move their labor sourcing to China. The ASF also put the Filipino Shipowners' Association to work on encouraging the Filipino government to facilitate compliance (*Lloyd's List* 16 Nov 1996).

Some domestic interests in the Philippines remained vested in the existing training school establishment. The training industry in the Philippines was notoriously corrupt. According to a Catholic Institute for International Relations report, many schools did "little more than issue a required certificate—for a fee, of course." (CIIR 1987: 110) Evidently, the government was reluctant to take on this lucrative industry. Faced with the prospect of their major labor source disappearing, shipowners had little patience with what appeared to be administrative incompetence. *Lloyd's List* quotes one Filipino manning agent as saying "The situation is very serious. Unless our maritime officials get their acts together soon a crisis situation could confront the manning industry and the country as a whole." (*Lloyd's List* 25 Feb 1999). Shipowners also acted to finance the upgrading of training in the Philippines. IMEC created a training fund to help bring the Philippines up to standard, financed by a levy of its members, and called upon others to donate as well (*Lloyd's List* 17 Feb 1998). In February, 1998, the ISF and the Filipino Shipowners' Association organized a fact-finding mission to meet with various government agencies and check on progress toward STCW 95 compliance (*Lloyd's List* 24 Feb 1998).

Finally, the Filipino government began to act in earnest. In 1998, the Philippines had 111 seafarer training schools of which only 9 met STCW 95 standards (*Lloyd's List* 24 June 1999). Although some non-STCW compliant institutions upgraded their standards, others simply lost their certification. The Philippines made it on the White List although with a reduced capacity to graduate and certify seafarers. STCW 95 compliance forced a reluctant Filipino government to take on its profitably corrupt training and manning establishment, or lose its status as a major labor supplier.

When STCW 95 finally came into full effect in 2002, it was not the labor supplier end that experienced difficulties in compliance so much as the flag states—some flags had administrative difficulties in supplying shipowners with needed certificates in time to meet the February 2002 deadline (*Business Times: Kuala Lumpur* 31 July 2002). In the end, the IMO granted a six month delay, during which it recommended that port state authorities give out warnings, but not detain vessels. STCW 95 then came into full force in August 2002 (*Marine Log, New York* June 2004).

INTERESTS OF CAPITAL

In the short term, the individual shipping firm competing in the global market has an incentive to find cheaper, less skilled seafarers—and to promote a global regulatory system which makes it possible for such seafarers to be employed on ships. On the other hand, in the long term, from the perspective of stabilizing the industrial environment, politically influential segments of maritime capital find it useful to have access to a highly skilled maritime workforce, in part to exclude low-standard competitors, in part to guard against the sort of public regulatory backlashes which often occur in response to major accidents such as oil spills, and in part because a high-skill paradigm improves shipping reliability and quality of service. The existence of a low cost option, however, makes the high-skill paradigm more difficult to achieve, because it undermines the institutional framework which produces and develops maritime skills.

Maintaining hegemony often has a price, in terms of the compromises hegemonic groups must make to obtain the consent of other groups, and to portray their interests as "public" interests. Not all capital fractions are equally willing to pay this price. Whether participation in and compliance with regulatory systems can be compelled, or whether non-compliant fractions can be ignored, depends on particular constellations of interest, and the means of compulsion available in specific circumstances. DeSombre, for example, notes that actors can use "clubs" to exclude non-compliant states or firms from desired resources. How, and how well, this works in practice, however, depends on the specific means of monitoring available, and the sanctions which can be applied to those flouting the rules of the club (DeSombre forthcoming). Within capital we see a struggle over the enforcement of regulation, with the battle lines drawn along the strategies and interests of firms.

There has been a clear shift in shipowner attitudes since the 1970s and 80s, when excited shipowners rushed to flag out and rid themselves of unwanted unions, taxes and regulations (Alderton *et al.* 2001: 27). However, as Haufler observes, regulation, as a collective good, is not necessarily beneficial to all industry participants, but rather can be used as a weapon by politically influential firms against those less well situated (Haufler 2000). High standard shipowners have good reason to support mechanisms extending high-cost regulation to those shipowners who have managed to escape ITF influence. Since the 1990s, these employers have talked of partnering with the ITF on some issues, instead of simply trying to avoid or undermine ITF demands and objectives. While the ISF criticized the ITF for "unilateralism," (*Lloyd's List* 9 May 1995) the ITF and ISF have built up a substantial common agenda. The ISF sees it as important that "quality" shipping is not inconvenienced by regulation, and emphasizes targeting "substandard" vessels. Juan Kelly, president of the ISF in 1994–95 states:

> Substandard employers operating rust buckets are fair game, and the ISF and ITF have a common cause in doing all we can to eliminate them. But the ITF approach is like a scatter gun, hitting everything in sight, the majority good as well as the minority bad (*Lloyd's List* 27 May 1994).

The ISF has common ground with the ITF in portraying shipping as a basically socially responsible industry, with a few bad apples that need to be tossed out. In the ISF's view, however, the ITF and port state control should focus on making those few bad apples disappear, and forget about forcing union contracts and unneeded inspections on high-standard employers. Above all, shipowners are keen to insure that FOCs and substandard shipping are not equated in the regulators' minds (Cremers 1998). However, some shipowners recognize they cannot have one thing without the other: the ITF "levels the playing field," and prevents substandard shipowners from competing with "quality" shipping.[5] STCW 95 and other enforceable regulatory initiatives have the same effect. Regulatory enforcement is needed for the continued health of the industry, but is something shipowners do not have the tools to do themselves (*Lloyd's List* 9 May 1995).

The ISF majority view rhetorically supports the ITF and IMO initiatives for quality shipping. However, the ISF is a bit more ambiguous when it comes to actual enforcement. The ISF can agree to regulations, and call for their enforcement, but this does not mean that actual shipowners will necessarily support or abide by the rules. Peter Cremers, of Anglo Eastern Ship Management, speaking at a manning and training conference, sums up the ambivalence of shipowners, "We all agree that we want to get rid of substandard shipping, though we prefer to keep the definition of this minimum standard somewhat vague—and some of us would not mind that the others start first—poor company, difficult marketing situation, etc." (Cremers 1998)

Furthermore, certain ISF affiliates evidently have misgivings about the way the "quality" versus "substandard" shipping debate is framed. These shipowners assert that compliance with international regulations, certified through existing regulatory channels, should be enough to avoid being labeled "substandard." "Quality" shipping will be rewarded by the market, and shipowners who wish to pursue that strategy are free to do so, but shipowners should not be punished for preferring a strategy of "minimal" adherence to international standards (see the Greek Shipping Association's submission to the International Commission on Shipping, for example (ICONS 2000)). A minority (or at least less well organized) voice from shipowners sees the drive to higher enforceable standards as favoring large companies at the expense of the small independent operator (with the implication that this is a bad thing).[6]

INTERESTS OF LABOR

STCW 95 is useful to the ITF and maritime unions generally, in that it limits labor market access to formally qualified seafarers, and reduces pressure on employers to push wages down. Unions have an intrinsic interest in being involved in the regulatory process, and in using regulatory issues for bargaining leverage. Belzer notes, for example, the introduction of commercial drivers' licenses in the US trucking industry favored the Teamsters' bargaining strength (Belzer 1993). Skill certification, like industry regulation generally, affects the competitive climate, as well as influencing industrial relations practices directly. Regulation therefore sets the framework in which bargaining about certain types of issues takes place, and the circumstances under which a union may portray itself as representing a public rather than particular interest.

In the IMO context the ITF relies on a discourse which emphasizes market stability, professionalism, shipping safety, environmental protection and long term investment. ITF representatives, and the representatives of certain affiliates, were heavily involved in the process of negotiating STCW 95, representing labor's viewpoint and providing expert advice. Like the shipowners, the ITF also mobilized organizational resources in support of STCW 95. Through its global network of ITF ship inspectors in ports around the world, the ITF influences IMO regulatory implementation, by accessing port state control officials on the local port level. As *Lloyd's List* states:

> . . . the ITF has also gained recognition and a voice at important shipping forums such as the IMO, ILO, the European Union and the US Coast Guard. Port state control authorities in Europe call in the ITF, the USCG organizes a joint safety seminar with it and the IMO draws upon the body of expertise in the ITF's global affiliates (*Lloyd's List* 9 May 1995).

Views of trade unionists are skeptical of the effectiveness of STCW 95 in practice, although there is broad support for the principle. In interviews of maritime unionists conducted from 1998 and 2003 in Europe and North America, many unionists expressed doubt about the effectiveness of STCW 95 in ensuring skill standards. Research lends some empirical support to this position: PSC, due to limited resources, is unable to thoroughly check all vessels (Bloor 2003). Fraudulent certificates are also a problem. To a certain extent, STCW 95 may even exacerbate this, because of increased demand from seafarers who do not want to go to the expense of upgrading their certification (Obando-Rojas *et al.* 2004). Some unionists were also concerned about the extra burden and expense STCW 95 presented for their members, who had to qualify for the new standards, although generally they regarded the acquisition of these skills as desirable. Despite the goal of standardized training norms and transparency in certification, some unionists suspect that seafarers from other countries are not being required to adhere to as rigorous a standard. However, none of those interviewed outright rejected STCW 95, but evidenced skepticism about what it can accomplish.

CONCLUSION

The growth of new transnational state forms creates new transnational spaces of contestation. Capital's escape from national regulation thus creates the conditions under which regulation, and perhaps eventually hegemony, is re-established globally. However, while public and quasi public transnational state forms provide some of the collective goods needed by transnational maritime capital, the global reconstitution of hegemony is much more questionable. Transnational and global state forms, such STCW 95 and the regime enforcing it, have very specific and contingent bases of authority, focusing around capital's immediate collective action dilemmas. Policy solutions, provided they are narrowly addressed to capital's collective action problems, can find a hearing in forums with real regulatory authority. But even naturally technocratic policy arenas, such as those regulating skill certification, provide room for class conflict. Within the technocratic context of the IMO, subordinate actors with the right kind of expertise still find room for generating power resources, making claims and influencing outcomes. Unions seek to use skill to delineate labor market boundaries, and to favor capitalists who manage with a high-skill paradigm. And even the exercise of such narrow authority as IMO's is contested by capital fractions seeking to continue down the "low-road," and avoid paying a share for the collective good.

In the global context, what is regarded as the appropriate use of state authority has been redefined quite narrowly in favor capital's direct short term interests, to perhaps the detriment of capital's long term hegemony. As the next chapter will show, policy solutions which go beyond addressing those narrow collective welfare issues to incorporate more fully the demands of subordinate actors are even more hotly contested.

Chapter Six
Global Regulatory Politics and Labor Standards in the ILO

Within the International Labour Organization (ILO), 177 member country governments and representatives of the 'social partners' (i.e. unions and employers) write the international conventions that are the basis for most of the current global labor rights regime. As with international regimes generally, ILO labor standards create normative pressure on governments to comply. In the case of the labor standards regime, compliance is generally accomplished by states implementing ILO conventions into national legislation (and then, presumably, enforcing the law to ensure that employers abide by this legislation). Recently, ILO standards have also become a basis for the construction of private firm-based systems of global labor standards articulation within TNCs and supply chains. In maritime shipping, neither the long established state centered articulation, nor the emerging private mechanisms, serves the functional requirements of the transnational labor market actors particularly well. As a result, within the maritime shipping section of the ILO, unions, shipowners and governments have been negotiating a very different mechanism in the form of a Consolidated Maritime Labour Convention (referred to herein as CMLC). This new instrument borrows elements both from the existing global labor rights regime, and the global maritime safety and environmental protection regime, centered on the International Maritime Organization.

The CMLC instrument could serve as the basis for what Trubek *et al.* (2000) describe as a "multi-level public-private regime," with various global, regional and national elements knit together in a transnational "web of rules"[1] to provide comprehensive labor standards enforcement. The CMLC paradigm applies different aspects of state authority in a fragmented manner, knit together by practices of maritime industrial regulation. Unlike the traditional member-state implementation model, the Consolidated Maritime Labour Convention will have member states enforcing labor standards directly on *each other's* ships through port state control. The CMLC negotiations show how the structure of the developing maritime labor standards regime is embedded in an ongoing struggle between organized labor and capital within the industry. CMLC outcomes are conditioned on the interests of the industry actors, the decision making rules of the ILO, and the precedents set by existing regimes.

The ILO tri-partite system structures the interactions between the shipping industry labor market actors, and the various ILO member governments. Political impetus for the convention came from pressure on shipowners to implement globally uniform standards in an industry deregulated through Flags of Convenience. A fraction among shipowners seeks to "level the playing field" with low-standard operators by re-regulating the industry on the global level. The emergence of this employer fraction has opened political opportunities for unions to push for enforceable global labor standards, and in particular to make the link between labor rights and port state control.

Within the ILO, unions and shipowners are organized into two "social partner" groupings of national associations. Unlike transnational pressure groups in other intergovernmental organizations (IGOs), union and employer representatives at the ILO have voting rights. The social partner groupings are led by representatives from among the ITF and ISF national affiliate organizations, although national social partner representatives need not be members of those organizations. Social partner group strategies are closely tied into the internal politics and global collective bargaining strategies of the unions' and shipowners' international associations. The leadership of the Shipowner group has been closely associated with IMEC, and IMEC's policy of *détente* with the ITF. Part way through the CMLC, an internal power struggle took place within the Shipowner group, resulting in a new 'hardline' leadership no longer as close to IMEC, which is unsure of whether it really wants the CMLC at all. As a result, the future of the convention is in doubt.

This case study demonstrates the ways in which pre-existing international regimes formed in the context of inter-state relations provide a terrain on which the global conflict between transnationally organized capital and labor takes place. This chapter will first explain the various existing models of labor standards articulation, and how the seafarers' rights convention fits into that. Then the configurations of actors and interests in the ILO, and the negotiations over Title V of the CMLC, on Enforcement and Compliance, are described. Finally, the chapter concludes by discussing what the labor market actors' (apparent) interests are and how these demonstrate the ways in which global class conflict has pushed traditional regulation by intergovernmental negotiation to one side, although the intergovernmental legacy still leaves an imprint on global industrial regulation. This chapter is based on personal observation of the meetings of the ILO High-level Tripartite Working Group on Maritime Labour Standards in July 2003 and January 2004, and the Preparatory Technical Maritime Conference in September 2004, semi-structured interviews at the offices of some of the participants, and informal conversations in the context of the meetings.

THE PROPOSED NEW SEAFARERS' LABOR RIGHTS CONVENTION

The introduction of the Consolidated Maritime Labour Convention would signal an important, though incremental, change in the way global labor rights are governed in maritime, but even more significant is the precedent it would set for labor rights and global governance generally. Although a logical continuation of current and ongoing developments, if passed it will codify maritime shipping's fundamentally new way of implementing labor standards. The CMLC builds on maritime regulatory experiences from port state control, STCW 95 and related initiatives, and on the realities and power relations of maritime industrial relations created by the ITF's collective bargaining strategy, and capital's responses to it. CMLC is different from the traditional *national regulation* model of labor rights articulation in that it is based not on the structure of the national states and the interstate system, but on the structure of the maritime shipping business. Although nation states enforce the standards, they do so not only on themselves as flag states in response to obligations to international treaties, but also on *each other and directly on private shipowners* as port states. Transnational enforcement machinery no longer looks like (officially) harmonized parallel sovereign systems, but more like a globally integrated network involving various levels of government authority. It is differs from the more recently developed *business standards* model of labor rights articulation in that authoritative external actors enforce the regime, and the CMLC's provisions have a better defined legal status than do business standards. Even when these are derived from ILO conventions and recommendations, or from the OECD codes of practice for TNCs, it is not always clear under private business standards precisely what rights and obligations are delivered, who has standing to claim them, who should comply with them, who should enforce them, and what penalties should apply to those who flout them (see Chapter Seven for a more extensive discussion of codes of conduct and private business standards). The CMLC draft text endeavors to specify all these things, although political disagreements may prevent the end result from being completely unambiguous.[2] Table 6.1 outlines the existing and proposed models of labor standards regulation:

Table 6.1: Models of Labor Rights Regime

Model	Normal ILO Nation-based enforcement Model	Corporate Social Responsibility: Employer Preferred Model	New Maritime Shipping Model: Union Preferred Model
Political Formulation Mechanism	Tri-partite model negotiation of conventions, entry into force through high number of ratifications.	Picking and choosing existing ILO conventions to adhere to. Driven by corporate strategy and the priorities of CSR partners.	Tri-partite model, driven by coherent "insider" social partner group.
Articulation Mechanism	Enforcement through shaming of national governments into implementing and enforcing in national law (Weisband 2001).	Enforced through corporate HRM policy, through pressure on suppliers, through the demands of marketing, and through relations with CSR partners.	Enforcement through fragmented state authority, building on top of existing maritime regulation: LSS, FS, and PSC.
Enforcement Problems	Fragmented by uneven geographical application. Enforcement limited by sovereignty, insufficient monitoring capacity, and inter-state competition for investment	Fragmented by uneven corporate application, limited by corporate enforcement in supply chains, effective application primarily limited to cooperative TNCs and their supply chains.	More comprehensive system than the others, with means of limiting geographical and inter-company fragmentation. Problems will persist in extending the instrument to ships not in international trade, and to ships operating only in regions where labor rights are not respected.

The maritime shipping model also differs from either of the other two models of labor rights articulation in the level of detailed guidance it provides. This last aspect is probably more due to the global uniformity of industrial relations practices in the industry and the special situation of seafarers than anything else. More than in other industries, in maritime, work organization, skills, and practices are fairly standard across flags, nationality of ownership, and national origin of the workforce. Regulation of living conditions adds an extra level of detail, because seafarers cannot go home at the end of the workday, so their living conditions and working conditions are much the same. As result, it is both feasible and necessary for the ILO to discuss labor rights at a greater level of detail than in other industries. Although particular to maritime shipping, these differences set precedents for how abstract and "aspirational" labor rights can be translated into practically applied and enforced regulations. While the parties have not yet agreed on all issues at the time of this writing, this is due to just a few (admittedly important) contentious paragraphs out of the 95 pages of text. Most of the text has been agreed. The draft instrument will combine and supersede most ILO seafaring labor conventions and recommendations, although the important recent Seafarers' Identity Document Convention (Revised) C185 is not included, nor are conventions deemed obsolete, nor those which have been superseded by IMO rules. Maritime conventions and recommendations related to seafaring are listed in Appendix D.

The draft instrument's structure introduces a number of innovations, some borrowed from the IMO experience, and some which resolve problems unique to the ILO's situation. The CMLC is divided into articles, regulations, and titles, as well as a preamble and appendices. Articles address administrative issues for managing the document, such as entry into force, amendments, definitions, and so on. Titles are substantive content, and consist of regulations, standards (called Code A), and guidelines (called Code B). Regulations set out the aims of each title, implemented in the way described in the code. Code A is mandatory, in that each ratifying country will be expected to change its legislation to be compatible with Code A. Substantial equivalence is allowed, so that national laws deemed to provide equivalent or superior protection to seafarers need not be changed. Code B contains a good deal of detail, but is only intended to provide guidance in implementing Code A and the regulations, and in that sense it is not mandatory. Code B is an innovation arising out of the CMLC negotiation process, and facilitates the inclusion of recommendations and poorly ratified conventions without giving those instruments greater status than they in effect already have. The CMLC draft's substantive content is listed in the Appendix E: Draft Consolidated Maritime Labor Convention Contents.

From the IMO experience, the convention borrows a "tacit amendment procedure," to allow tinkering with aspects of the rules without a full meeting of the ILO International Labor Conference. Negotiation participants consider this important because it is difficult to predict the impact of a convention as large and complex as this one. Revisions may be necessary, and these would be very time consuming under the normal ILO process. Inspection and enforcement procedures draw heavily on the IMO and PSC regime experience, as well as referencing the earlier ILO C178, Labour Inspection, Seafarers, 1996 (which in turn relied on IMO and PSC precedents in its formulation).[3]

ILO AS AN INSTITUTIONAL SETTING FOR LABOR STANDARDS NEGOTIATIONS

International relations scholars have shown that the bureaucratic and decision-making characteristics of international organizations have an effect on bargaining outcomes (Cox and Jacobsen 1973; Keohane 1984). This is certainly evident in the tri-partite structures of the ILO, where the social partners tend to be the driving force behind legislation. Governments only make up half the voting group, while each of the "social partners"—unions and employers—are allocated one quarter of the vote (a 2:1:1 voting ratio). Through a process resembling something between diplomatic negotiations and collective bargaining, the three groups negotiate conventions and recommendations. As with maritime conventions generally, the actual negotiation of the draft CMLC document is taking place in the ILO social dialogue/sectoral activities division (SECTOR). After being negotiated in SECTOR, the maritime conventions then go to the full International Labour Conference (ILC), which meets once a year, for a formal vote. This is a special procedure. Generally applicable conventions are negotiated and voted on in the ILC by representatives from national multi-sectoral union federations, business associations and governments and are not negotiated in SECTOR.

Because of the highly international nature of the shipping environment, the ILO, since its inception, has treated the welfare of seafarers as an area deserving of special attention, with industry specific machinery. 39 conventions and one protocol to a convention have been adopted in maritime, out of 185 conventions total. No other industry has received anywhere near this much attention—dock work and fishing are tied for second place with five conventions each. The rules of procedure and the institutional balance of power is the same, however, for general conventions and maritime shipping conventions. Presumably, if a proposed instrument is put forward by consensus from the maritime section of SECTOR, it will then be adopted at the ILC, since the required consensus between interested parties has already been mobilized. Few conventions are voted down in the ILC, although it does happen on occasion (Boockman 2001).

Because of the complexity of the CMLC, the convention has had an extended negotiating procedure. Special "High-Level Tripartite Working Group" meetings took place in December 2001, October 2002, July 2003, and January 2004, in order to have a mature document ready for the September 2004 Preparatory Technical Maritime Conference (PTMC), where the negotiations were supposed to be completed. The debates of the January 2004 working group, as well as the PTMC meeting, followed a multiple working group committee structure, because of the large numbers of issues to be addressed. This allowed for much more intensive discussions, moving forward at the same time on a variety of issues. After failure to come to agreement at the PTMC on certain aspects of the draft convention, the negotiators agreed to postpone consideration at the ILC to 2006, and held a supplementary meeting in April 2005 to work out the remaining points of disagreement.

The 2:1:1 voting configuration on the surface gives governments dominating influence. However, unlike the social partners, governments do not vote, strategize, or negotiate as a coherent block. The union side, and to a large extent the employers as well, have unified strategies, speak through designated group spokespeople, and tend to vote as blocks.[4] As a result, the social partners exercise a great deal of influence. The social partners treat governments as an audience to be influenced on issues where the social partners cannot find agreement. This is not to say that governments have no substantial influence. They are not only "swing" voters on key issues, but they are also the ones who determine the real world impact of the convention by ratifying it or failing to ratify. Their influence is, however, more passive than that of the social partners, in that the social partners shape the convention according to their preferences within the constraints of what they believe will be acceptable to a critical mass of governments.

Within negotiations, discussions are divided into plenary meetings, in which member governments, unions, and employer groups are all present. The ILO chairs plenary meetings. In plenary, group spokespeople are usually the only ones to speak from among the "social partners," meaning each social partner group speaks with one voice. Governments, however, generally speak for themselves. Although they have a group rapporteur, this is purely for reporting purposes. Plenary alternates with "group meetings," which are closed strategy sessions where each group attempts to arrive at a unitary position.

In the CMLC caucuses, the union and employer groups tend to be dominated by core constituents who are well networked and informed about the issues under discussion. The core groups include the group chairs, representative(s) from the groups' international associations (ITF and ISF), as well as some of the more interested leaders from national unions or employer associations. However, less central constituents provide input as well, particularly when representing their own national situations. Social partner delegates plan strategies for influencing the positions of specific national governments in the caucuses. Sometimes, this involves mobilizing a particular union or shipowner delegate to advise or pressure their national government representative, in hope of moving the government's position closer to that of the social partner group in question. The government group meetings, on the other hand, are not really strategy planning sessions at all, but rather serve as an extended plenary. Unlike the unions and employers, government views tend to be too divergent on contentious issues for a unitary strategy to emerge.

Between the larger and more formal meetings, much of the actual negotiation (particularly on complex issues) occurs in small specialized *ad hoc* working groups between social partner representatives and governments with a particular interest in the issue at hand. Overall coordination of the negotiations is provided by the "steering committee" consisting of the chairs and vice chairs of the various working groups. Many of the more contentious issues are resolved in small, informal groups of key players. These then report back to their caucuses to mobilize consensus around the solutions they bargain.

ACTORS AND INTERESTS

Space precludes full discussion of the CMLC negotiations, so this analysis will focus on the key, and still unresolved, issues in Title V, Compliance and Enforcement, the most contentious title of the convention. Until the July 2003 meeting, there seemed to be a consensus among the social partners that the convention should include a strong PSC element, even if there was disagreement on specific issues. In the January 2004 meeting, however, it became clear that the shipowners were having a change of heart. They began to question previously agreed text, and challenge each of the practical enforcement provisions as these came under discussion.

The Seafarer group's negotiating goals are clearly related to overall ITF collective bargaining strategy. From the union perspective, the main advantages of the convention are the extension of at least some minimum labor standards to non-union seafarers, and the involvement of government inspectors in labor inspection. By establishing enforceable standards for the still quite large non-union labor market segment, the ITF can take some of the cost pressure off of organized shipowners, making its bargaining job easier. The consensus in the Seafarers' group so far has been that the CMLC is worth the potential risk of legitimating the FOC system if it includes strong enforcement mechanisms.

Shipowners' stated interest in the convention has been to obtain a "level playing field" on labor costs, and a "one-stop shop," to certify compliance with international labor standards. They hope that by establishing standards based on uniform business practices, they can head off ITF and government action, as well as exclude lower-standard operators from the industry. Not all ship owner associations have the same priorities, however. Some would prefer that the CMLC, or at least a strictly enforced CMLC, not go forward. Others are skeptical about the prospects for wide ratification. These shipowners are concerned that if the convention is ratified by their own country, but not by others, they might be put at a disadvantage—particularly if enforcement provisions are weak. As a result of conflicting interests, the Shipowners' group has been in a state of disarray, with those skeptical about the convention on the ascendant.

Government views cannot be summed up as easily, although there are a few consistent trends. Governments prefer a convention which is easily compatible with their existing practice. There are budgetary concerns about the cost of inspections, and the need to train inspectors in labor rights issues. Many governments, it seems, oppose strong enforcement, and in particular oppose allowing PSC to detain ships on labor rights grounds. However, this apparent unwillingness, if that is what it is, has been camouflaged by unlikely sounding "practical" objections. These relate to the subjectivity of inspectors, the practical difficulties of labor inspection, and the drastic financial consequences for a shipowner of having a ship detained. It appears that some governments, for whatever reason, do not want labor rights and enforcement explicitly connected in the CMLC, but also do not wish to state their opposition outright. These views, however, only emerged after the shipowners' change of position, and probably in response to shipowner lobbying efforts (at least, this is the view of some Seafarer group members).

The Table 6.2 shows some of the areas of disagreement in the working group committee on certification and enforcement, the positions of the Seafarer and Shipowner group on each issue, and the consensus resolution as of September 2004 (if there was one).

Table 6.2: Positions of the Social Partners on Compliance and Enforcement Issues

Issue	Seafarer Group positions on inspection and compliance	Shipowner Group positions on inspection and compliance
Access of Flag State inspectors: some issues resolved for Seafarers' but key issue of withdrawal of certificate unresolved.	Serious breaches of "seafarer rights" as set out in convention should be grounds to detain a vessel. The term "rights" should be used.	The term "rights" should not be used as, in the words of the shipowner representative: "this convention is not a Bill of Rights for seafarers, but rather a consolidation of minimum maritime labor standards." Withdrawal of certification not justified on labor rights grounds alone.
Access of and authority of PSC—many areas of disagreement still unresolved, and more governments appear to support the shipowner position.	Inspectors are professionals who should have some leeway to decide whether or not to inspect a vessel. Any serious breach of the convention should be grounds for detention, including but not limited to health and safety of the seafarers.	Certificates should be *prima facie* evidence of compliance. Only if an inspector has clear grounds to believe the convention is being violated should an inspection occur. Inspectors should only inspect working and living conditions, and of the provisions of the convention, only health and safety issues should justify detention of a vessel.
Access of union officials—resolved in favor of seafarer position.	Union officials should be able to examine and verify certificates.	Only "authorities" should be able to examine and verify certificates.
Access of seafarers to convention text—resolved in favor of Seafarers.	Seafarers should have access to original text of convention and ship's certificates of compliance. The rights established by these should be visibly posted in public areas of ship.	Texts detailing seafarer rights and certificates of compliance should be kept with captain, only authorities should be able to examine and check validity of certificates.

(continued)

Table 6.2:—*(continued)*

Issue	Seafarer Group positions on inspection and compliance	Shipowner Group positions on inspection and compliance
Validity period of certificates—resolved through straight compromise	3 years	5 years
Access of seafarers to outside representation—resolved in favor of Seafarers	There should be clear on-board and on-shore complaints procedures. The seafarer should be allowed to pursue these through whatever employer, union and, flag and port state compliant mechanisms are available–whether internal or external to the employer. This should be clearly stated in the convention text, so that seafarers can see they have this right.	Want to narrow down seafarers' avenues of complaint to emphasize employer-based and flag state mechanisms, and insert language which might discourage seafarers from seeking redress.

In the end, the only points which could not be resolved were the role of the PSC, and the obligation of the flag state to withdraw certificates from ships not in compliance with the convention. Access of union officials, access of seafarers to the text of the document, and access of seafarers to outside representation could not be reasonably opposed, although a good deal of confusion resulted from attempts to find language which would limit the effect of these clauses. Other issues could be and were cleared up, usually after a concession from the Shipowners, when their apparently relatively inexperienced new leadership suddenly realized that their position contravened some important and obvious principle of human rights law or the ILO Constitution.[5]

When during the September 2004 PTMC, it became apparent that the shipowners and a number of governments would not approve language allowing PSC inspection and detention of a ship on purely labor rights grounds, the entire Seafarers' group stood up and walked out of the meeting. They accused the governments who disagreed with them of either not really understanding the issues, or of being opposed to including practical labor rights enforcement in the CMLC. As a result of the failure to reach agreement, the parties decided that areas not agreed would remain blank on the published draft. Interested parties would meet again to try and resolve their differences in a "special mechanism," and consideration of the document by the ILC would be put back from 2005 until 2006.

Statements by shipowners and governments continue to display optimism about prospects for the final disagreements to be resolved. Statements by the Seafarers' group are more skeptical.[6] For the Seafarers' group, weak enforcement provisions are a "deal-breaker." Unions see port state control and ship detention as the real back-stop to all other enforcement provisions, without which the rest of the convention is meaningless. For the Seafarers' group, codification of weak standards would essentially give a union seal of approval to the Flag of Convenience system without unions receiving their demand in return: a viable enforcement regime. Even without Seafarer support, the convention could theoretically be voted in and ratified. However, in the ILO context it would be unprecedented to pass a labor rights convention without the support of the Workers' group.

DISCUSSION

While ILO labor standards are built upon human rights norms, capital contests whether this is really the type of regime labor standards should be. Capital would prefer a regime in which implementation of human rights standards is conditional upon the compatibility of those standards with market competitiveness. It is not unusual for norm promoters within international organizations to adjust the content of their norms significantly in order to gain the consensus of other groups (Finnemore and Sikkink 1998), and this certainly is also a part of the process in the CMLC case. Unions support the continued basis of labor standards in human rights because of the universal and uncontingent nature of such rights. However, the opportunity for consensus around instituting specific practices may depend on presenting the regime in terms of "non-normative" business standards, supplanting formerly established "inalienable" human rights. For unions the price of moving the regime from one agreed in principle but ignored in practice (i.e. a regime based on "aspirational" human rights norms), to one enforced in practice, may involve allowing its underpinnings to be contested.

Shipowners wish to establish a functional convention, while continuing to contest the norms underlying the ILO labor standards regime (or at least this was their position before the change in leadership). Their original regulatory objectives of attaining a "level playing field," however, will not be achievable without strong PSC enforcement provisions. Even if the Seafarers' group can be persuaded to agree to a convention based primarily of flag state enforcement, shipowners from high-standard flags may find it undesirable—their low standard competitors will still have scope to cheat. On the other hand, if shipowners can successfully contest the ITF's capacity to regulate the shipping labor market, by, for example, contesting its capacity for industrial action in ports, or opening new labor supplier states like China, then they may be better off without the convention. However, if those ploys do not succeed, or if unions devise counter strategies, the ITF's industrial strength and bargaining power will continue to grow. The shipowners may find themselves back in the same negotiations in the near future, holding fewer cards in terms of being able to shape the CMLC. It is possible that the Shipowner groups' current position is not so much the outcome of considered strategy as a collective action problem.

Codifying accepted industry practice into a concrete set of rights and obligations under current conditions of "disciplinary neo-liberalism" (Gill 2003: 130–131) emboldens capital to question the constitutional basis of basic human rights. According to Gill, capital seeks to implement "the new constitutionalism," or the embedding of market principles into the very structure of the developing global polity. This is in order "to make transnational liberalism and if possible transnational liberal capitalism, the sole model for future development." (Gill 2003: 132) Part of this process involves denying or subordinating claims based on non-market principles, and rooting out of international law anything which might soften the disciplinary power of capital. Human rights in general, and labor rights in particular, provide room for claims based on non-market principles, which can interfere with capital's ability to impose discipline and operate as it pleases. Some of the Shipowners' objectives in the CMLC process can be seen in this light—i.e. as part of the deal they wish to see shipowners' explicitly freed from claims to rights not explicity provided in the CMLC, and then restrict the CMLC's contents to rights which are market compatible. The "one-stop shop" principle is essentially a denial of the validity of claims to rights not in the CMLC—a very valuable concession to capital should the convention be passed.

Turning negotiation of basic human rights into a global collective bargaining process may provide practical gains to workers and increase union power, but it also runs the risk of codifying a situation in which unions consent to the undermining of fundamental rights. Because of this, depending on the specific provisions of the deal, the Seafarers' group may have more to lose than to gain if a weak convention is passed. They may be better off waiting until greater pressure can be mobilized on governments and recalcitrant shipowners to establish a solid enforcement mechanism, than allowing this convention to proceed to a vote without rights based PSC enforcement language.

Although it is possible that the CMLC will never come into force, it also would not be surprising if it did. Maritime actors in the ILO certainly consider it within the realm of the achievable, and with a slightly different configuration of power in the Shipowners' group it could very well be realized. In that case, it will build on an already functioning global, transnational industrial governance system, and on a substantial maritime precedent of interlinked state sovereignty. Although the CMLC is, "small beer for the ILO" in terms of the number of workers directly impacted (*Lloyd's List* 22 Jan 2001), the precedent it sets for labor rights enforcement in the wider world will be explosive.

CONCLUSION

Both states and transnational non-state actors feature in maritime industry global governance, but it is the transnational class-based interests of the maritime industry actors which most decisively shape global maritime politics. Industry actors work on multiple levels, pursuing transnationally formulated strategies vis-à-vis each other, IGOs, and national governments. Although some autonomous state interests are clearly evident in concerns about inspection practicalities, budgets, national employment opportunities an so on, states are not always autonomous actors in their own right, but also serve as intermediaries for national or transnational private actors.

As the STCW 95 and CMLC cases show, the main actors in global maritime regulatory politics are transnational labor and capital, and not national governments. Nonetheless, national governments and the intergovernmental global legal framework remain crucial to the implementation of the maritime governance system. ILO agreements continue to be embedded in the formal structures of an international system based on relations between sovereign states. The ILO made this clear when in the January 2004 CMLC working group an ILO legal expert stated in response to a question about whether shipowners could violate the convention: "Member states adopt this convention. Only member states can violate this convention. A shipowner is not a member state. A shipowner cannot violate this convention. But a shipowner can violate the standards set out in this convention." The formal institution of sovereignty is important, and is retained, although the convention is aimed at influencing the behavior of shipowners more than governments.

Although the CMLC and STCW 95 contain the kind of detail one would expect to see in directly applicable national legislation or collective agreements, they are still intermediated as international treaties. States, not firms or individuals, are in the end the responsible parties. Each of the social partners is trying to bring the state back from its "retreat" (Strange 1996), but to do things in a different way than before, and only to do those things the social partner in question wants done, and not to do those things the other social partner wants done. This transnational reconstruction of the state does not provide the sort of all encompassing authority traditionally provided by states, but rather is fragmented and circumstantial, with its role defined by international agreement. These international agreements, in turn, are defined not so much by the relative influence and interests of states, as traditional international relations theory would have it, as by the interests, strengths and weakness of the social partners, and the characteristics of the existing regimes they build on. Political opportunity structures in global politics continue to be limited and defined by the immediate needs of global capital, constraining what subordinate actors can do with them. To a limited extent, regimes can be influenced by capital's need to establish hegemony, but the narrow basis of global regulatory authority inhibits a more substantial "global civil society" from stabilizing and legitimizing global capitalism.

Chapter Seven

Breaking No Eggs and
Making No Omelets

As has been shown, transnational working class capacities have developed within the maritime shipping industry, and these contribute to and influence the development of global state forms for transnational industrial governance. Workers and unions in many other industries also face increased capital mobility, resulting in declining union influence, worsening terms of employment, and reduced respect for labor rights. Globalization restructures production processes, creating new cross-national configurations of union influence within firms, which, since wage determination remains national, tend to result in competitive relations between unions at production sites. New transnational competitive pressures shape union strategy but do not pre-determine it, since unions can self-consciously seek to redefine the terms their transnational relations in solidaristic ways.

Outside maritime, the relative weakness of transnational inter-union coordination and lack of institutionalized industrial governance makes it more difficult to trace the ways in which transnational class struggle shape global industrial governance. It is clear that industry specific patterns of transnational coordination are emerging following the structure of competition and opportunities for union influence (Anner *et al.* 2006). Furthermore, unions are becoming increasingly interested in global regulatory governance (Anner 2001; Van Roozendaal 2002). However, the continuing national embeddedness of union authority and the tendency of transnational relations to focus on the firm level are persistent weaknesses in the structure of the global labor movement. It is not clear whether current trends in increasing transnational union activity can stem the global decline of the labor movement, or whether it is too little, too late.

Union responses to globalization have been purely reactive. In many cases, in the early stages of the transnationalization of production,[1] unions were not really aware of transnational inter-union competition in a concrete way. That is to say, they were aware of management demands and cost pressures, and ascribed these to import competition, capital mobility, or wage competition, but did not relate these to competition with specific production facilities, or local unions.[2] Nor were they aware of the opportunities and threats presented by global institutions and international regimes shaping the competitive dynamics in their industries. Over time, however, this situation changed, as unions began to learn about transnational competition between production sites—not least because management told them, often in quite specific terms. Management's use of "coercive comparisons" as a bargaining tactic prompted unions to develop transnational linkages to check claims about employment conditions elsewhere. Sometimes, these contacts have led to more developed strategies for transnational coordination, although this is by no means guaranteed. [3]

If maritime shipping is a guide, increasingly sophisticated global governance follows the need to contain and channel class conflict within an industry. Historically, organized labor served as a force for building and maintaining democratic institutions in advanced capitalist countries (Crouch 1993). Labor might play the same role in global politics through participation in industrial governance, if unions can coordinate their goals and mobilize transnational power resources. However, even if unions manage to globalize in specific industries, the route to a global polity via industry or issue specific governance could lead to a system based more on technocratic market regulation than on ideas of citizenship and justice. Union strength and patterns of transnational activity vary considerably across sectors and regions, so that some in some contexts significant progress has been made toward transnational unionism, while in others unions have remained substantially local. Unless there is a dramatic change in trajectory, very likely the near future will see sector and regionally specific patterns of governance incorporating transnational labor actors wielding a certain limited amount of influence. In other contexts, labor's capacity for resistance will continue a downward spiral, perhaps mitigated slightly by minimal global labor rights standards implemented primarily through the self-limiting and unreliable device of corporate social responsibility.

This chapter surveys the development of transnational unionism and its role in global governance, concluding that industry-specific patterns are in fact emerging. Idiosyncratic characteristics of specific capitalist globalization projects create competitive threats to national unions which structure transnational networking and strategies for resistance. The transnationalization of capital creates new productive structures and corporate hierarchies, provides new points of tension and opportunities for cooperation between trade unionists. The institutional structures of the global labor movement, the GUFs and other international union associations, serve as focal points, and contexts in which inter-union disputes are resolved and joint strategies contemplated. The GUFs' sectoral focus, and the weakness of the multi-sectoral organizations, reinforces the tendency toward sector-focused union strategies and governance.

Geographically specific factors also shape the global labor movement. The involvement of the now greatly expanded EU in labor regulation influences global labor standards. European-based TNCs transmit aspects of EU industrial relations practices to countries outside Europe. Because of the desire of the EU Commission to legitimate European integration, the EU has made an effort to co-opt unions into the European political process (Taylor and Mathers 2004). As result of EU subsidies, regional transnational union cooperation is far more systematic and widespread that elsewhere, providing the relatively stronger unions in Europe with opportunities to extend their influence across borders. Unions in Europe use their relative strength to establish labor rights protection systems within TNCs, and unions outside Europe leverage the relative strength of European unions vis-à-vis European TNCs.

On the other hand, the downward spiral of unionism in the USA, combined with the growth of China, and other low wage places like it, as a sites for TNC production, have broadened low wage production site alternatives outside the reach of effective union organization. The problems unions in Europe face are global, since conditions outside Europe tend to undermine efforts to maintain labor strength in the EU. In effect Europe serves as a reluctant power center for the global labor movement. The proliferation of Global Framework Agreements (GFAs) is the most obvious aspects of this trend, although one could argue that the GUF system itself is inherently Euro-centric. This is not to claim that unions in Europe are the solidaristic saviors of the global labor movement. Their relative strength vis-à-vis unions elsewhere does not necessarily make them less inclined to use their strength for egotistical ends. In any case, unions in Europe are also threatened by declining influence, as neo-liberalism takes root, undermining comfortably union-friendly national arrangements.

INSTITUTIONS OF THE INTERNATIONAL LABOR MOVEMENT

The institutional character of the global labor movement influences transnational inter-union cooperation, reinforcing sectoral patterns of activity. The global labor movement largely consists of the parallel structures of the International Confederation of Free Trade Unions (ICFTU), and the Global Union

Federations (GUFs). European-wide regional structures are also important, since they are actually in some ways more substantial than the global bodies. All these international union bodies are federations of national union affiliates, who fund them, govern them, and appoint their staff.

There has been considerable recent academic interest in network based, transnational "rank and file-ism"—with some advocating organizing the global labor movement along these principles instead of within the bureaucratic structures (Moody 1997). It clear that these rank and file networks, however, cannot, and in most cases do not intend to, replace the bureaucratic union structures. Rather, on some occasions, they supplement them, and on others seek to influence them. When they must, they stand in for them, but generally only to fight the battles which the bureaucratic labor movement has already abandoned (Castree 2000). Whatever the flaws of the institutionalized global labor movement, there is no clear alternative to it. Insofar as there are transnational working class capacities, these exist within, or at least in relation to, the formal international structures (Munck 2004: 10–11). This analysis therefore focuses on what could be labeled the "official" structures of the global labor movement.

Multi-Sectoral Organizations

Multi-sectoral organizations on the global stage serve a similar purpose to those on the national level, in providing a representative voice on issues of importance to the labor movement as a whole. The ICFTU formed in 1949, after US and UK delegates walked out of a World Federation of Trade Unions (WFTU) meeting and set up their own global organization. The new organization quickly attracted a following of non-communist unions from around the world. A strong rivalry between the ICFTU and WFTU developed, and continued throughout the Cold War. When communist regimes in Eastern Europe and the Soviet Union fell apart during the 1990s, the WFTU lost most of its affiliates, and new unions in those countries looked to the ICFTU and GUFs instead. Nowadays, the WFTU is a much more marginal organization than it was, although it still exists. There is also a relatively small World Confederation of Labor (WCL), which affiliates confessional unions.

Although there is an obvious structural symmetry in the relationship between the ICFTU and the GUFs at the global level, and national union centers and national affiliate unions, this symmetry conceals an important difference: the ICFTU does not affiliate the GUFs, and has little influence over them. An early attempt by the WFTU to assert authority over the GUFs and integrate them into the WFTU's sectoral Trade Union Internationals (TUIs), backfired in the face of strong GUF assertions of autonomy

(Lewis 2003), ensuring that the ICFTU would not make the same mistake. During the Cold War, ICFTU legitimacy with Third World and left wing unionists was compromised by its involvement in anti-communist politics, but with the end of the Cold War the ICFTU has realigned its activities in the direction of defending labor rights against the encroachments of globalization. The ICFTU operates as a global NGO lobbying the UN and other international organizations. For example, it helped coordinate union lobbying in the run up to the WTO Ministerial Meeting in Seattle in 1999, promoting the idea of enforcing labor standards through WTO trade sanctions (Anner 2001). It serves a coordinating and support function for the union side in ILO meetings. It occasionally has a supportive role in specific union disputes as well (Gordon 2000).

At the European level, national union centers are affiliated with the European Trade Union Confederation (ETUC) in Brussels, founded in 1973. This body focuses on influencing EU policy, on building European-level social dialogue with employers, and on building relationships between trade unions in Europe. Although focused on EU issues, its membership also includes unions from countries which are in Europe, but not actually in the EU. Since 2000, it has begun to promote the development of European level collective bargaining coordination, following discussions by the sectoral European Industry Federations along these lines (Broughton 2005b).

Sectoral Organizations

Most workplace related global level transnational labor union activity involves Global Union Federations in some way. The GUFs' primary tasks are to 1) develop contacts between national unions 2) advise and support international union campaigns and 3) represent union interests for particular industries or crafts in global political contexts. The most notable of their recent activities has been the establishment of union networks, and global framework agreements within particular TNCs. Except for the ITF, GUFs have little authority or direct mobilizing potential of their own, but, rather are networking and servicing organizations which national unions use for their own purposes. They do, however, derive independent influence as intermediaries, experts and information brokers. Appendix F lists the GUFs and the number of members each claims.

GUFs are governed by affiliates, who appoint their officers, decide their policies (in broad outlines), and decide to what extent they wish to participate in GUF organized activities. Most GUFs have their origins in 19th century craft based organizations, pre-dating the post-WWII formation of the ICFTU (and WFTU) by some time. Over time, these consolidated into a more industry-based structure, although some GUFs, and particularly departments of GUFs, retain a strong craft basis. They have expanded in resources and membership over time, as a result of national unions affiliating and making more resources available in response to concerns about globalization. With the exception of the ITF, GUFs have relatively small secretariats—perhaps 30 people at most, financed by dues from their affiliates.[4] Often, they receive grants from affiliates, governments or foundations, which are generally targeted to a specific project. Except for the ITF in London, their Secretariats are located either in Geneva or Brussels.[5]

GUFs often have regional offices. These structures are skeletal outside of Europe; in the EU context, however, regional structures are more substantial and often formally independent of the GUFs. The European regional structures, called European Industry Federations (EIFs), serve a similar role to the GUFs, but on the European level. Because of European Union Commission efforts to involve unions in European integration, EIFs receive significant subsidies from the EU for social partnership related activities, including setting up European works councils (EWCs), which are EU-wide employee representative bodies in TNCs, described below. With exceptions, the GUFs tend to be oriented toward global campaigns and solidarity actions, while the EIFs are more focused on European politics, and increasingly on trade union coordination.

On the global level, GUFs help unions set up company based union networks. Company based global union networks have their genesis in the 1960s, when United Autoworkers (UAW) then president Walter Reuther promoted the idea in International Metalworkers' Federation meetings. Councils formed in these early years met infrequently, generated little in the way of concrete action, and faded away over the years (Northup and Rowan 1979). The idea took off again in the early 1990s, however, and an increasing number of company level union networks have since been formed, mostly as a result of GUF activity, and sometimes as extensions of EWCs. Müller, Platzer and Rüb divide company level networks conceptually into those formed on the basis of a formal agreement with management, which they call world works councils (WWCs), those formed by unions without management's participation, or GUF networks, and those formed by rank and file workers, works councilors, and lower level union officials without official union sanction, or "grassroots networks." Without the legal backing the EWCs enjoy, GUF and grassroots networks come up against limited resources (Müller, Platzer and Rüb 2004: Ch17.1–17.3).

GUF networks have served as vehicles for global corporate campaigns. For example, the Rio Tinto company network, set up by the ICEM, has campaigned against the anti-union global mining giant Rio Tinto, bringing together unions, environmental groups, community activists, and indigenous rights groups (Goodman 2004). WWCs, despite their cooperative implications, have also facilitated mutual union support vis-à-vis management. For example, the Daimler-Chrysler world works council brings unions together to discuss concerns about management strategy. These contacts resulted in the negotiation of a global framework agreement, and have facilitated cooperation between German and Brazilian unions in responding to management initiatives (Anner *et al.* 2006)

At the EU level, EWCs facilitate the coordination of plant level representatives' reactions to transnational issues. The EWC directive gives the legal right for employees in TNCs in the EU to establish an EU-wide works council. The works council idea comes out of the industrial relations systems of certain European countries, where workers at firms of a certain size have legally established rights to in-firm representation. This is supplementary and parallel to any union representation. Germany is the country most noted for strong works councils, although they play a major role in French and Spanish industrial relations as well. Works councils and EWCs are not union bodies as such, although they are often union dominated. Not all firms in the EU which could have EWCs actually have them, and not all existing EWCs function at more than a very basic level—there were about 750 EWCs in all in 2004, while 2,169 firms qualified under the EWC Directive (Hall and Marginson 2004). Some EWCs are anchoring points for global level cooperation, with employee representatives from outside Europe being included.

There was initially some concern that transnational company level structures could actually speed the decline of national industry bargaining, by giving company level representatives access to resources that national unions do not have. It appears now, however, to have had the opposite effect in bringing unionists together, perhaps in part because of the dependence of EWCs on GUF and EIF resources. The WWCs, in particular, are union dominated bodies. While some EWCs have a life of their own (at Unilever, for example[6]), they do not seem to be particularly suited to bargaining coordination, or even to mobilizing solidarity (Wills 2001). Nonetheless, EWCs have served as channels for mobilizing transnational strikes. For example, the Renault EWC helped to mobilize French and Spanish unions to protest the closure of the Renault auto assembly plant at Vilvoorde, Belgium in 1997 (Lillie 1999). Generally, however, EWCs have been slow to develop the trust and sense of identity needed to assert an independent agenda, in part because of cultural differences and communication problems (Stirling and Tully 2004)

At the start of the 21st century, the institutional structure of the global labor movement is becoming more substantial, with industry level

GUFs more experienced and better resourced, and more company level inter-union networks being established. While there is a definite sense of a coherent global "movement," there is also a lack of consensus and coordination on specific issues. Authority within the GUFs remains invested in the national unions, and substantive contacts between plant level officials through transnational union networks produce conflict as well as cooperation. Inter-union conflict is probably inevitable, when jobs and living standards are at stake, so heated discussions may in some sense be a positive sign—i.e. in showing that unions are at least discussing their differences instead of undermining one another by default. However, the ability to consistently produce solidaristic rather than competitive outcomes is lacking. GUFs (or any transnational union organization for that matter) do not have authority to make binding decisions, or to enforce them. As long as there is no transnational source of union authority, common positions on wage levels will remain difficult to achieve and maintain.

GLOBAL AND REGIONAL TRANSNATIONAL BARGAINING

A key indicator of how successfully the international labor movement is coordinating its activities in a particular sector is the extent to which unions are able to induce employers to bargain collectively. Employers have proven reluctant to bargain with unions above the national level. Quite aside from the fact that employers are greatly advantaged by keeping negotiations as local as possible, to induce unions to compete with one another, there is probably not enough consensus on the union side in most cases to come up with a realistic unified collective bargaining agenda. Were employers to suddenly decide to sit across the table from them, unions would probably not be able to agree on more than basic issues. The big issue of wage cost competition, so important to the ITF's politics, is not discussed as such at the global level in other sectors. GUFs and EIFs do not have independent mandates to conclude collective agreements directly with employers, although there is now some discussion of coordinated bargaining in the EU.

The three most important types of transnational collective bargaining attempts which have occurred to date are (1) Global Framework Agreements (GFAs), sometimes know as International Framework Agreements (IFAs) (2) European Social Dialogue, and (3) European coordinated collective bargaining. The most significant of these so far in terms of real world impact are the GFAs. The European Social Dialogue is not widely thought to have produced much of concrete value to the labor movement. While it has produced, according to the Commission "over 40 joint texts," Hyman

(2001: 174) describes it as having "such limited content as to contain little of practical significance." European level coordinated collective bargaining, though potentially a very important development, has not actually come close to achieving its aims yet, and has therefore had little discernable real world impact (Hassel 2004). All of these attempts at transnational bargaining are either entirely Europe-focused, as with the European social dialogue and coordinated bargaining, or are essentially European projects applied in global contexts, as with the GFAs.

Global Framework Agreements

GUFs and GUF affiliates negotiate GFAs, which are essentially corporate codes of conduct which unions have signed on to, in exchange for influence over their content, and participation in their monitoring.[7] GFAs are an aspect of corporate social responsibility, intended to shield TNCs from negative publicity, foster positive relations with unions, and in some cases provide access to "socially responsible" niche markets (Christopherson and Lillie 2005). With a few exceptions, GFAs have only been signed by European based firms, with a heavy bias toward northern Europe. See Appendix G for a list of GFAs signed by GUFs.

Advocates of GFAs assert that union involvement makes them very different from normal corporate codes (Tørres and Gunnes 2003). From the perspective of usefulness to labor, this is certainly true, although the difference may be more nuanced than fundamental. As Tørres and Gunnes point out, codes of conduct usually have weak or nonexistent labor clauses. As documents of corporate policy, they have no legal weight, and are enforced, or not, at the discretion of the company. GFAs provide for union participation in monitoring, but the response to uncovered violations is at the discretion of the firm. There is, however, an assumption that the TNC will generally attempt to correct problems because to fail to do so would be to lose the benefit of the agreement, and invite a corporate campaign from the union side.

GFAs may cover the TNC's workforce, the supply chain, or both. As a matter of policy, they are supposed to be global, although the Chiquita GFA, which required a difficult campaign to achieve (Riisgard 2004), only covers Chiquita's Latin American operations. GFAs assert the intention of the firm in question to maintain certain standards, usually drawn from ILO conventions and recommendations, and elaborate on these standards in ways which make clear their implications for corporate policy. For example, the GFA between the International Federation of Building and Wood Workers (IFBWW) and IKEA sets forth IKEA's intention to follow the "IKEA Way" corporate code of conduct. This code sets out in great detail labor (and environmental) standard expectations for IKEA suppliers, although these do not apply in IKEA-owned retail outlets.[8] Despite the union signature, the "IKEA Way" deals with IKEA's obligations and intentions in relations to its supplier firms, rather than IKEA's or IKEA's suppliers' obligations to workers or labor unions.

ILO conventions and recommendations are at the basis of labor standards in the "IKEA Way." In some provisions, suppliers are additionally told they must comply with "applicable national legislation." The code does not set out wage levels, or grant specific rights or recourse to individual workers (IKEA 2002). If a supplier fails to observe the GFA's terms the IFBWW is expected to bring the matter to IKEA's attention, although the primary means of monitoring is through auditors hired by IKEA.[9] IKEA enforces the GFA through the threat of terminating its business arrangements with the supplier. This threat rarely comes into play, as IKEA works with suppliers to help them meet the standards, as long as the supplier is willing to make satisfactory efforts to do so.

GFAs sometimes serve as platforms for specific union demands in local and national contexts. For example, unions in Brazil and Turkey used the Daimler-Chrysler GFA to win union recognition (Anner *et al.* 2006). The US hotel union HERE (now merged with the Union of Needletrades, Textiles and Industrial Employees to form UNITE-HERE), leveraged the Accor hotel chain's GFA with the IUF[10] to pressure local management into recognizing a union at two New York hotels (Wills 2002). A major problem with this sort of strategic use of GFAs is that some affiliates lack awareness of the GFAs' existence and their possible strategic uses (Riisgard 2004). Furthermore, poor timing in negotiating a GFA can interfere with ongoing campaigns. For example, UNI signed a GFA with the H&M retail chain during a campaign by UNITE to organize H&M stores in the USA, creating the false impression that H&M's labor relations problems had been addressed.[11]

Corporate social responsibility (CSR) initiatives have received increasing attention in recent years, from companies, as well as from the labor movement. CSR may create a "union substitution" effect, by making it seem as if TNCs have addressed labor rights issues, while in fact they have not. GFAs represent an attempt to use the CSR discourse to union advantage. Potentially, CSR, particularly when implemented through GFAs, allows unions outside Europe to leverage the strength of European unions (by accessing rights which unions bargained in a European context). This gives GUFs and European unions some influence over working conditions and labor rights in places where union organization is weak or non-existent. The danger is that GUFs will become partners in the development of global union-substitution efforts.

European Social Dialogue

European social dialogue (ESD) an outgrowth of the EU Commission's perceived need to legitimate European integration by strengthening its "social dimension" (Schröder and Weinert 2004). ESD consists of negotiations between the ETUC and UNICE (the multi-sectoral employers' association, *Union des Industries de la Communauté européenne*), and between various sectoral employer organizations and EIFs. Employers have been reluctant to agree to anything substantive in the multi-sectoral ESD context. ESD has produced documents which have served as draft texts for EU Directives, so that in practice, the main leverage the ETUC enjoys is the possibility that if the employers do not agree to a text, the Commission will go ahead and draft a directive on its own. Obviously, this only works if there is a possibility that the Commission will draft something. Some see dependence on the Commission, which is not exactly known for its support of union goals, as a key weakness of the social dialogue process (Schröder and Weinert 2004). Given the ETUC's structural inability to muster independent power resource (Turner 1996; Taylor and Mathers 2004), multi-sectoral ESD is unlikely to be a building block for more substantial things. Resulting texts tend to be weakly worded from a labor perspective, and there is not always clear application to particular work situations.[12] Sectoral ESD has proven more fruitful, however, because of the greater potential within sectors for finding regulatory projects benefiting both capital and labor. Nonetheless, even this is topically limited to issues amenable to integrative bargaining.

European Collective Bargaining Coordination

In the late 1990s, unions became concerned about the impact of European Monetary Union, and increasingly tight monetary coordination by EU member states. With national governments less able to use fiscal and monetary policies to fine tune their national economies, unions in Europe might become locked in a competitive downward wage spiral.[13] Metalworking unions in the Benelux and northern Germany took the lead, sending observers to each others' negotiations starting in 1997 (Schulten 1999b). In 1998, at a European Metalworkers' Federation (EMF) meeting, unions set out a "coordination rule," establishing that unions should attempt to meet benchmarks in their bargaining. According to the rule, the benchmarks are not fixed wage costs, but are percentage increases based on productivity and inflation. The purpose is not to equalize labor costs, as with ITF agreements, but rather to ensure that unions do not deliberately "low-ball" their pay settlements to attract jobs. However, unions retained complete autonomy in bargaining policy (Schulten 1998), so that compliance with the benchmarks is voluntary.

Unions have not taken the benchmarks very seriously. Although of course the benchmarks are often met, there is no reason to believe that bargaining outcomes are different than they would have been without the benchmarks. There is no evidence of unions using the benchmark to make a case for higher pay settlements, or taking industrial action to ensure that pay settlements do not fall below the benchmark, as one would expect to see if transnational pattern bargaining were developing. National pressures are moving unions away from national level coordination, casting doubt on the ability of unions enforce the level of coordination they already have, let alone move to a new transnational level. For example, German unions have increasing difficulty maintaining national norms in the face of firm level concession bargaining by works councils (Schulten 2003). Voluntary benchmarks are unlikely carry much weight versus political pressure from national sources, or if unions feel they cannot strike successfully to maintain the standard.

Nonetheless the impetus for coordinated bargaining has grown, with the ETUC declaring support for the concept in 2000, and EIFs from other sectors creating their own coordination programs as well. The public service EIF, EPSU (European Public Service Union) has been pushing coordination since 2000 (Broughton 2000). Banking unions in UNI-Europa announced in 2004 their intention to engage in bargaining coordination (Broughton 2005a). It appears that, despite the lack of concrete results, unions feel bargaining coordination serves a purpose. At a minimum, it has expanded awareness among unionists that pay settlements in one country have an impact in other countries—demonstrating that these issues are legitimately transnational, and that ideally, unions *should* coordinate their demands (Broughton 2005a).

TRANSNATIONAL INDUSTRIAL ACTION

Crucial to labor movement strength is the ability of unions to mobilize workers, and to strategically channel class conflict to achieve economic and political goals. Globalization complicates this by restructuring industrial processes, and creating new and differently formed political spaces of contestation (Amoore 2002). These new spaces, at least initially, are less amenable to worker resistance—if nothing else because one motivating factor in capital's restructuring along transnational lines is to reduce the capacity of workers to resist. However, unions eventually devise new sources of leverage seeking out capital's new vulnerabilities. The usefulness, or at least the usability, of labor's traditional weapon of choice, the strike, is severely constrained by globalization, however, and even the innovative tactical developments of recent years have not been able to compensate fully for its loss. While unions occasionally engage in transnational sympathy strikes, this is not primarily as an economic weapon, but rather as part of overall "corporate campaign" tactics to embarrass and inconvenience targeted firms. Strikes, as contests of industrial strength, remain essentially national and local affairs, of declining frequency.[14]

In national settings, the national union often has some degree of control over company level negotiations. At the transnational level there is no equivalent to this authority. It is not unusual for unions outside the primary dispute to campaign and conduct sympathy strikes to show support, but the union involved in the primary dispute always formulates its bargaining demands and makes its settlement independently.

There are two basic categories of transnational union pressure tactic. The first is old-fashioned industrial action, deployed so as to exert influence across borders. The second is the corporate campaign,[15] or effort to tarnish a company's image and disrupt its business relationships in as many places as possible. These usually supplement primary industrial action, or in some cases occur instead of it—if, for example, workers at the primary site would be subject to reprisals were they to strike. These strategies overlap, and feed into one another in many cases. For example, a corporate campaign may involve some sympathy strikes—although the goal is usually publicity rather than industrial pressure.

Secondary Industrial Action

The transnationalization of production makes it strategically more important for unions to coordinate their industrial action. However, the national scope of union organization virtually ensures that any transnational strike will be "secondary" industrial action—meaning that it is not undertaken by workers on their own behalf, but rather in sympathy with workers elsewhere. Workers and unions undertaking secondary action are likely to be in violation of contract. As a result, the transnationalization of production in the absence of corresponding legal and institutional changes robs the strike weapon of its effectiveness.

The legal space and penalties for secondary industrial action vary greatly from country to country. In the United States or UK, a union can be held legally liable for an employer's losses from a secondary boycott. In the USA, however, under certain circumstances secondary strikes are legal. For example, unions in industries covered by the Railway Labor Act (i.e. railways and airlines) may vote to strike in sympathy. In Finland, even illegal strikes bring only mild financial penalties to the union conducting them, so secondary boycotts are an effective weapon if the issue is sufficiently important. Lobbying to make sympathy strikes legal in the context of European wage bargaining is an element in the European Metalworkers' Federations' 2003–2007 work program (EMF 2003).

There are three basic reasons unions want to engage in secondary industrial action. First is to prevent management from transferring production to facilities not on strike. Second is to target crucial elements of a transnational production chain. Third is to show broader support and build political momentum. While all of these transnational strike tactics provide useful leverage, they are not the same as coordinated strikes—i.e. they do not involve unions striking at the same time, with a unified strategy, and a coordinated set of demands.

Transnational production linkages are most often strategically exploited by unions in transport. For example, in civil aviation, unionized airplane mechanics sometimes refuse to service planes when the cabin crew are on strike. During the 1997 British Airways cabin crew strike, US-based International Association of Machinist mechanics refused to service British Airways aircraft. In other industries, it is unusual to do this. Unions more often cooperate to prevent shifts of production, since this can usually be accomplished through refusing to take on extra work, which is not necessarily a violation of contract, and does not require workers to actually walk off their jobs. For example, during the 2005 Finnish paper industry strike and lockout, Swedish paper unions refused overtime to prevent employers from shifting production to Sweden (*Paperiliitto* 5/2005).

Most transnational solidarity strikes, however, are short, symbolic sympathy strikes conducted as part of an overall campaign. The much vaunted Renault-Vilvoorde "euro-strike" is one example. When Renault announced the closure a factory in Vilvoorde, Belgium in 1997, the Belgian unions, helped by EWC activists in the French unions, launched a campaign to stop the closure. An effort to prevent Renault from shifting production to Spain failed, so that sympathy strikes ended up forming part of an effort which was primarily political and legal, rather than industrial. The campaign's strike actions involved a complete stoppage at Vilvoorde for several weeks, combined with short stoppages in French and to a lesser extent Spanish facilities. In the end, the unions forced the newly elected French Prime Minister Jospin to intervene save a portion of the Vilvoorde production (Lillie 1999).

Another example is the conflict between the USWA (United Steel Workers of America) and Bridgestone/Firestone tire company in the mid-1990s. The URW (United Rubber Workers' union), which organized Firestone plants, began the strike on July 12, 1994. Bridgestone/Firestone hired permanent replacements and refused to hire many of the strikers back when the URW called it off ten months later. The URW merged into the USWA, which began a corporate campaign to force Bridgestone to rehire the strikers. Unions in Argentina, Brazil, Belgium, France, Italy, Spain, Turkey, and Venezuela engaged in work stoppages and demonstrations against the company as part of this campaign. On November 4, 1996, the USWA reached an agreement with Firestone. Work stoppages, although no doubt a nuisance to management, served a more political than industrial purpose: i.e. to show worldwide support for the replaced workers, and demonstrate to management that the dispute was polarizing its relations with its global workforce.

Corporate Campaigns

In a search for new sources of leverage in an increasingly anti-union environment, unions in the United States developed the "corporate campaign" tactic in the 1970s and 80s. Corporate campaigns involve analyzing the power structure and vulnerabilities of a company, seeking to exert pressure in any way possible—usually through negative publicity, and disrupting relations with business partners, who do not want to be caught up in the dispute. Greven and Russo (2003: 6) define the three most important elements of the corporate campaign as "strategic research and planning, an effective media strategy and escalation." Although not a transnational tactic per se, when conducted against a TNC with a complex global structure, embedded in a web of transnational relations with investors, creditors, suppliers and customers, unions end up "following the money" across national borders, seeking allies, solidarity and additional leverage points. Since the 1990s, GUFs have been increasingly involved in corporate campaigns, initially to service US unions seeking to broaden domestic conflicts by bringing their disputes overseas.

Of all the GUFs, the ICEM (International Federation of Chemical, Energy, Mine and General Workers) has probably relied on corporate campaign tactics the most. Starting in 1995, it assisted the USWA in a corporate campaign to resolve a union-busting lockout at the Ravenswood aluminum plant, in West Virginia. The plant was part owned by international financier Marc Rich, now notorious for receiving a presidential pardon from Bill Clinton, through an offshore company structure. To pressure him, the USWA disrupted Rich's global interests and business partnerships, of which there were many in various countries around the world. [16] In another case, ICEM supported a corporate campaign by the Oil Chemical and Atomic Workers (OCAW, now merged into another union) against Crown Oil, over an industrial dispute at a Baltimore refinery. Among other things, this campaign involved leveraging the ICEM's GFA with the Norwegian oil firm Statoil. With the assistance of the ICEM and the Norwegian oil workers' union (NOPEF), OCAW was able to persuade Statoil to decline to renew a contract with Crown Oil, in order to uphold the principles in the GFA (Hickey 2004).

Corporate campaigns have also seen heavy use in retail. Retailers like the US-based Wal-Mart, the Belgian Delhaize, the French Carrefour, and the German Lidl, have all been targeted by transnational corporate campaigns. Some transnational corporate campaigns resulted from efforts by the North American United Food and Commercial Workers union (UFCW) to organize or make unprofitable new grocery store chains opening in the USA during the 1980s and 90s. These were usually European owned, resulting in the campaigns becoming transnational when the UFCW found it could request help from the usually more influential union in the corporation's home country. For example, in 1990 UFCW launched an organizing drive at a Carrefour store in Philadelphia, Pennsylvania. When management resisted unionization, the UFCW followed up with a corporate campaign, involving assistance from unions in France. Although Carrefour recognized the union in the end, the chain withdrew from the US market. The UFCW attributes the chain's failure to establish itself in the US market to damage done by the corporate campaign.

An example of a recent increasingly global campaign is the anti-Wal-Mart campaign. Wal-Mart's aggressive anti-union practices have made it the *bête-noir* of US retail unions. Its expansion overseas, and propensity to export its anti-union practices, have made it unpopular with unions in many other countries as well. As a result, Union Network International (UNI), the service sector GUF, and UNI affiliates have an ongoing campaign against the firm, spreading information about its practices and linking up with other anti-Wal-Mart campaign groups (Bibby 2005).

Corporate campaign practices are being increasingly adopted by unions outside North America. German discount retailer Lidl, for example, has resisted establishing a positive relationship with ver.di, the German service sector union. In an effort to stem Lidl's expansion, ver.di is using many of the same tactics used in the Wal-Mart campaign. Ver.di is documenting and publicizing worker rights violations at Lidl, as well as encouraging boycotts and building links with other anti-Lidl groups (ver.di 1/2005). Ver.di has transnationalized the dispute by drawing in unions from other countries, such as Finland, where Lidl has also had difficult relations with the retail union (*Palvelun ammattilaiset* 23 Apr 2004).

Corporate campaigns compensate for union weakness on the shop floor. If a union cannot legally strike, or does not have the leverage to win if it does, or if the company is not unionized in the first place, a corporate campaign can exert pressure anyway. Unlike sympathy strikes, which tend to run up against legal barriers and contractual obligations, campaigns are a flexible tool, which unions can adopt without major structural changes to national industrial relations systems. Both corporate campaigns and sympathy strikes, as tactics, can be executed without granting any authority to international union bodies, although unions have given GUFs greater resources to provide support for transnational campaigns.

INDUSTRIAL PATTERNS

General trends in tactics can be explained by organizational learning and the spread of new repertoires. As such, they reveal little about how union strategy relates to the changing structure of capital. This section, therefore, compares transnational labor market developments and patterns of union cooperation in construction, retail and civil aviation. One would expect that in sectors with international product markets and/or production, there would be more need, and more effort, for transnational coordination. The actual picture is more nuanced, however. Patterns of transnational inter-union competition and transnational opportunities for union influence shape cooperative union strategies (Anner *et al.* 2006). Management strategies are as important as actual product markets in defining how unions perceive competitive threats. Labor mobility, as well as capital mobility drives transnational union coordination.

Construction[17]

The construction industry is "local" in the sense that most construction work takes place on the site where a building is erected. This local rootedness has given way to global cost pressures and new forms of migration. Internationally active contractors create an ambiguous social space for migrant workers by isolating them from society, in which they are "illegalized" and unable to access social, political or legal protections (Hunger 2001). Core firms and union members work alongside workers and firms in this "shadow economy." Context-specific transnational configurations of interest, including unions, business enterprises, employer associations, civil society groups, and governments have emerged to regulate, or undermine regulation of, migrant work. The construction labor market is not as fully globalized as that for seafarers, but there are many strong regional labor flows which have developed at various points, including from Mexico to the United States, eastern to western Europe and South Asia to the Middle East.

In some places, better controlled labor markets have so far kept the number of migrant workers relatively small. In the Finnish construction industry, union density is about 80%, and migrant labor makes up about 10–15% of the labor force. This will probably change over the next several years, as it becomes easier to hire workers from the new EU member Baltic States. So far, however, the Finnish construction union has been able to keep control over the labor market and wage levels primarily by limiting the number of non-Finns employed. The migrant presence in the Finnish labor market is at a relatively small scale compared to, say, Germany, where the availability of migrant labor has undermined national collective agreements. Legal and illegal migrant work is now a regular feature of the German construction labor market, and the construction union has not been able to successfully organize enough of the new workforce to regain labor market control.

Nevertheless, even in Finland continuing signs of a growing underground labor market suggest that the union lacks the ability to monitor the work, due to the complexity of sub-contracting and a wide range of methods of contractors use to cover wrongdoing. Both Finnish and German unions have made efforts to establish ties to unions in labor-sending countries, and regularize the market for migrant labor. Construction unions are concerned about international migration policy, especially at the EU level, and have lobbied the Commission to establish the principle that host country rather than home country standards apply to migrant workers.

The sector GUF, the International Federation of Building and Woodworkers, has signed a number of GFAs with multi-national construction firms. However, the main strategy so far is for national unions to retain or regain control of local labor markets through exclusion of migrants when possible,[18] or organizing migrants when not. These strategies are combined with efforts to build links to unions in labor supply areas, so that migrant workers can enter the labor market in a controlled and legal way. GUF and EIF political efforts can be seen as extensions of this strategy to create a regulated transnational labor market. The European Federation of Building and Wood Workers (EFBWW) has lobbied the EU Commission against a proposed new Services Directive, which, in its proposed form, would make it legal for migrant workers to be employed under home country standards. Similarly, the IFBWW is involved with ILO discussions on the rights of migrant workers (IFBWW 2004).

Retail

Although giant transnational grocery and department store chains have expanded across Europe, the Atlantic, and increasingly into Asia as well, they continue to hire their retail workers in the same places they sell their products. Unlike construction, retail transnationals have not sought to lower wages by tapping into migrant labor markets. On the other hand, they have tried, and often succeeded, in lowering wages and working conditions in other ways.

Transnational retailers entered the US market during the 1980s from Europe and Japan. In many cases, these fought union organization, causing US retail unions such as the UFCW to develop a corporate campaign strategy. UFCW campaign tactics, as described earlier, focus not so much on supporting organizing drives, but rather on keeping non-union employers out of unionized local retail markets.[19] During the 1990s, Wal-Mart has become the paragon of anti-union retail employers. It has expanded throughout North America relying on its systematic, though sometimes legally dubious, procedures for reducing cost. Part of the savings comes from low pay for its retail staff, part from effective logistics and part from using market power to squeeze supplier firms. Wal-Mart's methods have proven imperfectly transferable to some settings, such as Germany (Christopherson 2001), but the firm has nonetheless managed to expand in many countries worldwide, threatening established retailers (Bibby 2005). Where Wal-Mart has not thrived, other versions of the anti-union hard-discount strategy have emerged, including the German Lidl supermarket.

Retail unions network through UNI, launch joint campaigns and pass information back and forth, but rarely take cooperation beyond this. Given the local nature of retail labor markets, coordinated bargaining is unlikely to become an urgent issue, unless firms begin to make use of migrant labor, as is occurring in construction. The actual impact of UNI's campaigns is unclear. The actions taking place are all more or less localized, although they are publicized globally.

Civil Aviation

The global airline industry has in the last 20 years become more concentrated and more transnational in structure. Nonetheless, airline regulation is still based on a system evolved from the 1944 Chicago Convention, which established the principle of bi-lateral division of routes between countries. Regulation restricted competition, allowing "rent sharing" between workers and airlines (Bylton *et al.* 2004). Airline deregulation, which began in the United States in 1978, and much more slowly Europe in the 1980s, has changed the impact of the regulatory regime on industry structure, while still leaving in place many of the basic forms of the old system. As a result of deregulation, low-cost carriers began to enter the market, airlines began to build transnational alliances, and many aspects of production were outsourced. Low-cost carriers have threatened the position of the established carriers causing them to look for new ways to reduce labor costs. Airline alliances have allowed airlines to share marketing, customer amenities and flight connections; more substantial alliance cooperation extends to profit and revenue sharing between airlines. Outsourcing has fueled the growth of transnational subcontracting firms, such as in-flight meal supplier Gate Gourmet. Accordingly, the contemporary civil aviation industry continues to be structured on a national basis, coordinated by international regime (Richards 1999). This national and international basis is cross-cut by increasingly transnational firms and firm networks.

The ITF has responded to the growth of airline alliances with its own "solidarity alliances." These are transnational networks of company-level union representatives from the airlines that have formed global alliances. Most of the focus is on flight attendant unions, although there has been some interest from ground staff as well, and pilots have created parallel networks of their own. There are currently four airline alliances with ITF networks: Star Alliance; oneworld, SkyTeam and TUI. These meet periodically, exchange information, and make policy statements. They are similar to GUF networks, but, because of the unique structure of the airline industry that inhibits the growth of TNCs, solidarity alliances involve workers from alliances of national companies, rather than from unified TNCs. They have not had a great deal of success in achieving recognition from management, although they have unsuccessfully pushed for GFAs.

Civil aviation unions see regulatory lobbying as very important, and efforts to influence regulation occur at the national, regional and global levels. For example, in the United States, airline unions have been very concerned to preserve cabotage, i.e. to ensure that flights from one US city to another must be on US owned carriers. In the EU context, the European Transport Workers' Federation is pushing for the Commission to mandate a clear division between skilled and certified flight attendants, and unskilled assistants, echoing the STCW 95 debate in shipping (see Chapter Five).

The structuring of inter-union relations along corporate lines (through alliances rather than TNCs), creates tensions because of sometimes competitive relations between the unions involved (Lillie and Martinez Lucio 2004: 174–5). However, there are also many concrete instances of transnational solidarity involving sympathy strikes and refusing "struck work." Opportunities to exert regulatory influence abound at the national level, and aviation unions are very much engaged in this. As these opportunities transfer to regional and global forums, the ETF, ITF and direct bilateral inter-union networks assume a steadily greater role.

UNIONS IN GLOBAL GOVERNANCE

As we have seen, union *tactics* have become global, although *structures* and *strategies* have not. Although union authority remains firmly vested in the national and local levels, unions are nonetheless increasingly willing to cross borders, and to consider the impact of their actions on groups of workers in other countries. Unions rely more and more on GUFs and transnational tactics to assist in times of crisis, but remain unwilling to permit an actual transfer of authority, or interference in core activities such as collective bargaining.

Transnational bargaining so far is notable for the degree to which it occurs at the labor movements' "lowest common denominator." GFAs focus on establishing very basic labor rights, on which all trade unionists more or less agree. Furthermore, GFA negotiations allow the unions with more central positions in the company to basically conduct the union side of negotiations, avoiding the problem of standardizing expectations between core unions and the peripheral ones, who are the ones most likely to actually make use of the agreement.

European collective bargaining and the coordination rule have the potential to develop into a system of transnational union benchmarking, with mandatory target wage increases backed up by the threat of transnational industrial action. According to Schulten, this could eventually become the basis for a "European solidaristic wage," involving narrowing wage differentials between countries and industries, countering the current neo-liberal trend toward divergence. Schulten continues, however, to explain that a lack of political commitment to follow through on these ideas has stalled progress. In particular, explicit "beggar thy neighbor" undercutting through participation in competition oriented national employment pacts show that national goals continue to be more important in union strategy than achieving real coordination (Schulten 2002). This is increasingly recognized as a problem, however. Concepts and strategies for bargaining coordination are in place, so all that is missing is national union commitment.

Outside maritime, the transnational working class has not developed sufficient capacities to challenge the dominance of the transnational capitalist class. Union coordination of bargaining and industrial action are not sufficiently developed to structure either union or employer interests in global industrial governance. While unions are involved in global industrial governance in some contexts—for example, in articulating ILO conventions into shop floor practice through the negotiation of GFAs, this participation does not have the strength and consistency of a unified union platform based on the transnationally defined interests of workers in an industry.

Chapter Eight
Conclusion

The Flag of Convenience campaign is a successful union attempt to reassert social control over an offshore industry. To make the campaign work required innovative organizational structures and strategies, turning the ITF-centered union network into a powerful global and transnational actor within the shipping industry. Class conflict in shipping serves as a basis for the creation of new transnational state forms, building on, and at the same time restructuring, the existing intergovernmental industrial regulatory system. Maritime industrial regulation is increasingly formed along the lines of the real existing transnational industry structure, rather than along the lines of insulated parallel national regulatory systems.

Palan observes that offshore expanded from a marginal phenomena to a major part of the world economy because it resolves some of the contradictions between the globalizing imperative of transnational capital, and an international system based on autonomous theoretically insular sovereign states. The growth of off-shore was not a deliberate project of transnational capital, but rather " . . . the contradictory nature of the nation state presented them [corporate lawyers and policy makers] with problems which they solved in ways that can now be seen to have laid the foundations of offshore . . ." (Palan 2003: 183). Transnational capital found the cracks in the nation state system and exploited them, to permit the growth of a global economy based on transnationally organized production. Offshore, however produces its own set of problems for capital (as well as for everyone else). First, there is the declining legitimacy of the nation state (Strange 1996). No longer capable of advancing the democratically determined interests of their citizens, states must instead commercialize their sovereignty, undermining their foundational myth of popular sovereignty (Palan 2003: 157, 187). The declining capabilities of the nation state also create new collective action dilemmas for capital. As the shipping industry case shows, the reproduction of the labor force, for example, is no longer assured when industry moves offshore to escape the unified state framework.

Offshoring, and the associated neglect of social issues and rights, generates resistance from society. This can lead to pressure for global re-regulation if there are social actors with access to the appropriate resources to channel the resistance. The outcome of this transnational class struggle depends on the configuration of interests supporting and opposing re-regulation and the leverage points available to compel offshore capital in a particular situation. As with the development of offshore itself, idiosyncratic factors come into play in specific situations, determining what strategies can be successful.

In the shipping industry, the actor configuration and availability of leverage points are relatively favorable. There is a global union organization which provides not only a consistent voice in favor of regulation, but also has its own independent means of enforcement. Although national governments have little interest in regulating and enforcing human rights standards, their use of port state control to protect national ports and shorelines provides a political opportunity for the transnational actors. Using the PSC structures and precedent, the transnational labor market actors seek to knit together a comprehensive maritime regulatory system. The success of transnational regulatory projects depends on the development of transnational class capacities, including strategies to reassert social control over transnational capital. By creating and channeling class conflict in the shipping industry, unions were able to motivate certain capital fractions to push for re-regulation. In industries besides maritime, unions lack sophisticated transnational capacities, and may not be able to play the same role as they do in maritime.

SOVEREIGNTY, CLUBS AND POLITICAL OPPORTUNITIES

New transnational state forms are emerging. These are based on the old national and intergovernmental forms, but function in different ways. The old organization of the world as a system of sovereign states, which coordinated their policies on international issues through issue specific regimes, shapes the current alternatives for building a new global polity. Current international structures tend to shunt transnational actors into issue specific regulatory contexts, with the price of admission to these discussions being the ability to participate constructively in obscure and highly technical debates. This is a legacy of the way international regulation has been managed, and it continues to influence the way global governance develops. Fortunately for the labor movement, many unions have this kind of expertise at hand. Unfortunately for the labor movement, technocratic discussions tend to restrict opportunities to bring up issues of social equality, justice and human rights, and channel solutions down paths which marginalize the interests of the groups least able to frame their demands in market-technical terms.

Context specific state and quasi-state forms can be sufficient to regulate an issue area if it is possible to construct a "club" to restrict access by non-compliant actors to desired goods (DeSombre forthcoming). The ability to restrict access, however, is highly context specific. Enforcement power can be exercised by both state and non-state actor, as long as they can 1) negotiate internally what compliance should look like, 2) monitor compliance, and 3) exclude the non-compliant from access to at least some desired goods. This can occur through a variety of means; the ITF uses industrial action to exclude non-compliant shipowners from certain ports, but other unions seek to create clubs of socially responsible firms, which then gain access to niche consumer markets (Anner *et al.* 2006). The ITF's system works better not only because it is more efficient at exclusion, but also because it involves more sophisticated and pervasive monitoring. What constitutes compliance is also set out clearly in specific and detailed employment contracts. The ability to agree on how compliance should be assessed is more important and difficult to achieve than it might seem: for the FOC campaign, this agreement required overcoming the North-South divide in inter-union politics.

Of course, states also create and enforce clubs, through PSC for example. PSC, although developed from a unilateralist precedent (Keslelj 1999), is implemented through what Slaughter (1997) calls transgovernmental cooperation, i.e. coordination among lower-level bureaucracies who are in direct transnational contact. Formally states created much of the maritime regulatory regime through intergovernmental treaties, although some of it is also descended from ancient maritime law, or developed from private practice. Provisions of formally constituted aspects of the maritime regime are, however, legally directed by states at states—for example, ILO or IMO conventions are legally addressed to states. However, transnational labor and capital are the real actors behind developing the regime, and these actors are also the real targets of the regime's provisions. Actually regulatory provisions influence the behavior of shipowners—states are, in a sense, providing capital with a regulatory service. This sort of global governance through clubs is fragmented, issue specific, and very much dependant on political opportunities and the capabilities of interested actors. It involves both states and non-state actors, as rule makers, subjects, and enforcers depending on the specific situation.

THE ITF AND TRANSNATIONAL CLASS CAPACITIES

Maritime industry governance is a response to the development of transnational class conflict in the industry. Transnational working class capacities in maritime are a political construct of the ITF union network. While there may be some truth to the abstract notion of a pure and true working class organically and spontaneously arising out of conditions of work and realities of everyday life, this idea of class is not endowed with power resources as such. Such a class would not be an actor, since actors must have goals and capacities to pursue them, implying organization and strategy. The organizational forms and strategies of the ITF and its affiliates cannot be separated from the development of class capacities in maritime: these things are one and the same. Creating viable global unionism means connecting transnational and global union structures to local work places, and building practical worker to worker solidarity across national borders. Formulating global goals and strategies to achieve them is just as important as building the structures to mobilize resistance. Resistance must be channeled toward certain goals to be effective—i.e. it must be targeted toward influencing the behavior of other actors, and must serve to either build union power or accrue material benefits to workers. The ITF builds on the leverage gained by dockworker action in ways which consolidate material gains and power resources for dockers and seafarers in a variety of contexts.

The ITF is now a *de facto* global trade union for seafarers, but this form of global unionism is different from traditional national unionism. Global unionism is built upon a multi-level transnational network. Inspectors connect together the shop floors of dock workers around the world, and tie together the links in global transportation chains. National union leaders in the Fair Practices Committee decide the policies to be implemented by the inspector network. The FPC balances the interests of national affiliate unions with the requirements of global bargaining leverage in deciding wage levels, and in labeling registers as Flags of Convenience. In labeling FOCs, the maritime unions specifically tackle the issue of offshore capital movement, and decide what it means in the context of their effort to reassert social control over transnational capital. They extend their own version of privately organized social regulation into the offshore world, although the offshore label becomes a bit confused when applied to processes where there is a real transnationalization of production, rather than just deregulation through fictional offshore techniques.

OFFSHORE GOVERNANCE, GLOBAL FACTORIES AND ALIENATION

Offshore and transnational production are very much interlinked processes, in that offshore provides the openings in the system which permit capital to move and coordinate globally (Palan 2003). Transnational production requires "command and control" functions which conglomerate in global cities (Sassen 2001) but also involves flows through offshore locations, at least in a legal sense (Palan 2003). The transnationalization of production involves movement and reorganization of physical production apparatus. Both offshore and transnational production tend to move capital's decision making out of the reach of nationally bounded labor unions, although transnational production can also extend the influence of well-situated core unions in TNCs beyond borders (Lillie and Martinez Lucio 2004), as occurs, for example, with global framework agreements (Christopherson and Lillie 2005).

Transnational production and offshoring are both extensions of the process of the alienation of labor from its product, which occurs, of course, in both purely national as well as in transnational contexts. Marglin demonstrates that capital only disseminates production innovations when these improve capital's ability to extract surplus. Hence, capital only changes production methods when the new methods allow it to exert greater control over the production process (Marglin 1974). Transnational production allows capital greater control over the production process, and helps to obscure the relations of production in such a way as to make it more difficult for collective action by workers to recover a share of the extracted surplus value. The geographical division of labor is as much determined by management's need to increase its control and extract surplus as is the organization of work on the shop floor.

Braverman, in his writing on scientific management and its effects, remarks that with the growth of capitalist factory production in the 19th and 20th centuries, the conception and execution of labor have been increasingly segregated. He notes that "a necessary consequence of the separation of conception and execution is that the labor processes is now divided between separate sites and separate bodies of workers . . . only during the past century . . . the scale of production, the resources available to the modern corporation by the rapid accumulation of capital, and the conceptual apparatus and trained personnel have become available to institutionalize this separation in a systematic and formal fashion." (Braverman 1974: 86–7) Transnational production is one aspect of a broader process of division of labor observed by Braverman, with bits of processes once comprehensively performed under one roof spread over the landscape. As a result, global factories develop, as different parts of inter-connected production processes locate in distant jurisdictions, and often in different countries. The coordination apparatus of the global factory strains under the confines of the nation state, fueling the impetus for capi-tal to move offshore.

Offshoring, as such, does not necessarily change the spatial division of labor. Offshore is not so much a physical move as a political and legal one, to remove certain spaces or contexts from social regulation. It is as much a strategy for alienation as transnational production is; through legal subter-fuge, wealth can be place beyond the grasp of workers, who may even have legal and contractual claims to it.[1] In concept, it is very similar to dereg-ulatory techniques used to manage industrial relations in other contexts. Employers abuse migrant domestic workers with impunity, for example, by employing techniques which isolate the workers and prevent them from having practical opportunities to seek remedy if their rights are violated (Lindio-McGovern 2004). In construction, layers of sub-contracting insu-late core firms from liability for the abusive practices of subcontractors. Although these practices may be illegal, capital insures that they take place in an effectively deregulated space beyond the reach of legal regulation and union protection (Hunger 2001). Instead of attacking fundamental human rights directly, capital removes specific work spaces, contexts, and catego-ries of powerless people from the protection they would normally enjoy as human beings within sovereign states. On-shore capital drives this process onward out of eagerness to deploy the effective technologies of discipline on display in offshore contexts.

LABOR PROTECTIONISM OR SOLIDARISTIC INTERNATIONALISM?

With the decline of northern welfare states and the increasing porosity of national boundaries, the geography of exploitation is no longer defined strictly by North versus South. Saskia Sassen, for example, notes that global cities, located both in the global North and the global South, have grown up as "command centers" of the global economy. These cities are at once concentrations of wealth (extracted from peripheral areas in both the North and South), as well as poverty, and are also focal points for class struggle (Sassen 2001). Simultaneous with the movement of capital to the periphery, production systems dependant on low wages have grown up within core countries, probably partly as a result of the need of the core labor force to compete with labor in the periphery. In a sense, the Flag of Convenience seafarers are just such a labor force; although they are isolated and invisible on their ships, they work partly within the borders of erstwhile "core" countries, on highly capital-intensive, sophisticated vessels, but are paid developing country wages.

A standard argument in the repertoire of many employers is that seafarers ought to be paid according to the standards of their home country (ISF Year 2000). According to employers, this concept is actually *more* sympathetic to the interests of the seafarers because those from more desperate circumstances will be more willing to accept low pay, and therefore more likely to receive the available jobs. The impoverished are actually harmed by high wages, out of context to their social circumstances. The story is sometimes embellished with anecdotes, such as Russian seafarers hiring bodyguards to protect their earnings, or otherwise dealing with the problems which sudden wealth can bring to those unaccustomed to the responsibility.[2] One article relates that some South Africans accuse the ITF of reinforcing the practices of "apartheid" in its maintenance of the minimum wage standard, because South African seafarers are not able to break into the market at ITF rates (*Lloyd's List* 26 Jan 2001). The flaw in this argument is obviously that if the ITF allowed South African seafarers into the market at lower rates, Filipinos, Russians, Poles and Indians would lower their rates as well. All seafarers would earn less money, and the South Africans would still be excluded because of the established market positions of the other nationalities, just as they are now.

Successful unionism involves the establishment of a labor cartel, which means that access to the labor market must be structured in some way. In the past, on the global scale this has been accomplished through protection of national markets via trade legislation, however this strategy is becoming less and less viable given the declining political influence of unions (Frank 1999). At the local scale, unions have restricted labor market access through skill certification (Cobble 1991), a concept which can be expanded to a larger geographic scale (by STCW 95, for example), but only really serves to solidify union control if appropriate union structures and global regulatory institutions exist. STCW 95 excludes many seafarers from developing countries from the maritime labor market, and there may have been some protectionist impulses behind the support of many ITF affiliates for its implementation. However, the beneficiaries are not so much the unions in industrialized countries, who are unlikely to see the return of their jobs as a result of the convention, but rather the unions in developing labor supply countries. These unions see their labor market position strengthened. These unions have members situated to upgrade their qualifications, and are concerned about competition from unqualified non-members, as well as the possibility that employers will shift their sourcing arrangements elsewhere. This is labor protectionism, surely, but it is South-South protectionism.[3]

Labor protectionism and internationalism are not necessarily at opposite ends of the same spectrum. The FOC campaign, for example, is based on egotistical parochial interests but nonetheless has established a private union-centered regime for regulating a global labor market. Effective internationalism depends on unions exercising monopolistic power over labor, which means maintaining distinctions within global labor markets. Serious internationalist strategies seeking to manipulate labor markets will inevitably run up against accusations of "protectionism," but these should be seen in their political context, rather than as serious and well-intended analytical critiques. The idea that labor standards can be protectionist has currency, and the word will inevitably continue to be used, both by employers, and by unions and governments attempting to undermine global standards to attract investment to their locations.

THE CHINA SYNDROME

In the first years of the 21st century, a series of dramatic plant closures and corresponding production moves to China made the Finnish public aware (a bit later than the rest of the world, perhaps) of the phenomena labeled in the Finnish popular press as "The China Syndrome" (*Kiina-ilmiö*). Quickly, the term began to be applied to the even more frequent shifts of production to Europe, so that China began to take at least some of the blame for just about any job losses occurring in Finland. From the Finnish end, these phenomena look quite similar, although China as a destination for Finnish firms actually represents a relatively smaller part of the problem than does Europe. Use of the "China Syndrome" label for all capital movements from Finland, however, conceals an important difference between China and Europe: in China, there are no established independent union partners for the world labor movement to deal with. Moving a factory from Finland to Europe results in inter-union bickering, or, much less frequently, inspirational solidarity, depending on the situation. Moving a factory to China takes it out of the effective reach of the global labor movement, because there is no union at the other end to bicker with.

To a lesser extent, the United States presents a similar problem. In the USA, unions are faced with the challenge of maintaining basic collective bargaining rights at any level. Although the labor movement is established and well resourced relative to labor in developing countries, there are also major firms and economic sectors with little or no union presence. There is also little transnational activity. US unions have become involved in transnational campaigns on occasion (usually to ask for help), but regional bargaining cooperation is not on the agenda at all, there is very little regional GUF presence, and there is not that much sectoral or pattern bargaining to begin with. In the context of George W. Bush's anti-union agenda, the American labor movement is in crisis, spiraling downward out of control.

The China Syndrome, and its US counterpart, are a problem for the global labor movement because these countries compete for investment with the rest of the world, set benchmarks and serve as laboratories for developing anti-union practices. Even if unions in the EU can work out their cooperation problems amongst themselves, they will still have to deal with competition from the US, China and elsewhere. Global union strategy ultimately needs to consider not only bargaining coordination, but also strategies for organizing the unorganized in those places where union are most difficult to organize. The ITF's solution for China has been largely to exclude it—but mostly China has excluded itself from the FOC labor market by employing its seafarers on its own ships. In other industries, unions have leveraged TNCs, forcing firms to enforce labor rights in their own facilities and in their supply chains. In the USA, GUFs and European unions have lent support to organizing campaigns by US unions, but as with transnational cooperation generally, these have really been domestic campaigns with some marginal transnational backing.

So far, unions have made little progress in the direction of strategically organizing from a global perspective. The international labor movement is built on the sovereign state system, and suffers from this structure in devising transnational solutions (Stevis 1998: 65–66). Transnational projects, such as organizing across global industries, are difficult to conceive, let alone conduct, within current union structures. The FOC campaign avoids this problem by organizing only in offshore spaces, outside the nation state system. It is difficult to see how global unions can cope with the problem of large non-union sectors within national boundaries if they remain confined to their current structures. Increasing use of offshore techniques to deregulate employment may resolve the issue.

THE ROAD MAP TO GLOBAL UNIONISM

The FOC campaign case demonstrates not only the possibility that unions can regulate global labor markets through unilateral bargaining coordination, but also the specific types of organizational changes needed to accomplish this. Specifically, national unions must cede bargaining autonomy to global organizations (Chapter Three), create, or allow to be created, autonomous horizontal transnational structures, to implement uniform procedures (Chapter Four), and pursue transnationally formulated political demands to restrict labor market access and protect labor rights (Chapters Five and Six). Unfortunately, these organizational changes threaten the power of national union leaderships, and will therefore be very difficult to implement until substantial further union decline has taken place. The ITF developed a system of side-payments to take care of this, but this system arises out of the particular circumstances in maritime shipping, and in any case is a solution with its own set of problems. Dock unions provide an excellent example of solidaristic internationalism, but this occurs in the context of minimal inter-port wage competition, a strong radical syndicalist ideology, and a preexisting global network through which to pursue this internationalism.

Dimitris Stevis poses the question "Activists would like to know whether labor organizations are basically sound but need to be reformed or are fundamentally unsuitable for a vital international labor politics." (Stevis 1998: 52) Current efforts at labor transnationalism in industries other than maritime indicate that national union leaders are grappling, though so far unsuccessfully, with the difficult political compromises and resource commitments real transnational structures and capabilities require. Transnational structures take time to develop, and it may be that the labor movement simply cannot restructure itself quickly enough to stem its decline. It may also be that the creation of a global labor movement is simply beyond the limited capabilities of bureaucratic trade unions.

It could be that we have to wait for the wheel to come around again— for unions to decline and perhaps disappear, and then be reborn, with structures better suited to the new global political economy. John Kelly, while not exactly advocating the preceding viewpoint, writes that worker collectivism is determined by autonomous social and economic factors. Union power in society is influenced by the extent to which workers think collectively. There is not much that unions can do about this except respond intelligently to the spirit of the times. Collectivism, according to Kelly, is currently at a low ebb, but we have only to wait for workers to become increasingly angry over the failure of capitalist society to fulfill their life expectations for unionism to be again revitalized from the bottom up (Kelly 1998). If Kelly is right, and the ebbs and flows of collectivism determine union strength in society, union strategy should not matter except perhaps in the margins, since the great forces of history determine working class power, and not the stratagems of a small circle of ITF staffers in London.

The question, then, is whether ITF strategy is just a cleverly executed rear-guard action to delay union decline, or whether it represents a major strategic innovation, which other unions will perhaps imitate, setting off labor movement revitalization from above. Of course, the answer may not be entirely one choice or the other. More likely, opportunities to engender collectivism, and to use it strategically to create power resources will appear from time to time, but will only be seized by those union leaders ready to make use of them.

Appendix A

LIST OF FOC AND OPEN REGISTERS

Flag	Number of Ships in Register	Number of Foreign Owned Ships
Antigua and Barbuda	980	923
Bahamas	1119	968
Barbados	58	51
Belize	295	153
Bermuda (UK)	108	103
Bolivia	32	11
Burma	37	20
Cambodia	479	193
Cayman Islands	129	126
Comoros	79	35
Cyprus	972	899
Equatorial Guinea	1	0
French International Ship Register (FIS)	56	6
German International Ship Register (GIS)	332	5
Georgia	175	105

(continued)

(continued)

Flag	Number of Ships in Register	Number of Foreign Owned Ships
Gibraltar (UK)	161	142
Honduras	137	44
Jamaica	9	8
Lebanon	44	6
Liberia	1465	1392
Malta	1140	1080
Marshall Islands (USA)	540	462
Mauritius	8	6
Mongolia	65	38
Netherlands Antilles	168	158
North Korea	238	52
Panama	5005	4388
Sao Tome and Príncipe	15	2
St Vincent	657	554
Sri Lanka	23	10
Tonga	29	7
Vanuatu	52	52

REGISTERS LABELED AS "OPEN" BY LLOYD'S BUT NOT LABELED FOC BY THE ITF

Flag	Number of Ships in Register	Number of Foreign Owned Ships
Hong Kong	837	453
Norway (NIS)	740	174
Isle of Man	267	253
Luxembourg	40	40

Sources: ITF Website, www.itf.org.uk, examined September 12, 2005, for FOCs, and CIA World Factbook, accessed July 14, 2005, for ship statistics.

Appendix B

DEPLOYMENT OF ITF INSPECTORS IN THE YEAR 2000

Part time inspectors are counted as .5 inspectors

Argentina	2	Latvia	1
Australia	4	Malta	.5
Belgium	2	Mexico	1
Brazil	3.5	Netherlands	2
Canada	2.5	New Zealand	1
Chile	1	Norway	4
Columbia	1	Panama	.5
Croatia	1.5	Poland	2
Denmark	2	Portugal	1
Finland	2.5	Romania	1
France	4	Russia	3
Germany	4	Singapore	1
Greece	2	Slovenia	.5
Iceland	.5	South Africa	2.5
India	4.5	Spain	5.5
Indonesia	1	Sri Lanka	1
Israel	1	Sweden	4
Italy	5.5	Taiwan	2
Kenya	1	UK	2.5
Korea	4	USA	15.5
Japan	2		

Source: ITF FCR (2001).

Appendix C

LIST OF INTERNATIONAL DOCKWORKERS COUNCIL MEMBER ORGANIZATIONS

International Longshore and Warehouse Union (ILWU)	USA
ILA Local 273—St. John's	Canada
ILA Local 1414—Savannah	USA
ILA Local 1291—Philadelphia	USA
ILA Local 1422—Charleston	USA
ILA Local 1771—Charleston	USA
Trade Union of Port Workers of Bulgaria	Bulgaria
Cyprus Agricultural Forestry, Transport, Port, Seamen and Allied Occupations Trade Union Peo (Segdamelin—Peo)	Cyprus
Federación de Trabajadores Marítimos Portuarios de San Antonio	Chile
Federación de sindicatos de trabajadores portuarios (FETRAPI)	Chile
Federación Nacional de Trabajadores Marítimos y Portuarios del Perú (FEMAPOR)	Peru
UGTA Syndicat des dockers d'Alger	Algeria
Syndicat UMT des dockers du Maroc	Morocco
M.U.A—Sydney Branch Retired Maritime Union of Australia	Australia

(continued)

(continued)

Dockers in Freeport Copenhagen	Denmark
The Initiative Factory/Liverpool Dockers & Stevedores	UK
Fédération Nationale des Ports et Docks C.G.T.	France
Union Dockworkers Port of Piraeus	Greece
Federação Nacional dos Sindicatos de Trabalhadores Portuários	Portugal
Coordinadora Estatal de Trabajadores del Mar	Spain
Swedish Dockworkers Union	Sweden

Source: http://www.idcdockworkers.org/ accessed 23 Sept 05.

Appendix D

LIST OF ILO CONVENTIONS RELATED TO SEAFARING

Name	Number	Year	Ratifications
General			
National Seamen's Codes Recommendation	R9	1920	
Seafarer's Engagement (Foreign Vessels) Recommendation	R107	1958	
Social Conditions and Safety (Seafarers) Recommendation	R108	1958	
Employment of Seafarers (Technical Developments) Recommendation	R139	1970	
Continuity of Employment (Seafarers) Convention	C145	1976	17
Continuity of Employment (Seafarers) Recommendation	R154	1976	
Merchant Shipping (Minimum Standards) Convention	C147	1976	51
Protocol to the Merchant Shipping (Minimum Standards) Convention	P147	1976	
Merchant Shipping (Improvement of Standards) Recommendation	R155	1976	

(continued)

(continued)

Name	Number	Year	Ratifications
Training and entry into employment			
*Placing of Seamen Convention	C9	1920	40
Recruitment and Placement of Seafarers Convention	C179	1996	9
Recruitment and Placement of Seafarers Recommendation	R186	1996	
Seamen's Articles of Agreement Convention	C22	1926	58
Seafarers' Identity Documents Convention	C108	1958	64
Vocational Training (Seafarers) Recommendation	R137	1970	
Conditions for admission to employment			
*Minimum Age (Sea) Convention	C7	1920	53
Minimum Age (Sea) Convention (Revised)	C58	1936	51
Medical Examination of Young Persons (Sea) Convention	C16	1921	81
Medical Examination (Seafarers) Convention	C73	1946	44
Certificates of competency			
Officers' Competency Certificates Convention	C53	1936	36
Certification of Ships' Cooks Convention	C69	1946	37
Certification of Able Seamen Convention	C74	1946	28

(continued)

(continued)

Name	Number	Year	Ratifications
General conditions of employment			
Seafarers' Hours of Work and the Manning of Ships Convention	C180	1996	17
Seafarers' Wages, Hours of Work and the Manning of Ships Recommendation	R187	1996	
*(Shelved) Paid Vacations (Seafarers) Convention (Revised)	C91	1949	24
Seafarers' Annual Leave with Pay Convention	C146	1976	15
*Repatriation of Seamen Convention	C23	1926	46
Repatriation (Ship Masters and Apprentices) Recommendation	R27	1926	
Repatriation of Seafarers Convention (Revised)	C166	1987	12
Repatriation of Seafarers Recommendation	R174	1987	
Protection of Young Seafarers Recommendation	R153	1976	
Safety, health and welfare			
Food and Catering (Ships' Crews) Convention	C68	1946	25
Bedding, Mess Utensils and Miscellaneous Provisions (Ships' Crews) Recommendation	R78	1946	
Accommodation of Crews Convention (Revised)	C92	1949	45
Accommodation of Crews (Supplementary Provisions) Convention	C133	1970	29

(continued)

(continued)

Name	Number	Year	Ratifications
Crew Accommodation (Air Condition-ing) Recommendation	R140	1970	
Crew Accommodation (Noise Control) Recommendation	R141	1970	
Prevention of Accidents (Seafarers) Convention	C134	1970	29
Prevention of Accidents (Seafarers) Recommendation	R142	1970	
*Seamen's Welfare in Ports Recommen-dation	R48	1936	
*Seafarers' Welfare Recommendation	R138	1970	
Seafarers' Welfare Convention	C163	1987	15
Seafarers' Welfare Recommendation	R173	1987	
Health Protection and Medical Care (Seafarers) Convention	C164	1987	14
*Ships' Medicine Chests Recommendation	R105	1958	
*Medical Advice at Sea Recommendation	R106	1958	
Labour inspection			
Labour Inspection (Seafarers) Convention	C178	1996	11
Labour Inspection (Seafarers) Recommendation	R185	1996	
Social security			
Unemployment Indemnity (Shipwreck) Convention	C8	1920	59

(continued)

(continued)

Name	Number	Year	Ratifications
Unemployment Insurance (Seamen) Recommendation	R10	1920	
Shipowners' Liability (Sick and Injured Seamen) Convention	C55	1936	18
Sickness Insurance (Sea) Convention	C56	1936	19
Social Security (Seafarers) Convention (Revised)	C165	1987	3
Seafarers' Pensions Convention	C71	1946	13

Source: ILO Website, accessed 23 Sept 05.

Appendix E

**DRAFT CONSOLIDATED MARITIME LABOR
CONVENTION CONTENTS**

Substantive Titles, text available at: www.ilo.org/public/english/standards/
relm/ilc/ilc94/ptmc/pdf/cmlc-draft.pdf

Title 1. Minimum requirements for seafarers to work on a ship
    Regulation 1.1—Minimum age
    Regulation 1.2—Medical certificate
    Regulation 1.3—Training and qualifications
    Regulation 1.4—Recruitment and placement
    Regulation 1.5—Seafarers' identity document

Title 2. Conditions of employment
    Regulation 2.1—Seafarers' employment agreements
    Regulation 2.2—Wages
    Regulation 2.3—Hours of work and rest
    Regulation 2.4—Entitlement to leave
    Regulation 2.5—Repatriation
    Regulation 2.6—Seafarer compensation for the ship's loss or
                foundering
    Regulation 2.7—Manning levels
    Regulation 2.8—[Continuity of] [Career development and regularity
                of] employment in the maritime sector

Title 3. Accommodation, recreational facilities, food and catering
    Regulation 3.1—Accommodation and recreational facilities
    Regulation 3.2—Food and Catering

Title 4. Health Protection, medical care, welfare and social protection
  Regulation 4.1—Medical care on board ship and ashore
  Regulation 4.2—Shipowners' liability
  Regulation 4.3—Health and safety protection and accident
        prevention
  Regulation 4.4—Access to shore-based welfare facilities
  Regulation 4.5—Social security

Title 5. Compliance and enforcement
  Regulation 5.1—Flag state responsibilities
  Regulation 5.1.1—General principles
  Regulation 5.1.2—Authorization of recognized organizations
  Regulation 5.1.3—Maritime labour certificate and declaration of
        compliance
  Regulation 5.1.4—Inspection and enforcement
  Regulation 5.1.5—On-board compliant procedures
  Regulation 5.1.6—Marine casualties
  Regulation 5.2—Port state responsibilities
  Regulation 5.2.1—Inspections in port
  Regulation 5.2.2—Onshore complaint-handling procedures
  Regulation 5.3—Labour-supplying responsibilities

Appendix F

LIST OF GLOBAL UNION FEDERATIONS

Name	Number of members
Education International	29+ million
International Confederation of Free Trade Unions	145 million
International Federation of Building and Wood Workers	10+ million
International Federation of Chemical, Energy, Mine and General Workers' Union	20+ million
International Federation of Journalists	0.5 million
International Metalworkers' Federation	25 million
International Textile, Garment and Leather Workers' Federation	10+ million
International Transport Workers' Federation	4.5 million
International Union of Food, Agricultural, Hotel, Restaurant, Catering, Tobacco and Allied Workers' Association	12 million
Public Services International	20 million
Union Network International	15 million

Source: All links available through the ICFTU website, accessed 23 Sept 05.

Appendix G

LIST OF GLOBAL FRAMEWORK AGREEMENTS

BMW	Germany	Auto Industry	IMF	2005
Bosch	Germany	Automotive / Electronics	IMF	2004
Carrefour	France	Retail Industry	UNI	2001
Chiquita	USA	Agriculture	IUF	2001
DaimlerChrysler	Germany	Auto Industry	IMF	2002
Danone	France	Food Processing	IUF	1988
EADS	Netherlands	Aerospace	IMF	2005
EDF	France	Energy Sector	PSI	2005
Endesa	Spain	Power Industry	ICEM	2002
Eni	Italy	Energy	ICEM	2002
Faber-Castell	Germany	Office Material	IFBWW	1999
Fonterra	New Zealand	Dairy Industry	IUF	2002
Freudenberg	Germany	Chemical Industry	ICEM	2000
GEA	Germany	Engineering	IMF	2003
H&M	Sweden	Retail	UNI	2004
Hochtief	Germany	Construction	IFBWW	2000

(continued)

(continued)

IKEA	Sweden	Furniture	IFBWW	1998
Impregilo	Italy	Construction	IFBWW	2004
ISS	Denmark	Cleaning & Maintenance	UNI	2003
Leoni	Germany	Electrical/ Automotive	IMF	2003
Lukoil	Russia	Energy / Oil	ICEM	2004
Merloni	Italy	Metal Industry	IMF	2002
Norske Skog	Norway	Paper	ICEM	2002
OTE Telecom	Greece	Telecommunication	UNI	2001
Prym	Germany	Metal Manufacturing	IMF	2004
Renault	France	Auto Industry	IMF	2004
Rheinmetall	Germany	Defence /Auto/ Electron.	IMF	2003
Rhodia	France	Chemical Industry	ICEM	2005
Röchling	Germany	Auto industry, plastics	IMF	2005
SCA	Sweden	Paper Industry	ICEM	2004
Skanska	Sweden	Construction	IFBWW	2001
SKF	Sweden	Ball Bearing	IMF	2003
Statoil	Norway	Oil Industry	ICEM	1998
Telefonica	Spain	Telecommunication	UNI	2001
Triumph	Germany	Textiles	ITGLWF	2001
Veidekke	Norway	Construction	IFBWW	2005
Volkswagen	Germany	Auto Industry	IMF	2002

Sources: List compiled from GUF websites and European Industrial Relations Observatory (www.eiro.eurofound.eu.int).

Notes

NOTES TO CHAPTER ONE

1. In maritime shipping employers are referred to as "shipowners." This designation is not always strictly accurate, because of complexities of shipping ownership and management, but this book follows common usage of the term "shipowner" to designate employer interests in the maritime industry.
2. In the sense that they accept registration by ships beneficially owned by foreign nationals
3. The ISF is associated with the International Chamber of Commerce for Shipping, which represents shipping's broader political interests on the global stage.
4. i.e. in the Joint Maritime Committee wage sub-committee at the International Labour Organization, detailed in Chapter Three.
5. This position is supported by the empirical development of labor transnationalism. There have been some important transnational shop floor networks created outside "official" unions, involving activist workers and dissident union officials. These have, however, been more aimed at engagement with established unions, rather than at undermining them. Independent structures generally interact willingly, if critically, with established unions, in order to improve their own possibilities to act (Castree 2000; Müller, Platzer and Rüb 2004: 241–248).
6. The UK ship officers' union, NUMAST, and the Dutch seafarers' union, FWZ, are currently discussing a merger. To the unionists involved, at least, this merger seems a realistic and workable possibility.
7. Voss and Shermann, for example, demonstrate that the implementation of an intensive union organizing agenda by union locals in California resulted in internal strife, complicating the organizational change—although not always stopping it (Voss and Shermann 2000).
8. Until recently, these union bodies were referred to as International Trade Secretariats, but this was changed.

9. There are also some competing international federations and less institutionalized networks, but none of these are anywhere near as influential as the mainstream international trade union movement.

10. In summary, the consensus within the WTO maintains that labor standards are the responsibility of the ILO, and should remain within that body. Therefore, labor standards violations should result only in such sanctions as the ILO is capable and authorized to apply. Although ILO "shaming" appears to have some effect (Weisband 2001), in general ILO sanctions are not considered very effective relative to WTO sanctions.

11. An often cited OECD report on the effects of sub-standard shipping does just that (OECD 2001).

NOTES TO CHAPTER TWO

1. This is not to imply there were no struggles over wages before WWII. Shipowners kept wages low through a variety of techniques, including hiring cheaper foreigners, and repressing union organization (Markholt 1998).

2. Some shipowners in the United States, for example, have become less dependent on the "Jones Act" cabotage shipping. The Jones Act mandates that shipping between US ports be on US-flagged ships which were also built in the USA. Shipowners can apply for waivers, however, if there is not enough qualified tonnage, so the strategy has been to not build enough tonnage, and apply for waivers.

3. High tonnage ships tend to have more crew than low tonnage ships, but not proportionally more. If the same number of tons of cargo is carried in fewer ships, fewer seafarers will be needed to carry it.

4. This is important, because it means the number of ships is somewhat more indicative of the employment impact than the tonnage number, although neither figure is exactly proportional. It is necessary to look at ship numbers rather than employment figures directly because employment figures are only available for certain countries, and are rarely available for FOC registers.

5. dock work (cargo handling)

6. See Chapter Five for an explanation of White-Listing.

NOTES TO CHAPTER THREE

1. Extracts from this chapter were original published in "Global Collective Bargaining on Flag of Convenience Shipping," *British Journal of Industrial Relations* , 42:1 March 2004 pp. 47–67.

2. For example, there is the European "Social Dialogue," described in Chapter Seven.

3. Capital supplier countries are countries in which relatively large numbers of shipowners reside, but which provide relatively fewer seafarers to the global labor market.

4. Labor supplier countries are countries which provide relatively large numbers of seafarers to the global labor market, but in which relatively fewer shipowners reside.

5. The ITF Total Crew Cost (TCC) agreement sets forth minimum wage standards, overtime rates, benefits, and standards of accommodation and safety. Repatriation, termination procedures, and insurance for death or disability are also provided for, as well as some safeguards against common employer tactics for circumventing ITF contracts. The agreements specify safe manning scales, including number of seafarers in each job category, for different types of vessels.

6. Number of ships covered is a better guide to the level of union density in the FOC labor market covered, because there are more reliable statistics. The 85,000 seafarers figure is from the ITF contracts database in June 2001, and is probably accurate; however, there is no accurate number available for the denominator in the union density figure (i.e. there is no accurate figure for the total number of working seafarers in the world).

7. There were 18,630 FOC ships in 2000 according to the ITF. Of these, 5984 had ITF-acceptable collective agreements at the end of 2000. This would put ITF coverage at 32%. The ITF treats as FOCs some registers listed in its database as national flags and second registers. Potentially, these could add about 3,000 FOC ships, dropping coverage to 27%. However, a portion of the FOC fleet is not in the maritime cargo market. There are around 3,000–4,000 FOC fishing vessels, as well as research, passenger, and miscellaneous ships (perhaps another 1000 vessels). While fishing and cruise ships are important labor markets, they are not in the cargo shipping market from the perspective of industrial leverage. The ITF also has a negligible number of these ships under contract. Depending on the assumptions one makes, the ITF has around 30–40% (or slightly more) of ships in the maritime shipping market under contract. This approximate figure is sufficient to demonstrate that a substantial portion of the FOC fleet is under ITF contract.

8. At times, because of unusual situations, the ITF grants minor exceptions, but these occasions are carefully controlled to ensure they will not destabilize the labor market, and undermine the ITF wage consensus. For example, the ITF has allowed Columbus Lines, a German employer, to pay less than TCC rates to Kiribatan and Tuvaluan seafarers, because of the unusual circumstances of their recruitment.

9. China is a major maritime country, but most of Chinese seafarers work on Chinese flag ships. Some shipowners see China as a potential new major labor supplier country for international shipping. Despite the ITF's abortive attempts to initiate discussions with the Chinese labor movement, so far it has not been possible to reach an accommodation. There appears to be some low-key international sourcing of Chinese labor through the Singaporean ITF affiliate, which is apparently acceptable to the ITF.

10. There is still a minimum AB rate, however, set at USD 1300 in the 2003 agreement.

11. Seafarers have overtime work built into their regular schedule. A relatively large amount of overtime pay is also calculated into wage scales under ITF agreements.

12. As part of the Philippine's government's labor export promotion policy, the POEA is a government department involved among other things with regulating the export of Filipino seafarers.

13. These ISF figures also probably overstate the size of the labor force for some countries. For the Philippines and Indonesia, a great many of the seafarers counted in the survey are probably under-qualified and unemployed. This is a less severe problem in India and the Eastern European countries. China employs the better part of its seafarers on its own fleet. It has an enormous potential to export seafarers and destabilize the labor market, but only if serious institutional and linguistic problems can be overcome. The effective sizes of the capital supplier country labor forces are probably relatively smaller than indicated because of unemployment and because many work under contracts which allow for long paid leaves ashore (up to half the time under some contracts).

14. The Seafarers' International Union's (SIU) in particular is considered by many a corrupt union. Evidence of this is historical, but continues to reflect in how the union is perceived. For example, former president Paul Hall was known for his friendship with one of his "most trusted muscle men" Hal Banks, who ran the SIU Canadian Section. Banks was convicted for ordering the murder of a union organizer in Canada, but fled to the US and never served his sentence because of US State Department intervention (Lewis 2003: 146–151).

15. This was accomplished by having locals sign affidavits on behalf of foreign shipowners. For example, one Cypriot secretary "with a monthly salary of Cpounds 500 (Dollars 260) was alleged to own 23 vessels." (*Lloyd's List* 9 May 1998)

16. According to some interviewees, as of 2001, the Cypriot maritime union refused to acknowledge Cyprus as an FOC, and insisted that Cyprus flag ships be treated as traditional national flags.

17. In 1997, 71% of the ships in the Cyprus register were Greek-owned, 7.8% German, and 4% Russian (UNCTAD 1997). Additionally, Latvian, Estonians, and Russians frequently crew Cyprus flag vessels. Israel and Sweden have strong records of obtaining ITF contracts through industrial action.

18. This is not to imply that governments protect national fleets solely or primarily to protect domestic jobs. National defense and industrial policy often justify national flag protections. However, the end effect from the union perspective is the maintenance of national employment levels, and the protection of domestic jobs.

19. This strategy only works for ships in local trades which call in Finnish ports, and is effectively equivalent to union-imposed cabotage. Fortunately for Finnish seafarers, important Finnish exports, such as wood products, are usually destined for markets in central Europe. Unlike Finnish short-sea shipping, Finnish-owned oil tankers involved in cross trading were easily able to flag out and replace their crews at international rates (Kaukiainen

1993). Because they do not call in Finnish ports, they could not be boycotted by Finnish dock workers.

20. On the other hand, by maintaining consistently close to ITF rates, NIS wage norms did a great deal to stabilize ITF wages as the "industry norm" in the 1990s.

NOTES TO CHAPTER FOUR

1. Extracts from this chapter originally appeared in "Union Networks and Global Unionism in Maritime Shipping," *Relations Industrielles/Industrial Relations*, 60:1 Winter 2005, pp. 88–111.
2. Usually this means dock workers (longshoremen), but tug boat pilots and other workers sometimes have a role as well.
3. Sampson and Wu, for example, describe the way in which the organization of modern port work has speeded up the turnaround time for ships, decreasing the opportunities for seafarers to go ashore (Sampson and Wu 2003).
4. According to the ITF "Message to Seafarers," directory examined in December 2004.
5. The extent to which this is true, however, seems to vary from place to place. In Sweden and Finland, where the maritime unions are influential within the ITF, and the inspectors are in any case very effective, there seems to be a high degree of national autonomy. In the USA, on the other hand, where corrupt inspectors from certain seafaring unions have caused problems in the past, and there is strong rivalry between maritime unions, the ITF exerts more direct control (*Journal of Commerce* 23 Aug 1987; *Journal of Commerce* 26 Dec 1995).
6. According to former ITF General Secretary Harold Lewis, the then newly affiliated Waterside Workers' Federation of Australia played a crucial role in the decision to intensify the campaign (email, Sept. 2005).
7. According to B.L. Williamson's account this appears to have been the case in Belgium, Canada, Germany, the Netherlands, and the United States (Northup and Rowan 1983: Appendix B).
8. Blacklisting and employer attempts to recover ITF wages after the fact continue to be a problem although there are now institutions and routines for dealing with this.
9. Ver.di (*Veriente Dienstleistungsgewerkschaft*) is the result of a merger between ÖTV (*Gewerkschaft Öffentliche Dienste, Transport und Verkehr*), DAG (*Deutsche Angestellten-Gewerkschaft*), DPG (Deutsche Postgewerkschaft), HBV (*Gewerkschaft Handel Banken und Versicherungen*) and IG Medien in 2001.
10. In interviews, Swedish and Finnish dock union officials sometimes complained that the ÖTV would come to them with requests for secondary action, which could equally as well have been conducted in German ports. However, the German unionists have difficulty persuading German dockers to undertake solidarity actions, whereas that has not been a problem in Sweden or Finland.

11. At the 1998 Congress, the Dockers' Section praised Germany and Chile for introducing cargo-handling clauses into their collective agreements, and urged other countries to follow this example (ITF 1998b: 59), indicating that application had not been widespread.
12. For more details on this case, see Lillie and Martinez Lucio (2004)
13. Brian McWilliams, former President of the ILWU, is somewhat cynical about the ITF, but believes it is better to influence the ITF from the inside, rather than remain on the "outside throwing stones." Likewise, he justifies his organization's dual membership in the ITF and IDC by the desire to support anyone who is doing any kind of constructive international work (Telephone interview 2/2001).
14. Four of the Charleston Five were black, and in the racially charged climate surrounding the then-ongoing campaign to remove the Confederate flag from the state capital, apparently Condon thought the high-profile prosecution of black trade unionists made good politics.
15. ILA Local 1422 President Kenneth Riley has become increasingly popular with ILA rank and file as a result of his handling of the dispute, threatening the old-guard ILA International President John Bowers. Accusations that the ILA was playing internal politics at the expense of mounting an aggressive defense of the Charleston 5 came from all the usual suspects, including radical activists within the ILWU. The ILA's weak and inconsistent response to the accusations, as well as its attempts to delegitimate, rather than join, IDC and ILWU solidarity activities suggest that the ILA's critics are justified.

NOTES TO CHAPTER FIVE

1. Known as substandard shipowners, these shipowners evade safety, environmental and labor standards in a systematic effort to reduce costs and in doing so make it economically more difficult for other shipowners to maintain standards (OECD 2001).
2. The Paris (MoU) Memorandum of Understanding, a regional organization coordinating port state inspections in Europe, for example, assigns points to ships to determine the likelihood of inspection. Ships flying "problem" flags are more likely to be inspected (Paris MoU website).
3. Under STCW and STCW 95, there are specific safety procedures ratings are expected to know, and ratings filling specialized jobs should also have certificates showing they are qualified.
4. According to the 1990 BIMCO/ISF survey "current recruitment and training levels are unlikely to be adequate and the industry will have to expand the number of trainees significantly if serious problems are to be avoided." (*Lloyd's List* 11 Apr 1991)
5. Jeremy Smith, Chairman of the Liberian Shipowners Council, made a statement to this effect at a 1995 conference cited in (*Lloyd's List* 17 Oct 1995).
6. David Kinvade of Denholms Ship Management in Hong Kong, expressed this view at the 1995 Liberian Shipowners conference (*Lloyd's List* 17 Oct 1995).

NOTES TO CHAPTER SIX

1. Here, Trubek *et al.* reference Dunlop (1958).
2. For example, shipowners, some governments, and apparently even some unions want to exclude certain ship types, trade routes, and crafts from the scope of the convention. Shipowners seek a higher tonnage cut-off, so that seafarers on very small ships are not covered. They also wish certain job categories, such as catering staff, not to be covered, on that basis that the convention should only apply to "professional seafarers." Developing countries wish to see ships of traditional build (i.e. sailing vessels) excluded. Solutions have yet to be devised on some issues.
3. The convention draft texts, some of the minutes of the meetings, and various position papers on it are available at: http://www.ilo.org/public/english/dialogue/sector/sectors/mariti/consol.htm
4. Boockman (2003) shows that unions always vote with their group, and always vote "yes" for every convention. This is not as surprising or one sided as it may seem—if a labor rights convention were unacceptable to the union side, it would be unlikely to go forward to a vote in the first place. Employers, however, do not always vote together, nor do they always support every convention.
5. This was the situation, for example, during the discussion of the seafarer right of access to outside representation, where the employers' proposed language would have put very significant restrictions on seafarers' rights to free assembly, which would have contravened the ILO Constitution and the UN Charter.
6. See, for example, the Seafarers' and Shipowners' submissions to the Tripartite Intersessional Meeting on the Follow-up to the Preparatory Technical Maritime Conference, ILO, Geneva, 21–27 April 2005, available at http://www.ilo.org/public/english/dialogue/sector/sectors/mariti/consol.htm.

NOTES TO CHAPTER SEVEN

1. The assumption here is that globalization, as commonly understood, is related to the transnationalization of production in the current era. While some have pointed out that there were substantial trade flows in previous eras, such as the 19th century (Hirst and Thompson 2002), contemporary globalization, with its coordinated transnational production networks and precise global control, is a different phenomenon altogether.
2. Dana Frank's history of economic nationalism in the USA shows this process occurring in the 1970s and 80s (Frank 1999).
3. Sharing bargaining information can be used to prevent unions undercutting one another, but unions can also use it to tailor concessionary offers to management, undercutting the union which gave the information in the first place (Martinez Lucio and Weston 1997). Much depends therefore on the level of trust which unions at competing production sites build with one another, but trust and solidarity are difficult to achieve among workers

divided by nationality, language and culture, even when they are in direct contact with one another (Stirling and Tully 2004; Wills 2004).

4. The ITF's staff is quite a bit larger, financed in part by FOC campaign money, although one could argue that it is still small for a union organization covering the whole globe and several industries.

5. Much of the information about GUFs in this paragraph is taken from Windmuller (2000), who gives a more complete account of the history and institutional structure of the GUFs.

6. Günter Baltes, EWC Coordinator for Unilever, for example, envisions EWCs as structures for representation independent from unions (Personal Interview 1999).

7. Many GFAs have been set up on the initiative of EWCs, but with the involvement of the GUFs.

8. IKEA suppliers are generally under the jurisdiction of IFBWW unions, while retail outlets would fall under UNI's area of responsibility. UNI has not established a GFA with IKEA.

9. The IKEA case is described in more detail in Christopherson and Lillie (2005).

10. International Union of Food, Agricultural, Hotel, Restaurant, Catering, Tobacco and Allied Workers' Associations

11. Thanks is due to Marco Hauptmeier for his detective work in uncovering the details behind this incident, and for his letting me use this work here.

12. The texts of these agreements can be viewed on http://www.etuc.org/r/615.

13. Some argue that at that time, unions were already locked into a competitive downward wage spiral regardless of the approach of EMU (Schulten 1999a).

14. This may or may not make strikes less important. During the post-WWII period, strikes in many countries became ritualized activities—extensions of normal collective bargaining, regulated to be fairly predictable, while allowing an outlet for industrial conflict. In the 1980s in most countries they became less common, and in practice less a part of normal industrial relations. Therefore, strikes which do occur may take on greater political importance since they represent a breach of organized labor's now much more confined space for action.

15. The term "corporate campaign" refers to a specific type of strategically oriented campaign aimed at a company in support of an industrial dispute. In practice, corporate campaigns tend to have a limited set of workplace oriented goals.

16. See Juravich and Bronfenbrenner (1999) for a description of this campaign.

17. This section on construction work was originally drafted in collaboration with Ian Greer. It appears here with his permission

18. Construction unions do not frame their strategy in these terms, but rather in terms of legal versus illegal work. This takes the politically difficult decision of who is "illegal" and who not out of the labor movement's hands, which from the union perspective is probably just as well.

19. For example, in the early 1980s, Belgian retailer Delhaize entered the US market under the name Food Lion. Food Lion began expanding out of its initial base in South Carolina in 1980, moving into local labor markets well organized by the UFCW. When the UFCW tried to organize Food Lion, management fought back. In the late 1980s, UFCW began asking European unions for help. Corporate campaign tactics became more aggressive as time went on, and by the 1990s each side focused more on putting the other out of business than anything else. UFCW publicized Food Lion's health code violations. In one case, the union went together with a TV camera crew to the meat department of a Food Lion. As a result of this, Food Lion's stock price fell. Food Lion sued, and won, on the basis that the publicity campaign constituted an illegal conspiracy in restraint of trade.

The transnational element of the campaign consisted of cooperation with the Delhaize union in Belgium. The Belgians organized sympathy strikes and accompanied UFCW organizers on organizing rounds in the USA. Belgian unionists were concerned that management anti-union practices developed in the USA might be used in Europe.

NOTES TO CHAPTER EIGHT

1. An example of this is the way in which many ship owners use one-ship companies anonymously held in tax haven jurisdictions to protect themselves from claims of unpaid wages by seafarers. When seafarers find they haven't been paid for an extended period of time, sometimes they will pursue legal claims against the shipowner. If the owner has had the foresight to set up a one-ship offshore corporate structure to protect anonymity, often it will be impossible to legally attach claims to him or her. Since the company owning the ship has no assets but the one ship, legal action to recover the unpaid wages will at most result in the sale of the ship to cover the debts. Any debts over and above the value of the ship will go unpaid.

2. In this version of reality, shipowners are never handicapped by excessive wealth, regardless of their national origin.

3. Furthermore, unqualified seafarers are, objectively, a hazard to public safety and the environment, and shipping may not be the best place to find jobs for unqualified people, regardless of how needy. Few would suggest hiring uneducated and untrained sheep herders or rice farmers from developing countries as jet airline pilots or brain surgeons, although the certification requirements of those professions certainly restrict access by the underprivileged.

Bibliography

Alderton, T., Bloor, M., Kahveci, E., Lane, A.D., Sampson, H., Thomas, M., Obando-Rojas, B., Winchester, N., Wu, B., and Zhao, M. (2001) *The Impact on Seafarers' Living and Working Conditions of Changes in the Structure of the Shipping Industry*, Geneva, Switzerland: ILO Sectoral Activities Programme.

———. (2004) *The Global Seafarer: Living and Working Conditions in a Globalised Industry*, Geneva: ILO.

Alderton, T. and Winchester, N. (2002) "Globalization and De-regulation in the Maritime Industry," *Marine Policy*, 26: 35–43.

Amante, M. (2004) "Industrial Democracy in the Rough Seas: The Case of Philippine Seafarers," *Proceedings of the Industrial Relations Research Association Conference*, January 3–5, San Diego.

Amoore, L. (2002) "Work, production and social relations: Repositioning the firm in the global political economy," in J. Harrod and R. O'Brien (eds) *Global Unions: Theory and strategies of organized labour in the global political economy*, London: Routledge.

Anner, M. (2001) "The Paradox of Labor Transnationalism: Northern and Southern Trade Unions and the Campaign for Labor Standards in the WTO," Working Paper, Workshop on Transnational Contention, Cornell University. http://falcon.arts.cornell.edu/sgt2/contention/working_papers.htm (accessed 23 September 2005)

———., Greer, I., Marco, H., Lillie, N. and Winchester, N. (2006) "The Industrial Determinants of Transnational Solidarity: Global Inter-Union Politics in Three Sectors," *European Journal of Industrial Relations*, Vol 12, No. 1.

Arora, A.G. (1997) *Voyage: Chronicle of the Seafarers' Movement in India*, Mumbai, India: NUSI.

Arthurs, H.W. (2001) "Private Ordering and Workers Rights in the Global Economy: Corporate Codes of Conduct as a Regime of Labour Market Regulation," in J. Conaghan, K. Klare, M. Fischl (eds), *Transformative Labour Law in an Era of Globalization*, Oxford University Press: Oxford.

Baltic News Service, various issues.

Beasley, M. (1996) *Warfies: The History of the Waterside Workers' Federation,* Rushcutters Bay, Australia: Halstead Press.

Behrens, M., Hurd, R., and Waddington, J. (2004) "How Does Restructuring Contribute to Union Revitalization," in C. Frege and J. Kelly (eds), *Varieties of Unionism: Struggles for Union Revitalization in a Globalizing Economy ,* Oxford: Oxford University Press, pp. 117–136.

Belzer, M. (1993) *Collective Bargaining in the Trucking Industry: The Effects of Institutional and Economic Restructuring,* PhD Thesis, Cornell University, Ithaca, NY.

Bergantino, A. and Marlow, P. (1998) "Factors influencing the choice of flag: empirical evidence," *Maritime Policy and Management,* 25(2): 157–174.

Bertzbach, J. and Edin Mujkanociv, E. (1997) *Studie zur Zukunft der Hanfenbeschäftigten am Beispeil der Le Havre-Hamburg Range zum Beginn der 21. Jahrhunderts,* Bremen: ÖTV.

Bibby, A. (2005) "The Wal-Martization of the world: UNI's global response," Geneva: Union Network International.
http://www.union-network.org/UNIsite/Sectors/Commerce/Multinationals/Wal-Mart_UNI_Report_Walmartization_2005.htm (accessed 23 Sep. 05).

BIMCO/ISF (1995) *1995 Manpower Update,* Warwick, UK: University of Warwick, Institute for Employment Research.

BIMCO/ISF (2000) *2000 Manpower Update,* Warwick, UK: University of Warwick, Institute for Employment Research.

Bloor, M. (2003) "Problems of Global Governance: Port State Control and ILO Conventions," Paper presented at *2003 SIRC Symposium,* Cardiff University, 19 Sept. http://www.sirc.cf.ac.uk/Publications/Symposium%20Proceedings% 202003.pdf (accessed 23 Sep. 05)

Blyton, P., Lucio, M. M., McGurk, J., Turnbull, P. (2004) "Globalisation and Trade Union Strategy: Evidence from the International Civil Aviation Industry," in R. Munck (ed.), *Labour and Globalisation: Results and Prospects,* Liverpool: Liverpool University Press.

Boockman, B. (2003) "Mixed Motives: An Empirical Analysis of ILO Role-Call Voting," *Constitutional Political Economy,* 12, pp.263–285.

Brand, U. (2005) "Order and regulation: Global Governance as a hegemonic discourse of international politics?" *Review of International Political Economy,* 12:1 pp. 155–176.

Braverman, H. (1974) *Labor and Monopoly Capital,* New York: Monthly Review Press.

Bronfenbrenner, K. (ed.) (1998) *Organizing to win: new research on union strategies,* Ithaca, NY: ILR Press.

Broughton, A. (2000) "EPSU agrees framework for coordinated action," European Industrial Relations Observatory, 28 July, http://www.eiro.eurofound.eu.int/. (accessed 23 Sept 05)

———. (2005a) "Joint collective bargaining declaration in banking" European Industrial Relations Observatory, 1 April, http://www.eiro.eurofound.eu.int/. (accessed 23 Sept 05)

———. (2005b) "ETUC issues report on collective bargaining," European Industrial Relations Observatory, 31 January. http://www.eiro.eurofound.eu.int/. (accessed 23 Sept 05)

Burawoy, M. (1985) *The Politics of Production*, London: Verso.

Burgess, K. (2004) *Parties and Unions in the New Global Economy*, Pittsburgh: University of Pittsburgh Press.

Business Times: Kuala Lumpur, 31 July 2002.

Castree, N. (2000) "Geographical scale and grass-roots unionism: the Liverpool dock dispute, 1995–98," *Economic Geography* 76, 3, 272–92.

Chapman, P. (1992) *Trouble on Board: The Plight of the International Seafarers*, Ithaca, NY: ILR Press.

Christopherson, S. (2001) "Can Walmartization be Stopped?? Barriers to the Globalization of Retailing, " Paper presented at the *Conference on Global Economic Change*, Graduate School of Geography, Clark University, Worcester, MA, 14 Oct. http://www.clarku.edu/leir/christopherson.htm. (accessed on 23 September 2005).

———. and Lillie N. (2005) "Neither Global Nor Standard: Corporate Strategies in the New Era Of Labor Standards," *Environment and Planning-A* Vol 37, pp. 1919–1938.

Catholic Institute for International Relations (CIIR) (1987) *The Labour Trade: Filipino migrant workers around the world*, London: Russell Press.

Central Intelligence Agency (CIA) *World Fact Book* Washington, D.C.: CIA http://www.cia.gov/cia/publications/factbook/ (accessed Sept. 23, 2005)

Cobble, D. S. (1991) "Organizing the Postindustrial Work Force: Lessons from the History of Waitress Unionism," *Industrial and Labor Relations Review*, (44)3: 419–435.

Commons, J. R. (1909) "American Shoe Makers 1648–1895," *Quarterly Journal of Economics*, pp. 39–83.

Containerisation International, various issues.

Couper, A., Walsh C.J., Stanberry, B.A., Bourne, G.L. (1999) *Voyages of Abuse: Seafarers, Human Rights, and International Shipping*, London: Pluto Press.

Cowie, J. (1999) *Capital Moves: RCA's seventy year quest for cheap labor*, Ithaca, NY: Cornell University Press.

Cox, R. (1971) "Labor and Transnational Relations," in R. Keohane and J. Nye, Jr. (eds), *Transnational Relations and World Politics*, Cambridge: Harvard University Press, pp. 204–234

Cox, R. (1987) *Production, Power and World Order: Social Forces in the Making of World History*, New York: Columbia University Press.

———. (1996) "Social forces, states and world orders: beyond international relations theory," in R. Cox and T. Sinclair, *Approaches to World Order*, Cambridge University Press: Cambridge.

Cox, R. and Jacobson, H. (1973) *The anatomy of influence: decision making in international organization*, New Haven: Yale University Press.

Cremers, P. (1998) Presentation to the *ISF Manning and Training Conference*, 9 September.

Crouch, C. (1993) *Industrial Relations and European State Traditions*, Oxford, UK: Clarendon.

Cutler, A., Haufler V., and Porter, T. (eds) (1999) *Private Authority and International Affairs*, Albany: State University of New York Press.

Desombre, E. (forthcoming) *Globalization and Environmental, Safety and Labor Regulation at Sea*, Book manuscript cited with permission.

Dirks, J. (2001) *Internationales positives Regulieren in der Handelsschifffahrt im Kontext der Globalisierung : Eine Untersuchung der STCW 95 Konvention*, Münster-Hamburg-Berlin-Wein-London: Lit Verlag.

Donn, C. (1989) "Concession bargaining in the ocean-going maritime industry." *Industrial and Labor Relations Review*, January Vol. 42, No. 2, Pg. 18.

Dølvik, J. E. (1997) *Redrawing the Boundaries of Solidarity?: The ETUC Social Dialogue and the Europeanisation of Trade Unions in the 1990s*, Oslo: FAFO.

Dunlop, J. (1958) *Industrial Relations Systems*, New York: Holt.

European Metalworkers' Federation (EMF) (2003) *EMF Work Programme 2003–2007*, http://www.emf-fem.org/ (accessed 23 Sep. 05).

Fichter, M. and Greer, I. (2004) "Analyzing Social Partnership: A Tool for Revitalization?" in C. Frege and J. Kelly (eds), *Varieties of Unionism: Struggles for Union Revitalization in a Globalizing Economy* , Oxford: Oxford University Press, pp. 71–92.

Finnish Maritime Administration (1993) *Shipping and Seafarer Statistics.*

Finnish Maritime Administration (1999) *Shipping and Seafarer Statistics.*

Finnemore, M. and Sikkink, K. (1998) "International Norm Dynamics and Political Change," *International Organizations*, Vol. 52 No. 4 pp. 971–991.

Frank, D. (1999) *Buy American: Untold Story of Economic Nationalism*, Boston: Beacon Press.

Frege, C., Hurd, R. and Turner, L. (2004) "The New Solidarity? Trade Union Coalition Building in Five Countries," in C. Frege and J. Kelly, (eds), *Varieties of Unionism: Struggles for Union Revitalization in a Globalizing Economy*, Oxford: Oxford University Press.

Frege, C. and Kelly, J. (eds) (2004) *Varieties of Unionism: Struggles for Union Revitalization in a Globalizing Economy*, Oxford: Oxford University Press.

Gereffi, G. and Korzeniewicz, M. (1994) *Commodity Chains and Global Capitalism*, Westport, CT: Praeger Publishers.

Gill, S. (1995) "The Global Panopticon? The Neoliberal State, Economic Life, and Democratic Surveillance," *Alternatives*, 20, 1, Jan-Mar, 1–49.

———. (2003) *Power and Resistance in the New World Order*, New York: Palgrave.

Goldstein, J., Kahler, M., Keohane, R., and Slaughter, A. M. (2000) "Introduction: Legalization and World Politics," in *International Organization*, 54, 3, Summer, pp. 385–399.

Goodman, J. (2005) "Australia and Beyond: Targeting Rio Tinto," In R. Munck (ed.) *Labour and Globalisation: Results and Prospects*, Liverpool: Liverpool University Press.

Gordon, M. (2000) "The International Confederation of Free Trade Unions: Bread, Freedom and Peace," in Gordon, M. and Turner, L. (eds) *Transnational Cooperation Among Labor Unions*, Ithaca, NY: ILR Press.

Green, D. (1996) "Port Reform in New Zealand," *H.R. Nichols Society XVII Conference 1996: Tenth Anniversary of the Society Conference* May 17, Brighton, Australia. http://www.hrnicholls.com.au/nicholls/nichvo17/volxv010. htm (accessed on 23 September 05)

Green, F. (1992) "On the political economy of skill in the advanced industrial nations," *Review of Political Economy*, 4.4, pp. 413–435.

Greven, T. and Russo, J. (2003) "Transnational 'Corporate Campaigns': A Tool for Labour Unions in the Global Economy?" Paper Presented at the *13th Annual International Industrial Relations Association Conference*, Berlin, Germany Sept 8–13.

Hall, Mark and Paul Marginson. (2004) "Developments in European Works Councils," European Industrial Relations Observatory, 11 November, http://www.eiro.eurofound.eu.int/. (accessed on 23 Sept 05)

Hall, P. and Soskice, D. (2001) *Varieties of Capitalism: The Institutional Foundations of Comparative Advantage*, Oxford: Oxford University Press.

Hamann, K. and Kelly, J. (2004) "Unions as Political Actors: A Recipe for Revitalization?" in C. Frege and J. Kelly (eds), *Varieties of Unionism: Struggles for Union Revitalization in a Globalizing Economy* , Oxford: Oxford University, pp.93–116.

Harlaftis, G. (1996). *A History of Greek-owned Shipping: The making of an International Tramp Fleet, 1830 to the Present Day*, London and New York: Routledge.

Harrigan, J. (1984) "Flags of Convenience and Maritime Labor," *Industrial Relations Journal*, 15, 2 pp. 35–40.

Harrod, J. and O'Brien, R. (2002) "Organized labour and the global political economy," in J. Harrod and R. O'Brien (eds), *Global Unions?: Theory and strategies of organized labour in the global political economy*, London: Routledge.

Hassel, A. (2004) "Europeanisation by co-ordination? The merits of the co-ordination rule in European wage bargaining," in *European Trade Union Year Book*, H. Jørgensen, M. Bærentsen, and J. Monks, (eds) Brussels: European Trade Union Institute.

Haufler, V. (2000) "Private Sector International Regimes," in *Non-state actors and authority in the global system*, R. Higgot, G. Underhill and A. Bieler (eds) New York: Routledge.

Haworth, N. and Hughes, S. (2002) "Internationalization, industrial relations theory, and international relations," in J. Harrod and R. O'Brien, (eds), *Global Unions?: Theory and strategies of organized labour in the global political economy*, London: Routledge.

Heery, E. and Adler, L. (2004) "Organizing the Unorganized," in C. Frege and J. Kelly (eds), *Varieties of Unionism: Struggles for Union Revitalization in a Globalizing Economy* , Oxford University Press, pp. 45–70.

Hensman, R. (2001) "World Trade and Workers' Rights: In Search of an Internationalist Position," in P. Waterman and J. Wills (eds) *Place, Space and the New Labour Internationalisms*, Oxford, UK: Blackwell Publishers.

Herod, A. (1992) *Towards a labor geography: the production of space and the politics of scale in the East Coast longshore industry, 1953–1990*, PhD Thesis, Rutgers University, New Jersey, USA.

———. (1998) *Organizing the Landscape: Geographical Perspectives on Labor Unionism*, Minneapolis, MN: University of Minnesota Press.

Hewson, M. and Sinclair, T. (1999) "The Emergence of Global Governance Theory." in M. Hewson and T. Sinclair (eds) *Approaches to Global Governance Theory*, Albany, NY: State University of New York Press.

Hickey, R. (2004) "Preserving the Pattern: Membership Mobilization and Union Revitalization at PACE Local 4–277," *Labor Studies Journal*, 29:1 (Spring) pp.1–20.

Hirst, P. and Thompson. G. (2002) "The Future of Globalization," *Cooperation and Conflict*, Vol. 37, No. 3, 247–265.

Hunger, U. (2001) "Globalisierung auf dem Bau," *Leviathan: Zeitschrift für Sozialwissenschaft*, Vol 1, pp. 70–82.

Hyman, R. (1987) "Strategy or Structure? Capital, Labour and Control," *Work, Employment and Society*, 1(1): 25–55.

———. (2001) *Understanding European Trade Unionism: Between Market, Class and Society*, London: Sage.

IKEA (2002) *IWAY Standard: Minimum Requirements for Environment, Social and Working Conditions and Wooden Merchandise*, http//www.ifbww.org/files/iwayst.pdf (accessed on 23 Sep. 05)

International Chamber of Commerce for Shipping/ International Shipping Federation (ICS/ISF) *Annual Review 2005*, London: ICS/ISF

International Commission on Shipping (ICONS) (2000) *Ships, Slave and Competition: Inquiry into Shipping Safety*, Charlestown, Australia: International Commission on Shipping.

International Confederation of Free Trade Unions (ICFTU) *Annual Survey of Violations of Trade Union Rights*, Brussels: ICFTU, http//www.icftu.org/survey2004.asp?language=EN (accessed on 23 Sept. 05)

International Dockworkers Council (IDC) website, http://www.idcdockworkers.org/, (accessed 23 Sept 05)

International Federation of Building and Woodworkers (IFBWW) (2004) *Exploitation of construction, forestry and wood workers in connection with migrant and cross border work*, http://www.ifbww.org/files/migrantworkers.pdf (accessed 23 Sep. 05)

International Labour Organization (ILO) (1998) *World Labour Report 1997–1998: Industrial Relations, Democracy and Social Stability*, Geneva, Switzerland: International Labour Organization.

International Longshore and Warehouse Union (ILWU) (1996) *Six Decades of Militant Unionism*, San Francisco: ILWU.

International Shipping Federation (ISF) (1999) *The ISF Year*, London, UK: ISF.

International Shipping Federation (ISF) (2000) *The ISF Year*, London, UK: ISF.

International Shipping Federation (ISF) (2001) *The ISF Year*, London, UK: ISF.

International Transport Workers' Federation (ITF) (1990) *Congress Proceedings* London: ITF.

International Transport Workers' Federation (ITF) (1994) *Congress Proceedings* London: ITF.

International Transport Workers' Federation (ITF) (1998a) *Oslo to Dehli: A Comprehensive Review of the ITF FOC Campaign*, London: ITF.

International Transport Workers' Federation (ITF) (1998b) *Congress Proceedings* London: ITF.

International Transport Workers' Federation (ITF) (2004) *Message to Seafarers*, http://www.itfglobal.org/seafarers/msg-contacts.cfm, (accessed 12 Dec 2004)

International Transport Workers' Federation Flag of Convenience Campaign Annual Reports (ITF FCR) (1997). London: ITF.

International Transport Workers' Federation Flag of Convenience Campaign Annual Reports (ITF FCR) (1998). London: ITF.

International Transport Workers' Federation Flag of Convenience Campaign Annual Reports (ITF FCR) (1999). London: ITF.

International Transport Workers' Federation Flag of Convenience Campaign Annual Reports (ITF FCR) (2000) London: ITF.

International Transport Workers' Federation Flag of Convenience Campaign Annual Reports (ITF FCR) (2001) London: ITF.

International Transport Workers' Federation Flag of Convenience Campaign Annual Reports (ITF FCR) (2002) London: ITF.

International Transport Federation Report on Activities (ITF ROA) 1974 (for 1971–73), 1977 (for 1974–1976), 1980 (for 1977–1979), 1983 (for 1980–1982), 1986 (for 1983–1985), 1990 (for 1985–1989) and 1994 (for 1991–1993), London, ITF.

International Transport Workers' Federation Press Release 19 April 2005.

James, R. and James, E. (1963) "Hoffa's Leverage Techniques in Bargaining," *Industrial Relations*, Vol 2, No. 3 May.

Japanese Seamen's Union (JSU) website, "JSU's Welfare Services to its Non-Domiciled Special Members," www.jsu.or.jp/eng/e-iss.htm (accessed 23 Sep. 05)

Jessop, B. (2002) "Time and Space in the Globalization of Capital and their Implications for State Power," *Rethinking Marxism*, 14:1 Spring pp. 97–117.

Johnsson, L. (1996) *Funny Flags: ITF's Campaign—Past, Present and Future.* Falköping, Sweden: SEKO.

Journal of Commerce (JOC), various issues.

Juravich, T. and Bronfenbrenner, K. (1999) *Ravenswood: the steelworkers' victory and the revival of American labor,* Ithaca, NY: ILR Press.

Kahveci, E. and Sampson, H. (2001) "Findings from the Shipboard Based Study of Mixed Nationality Crews," Paper presented at the *2001 SIRC Symposium*, 29 June, Cardiff, UK.

Kapstein, E. (1996) "Workers and the World Economy," *Foreign Affairs*, May/June.

Kaukiainen, Y. (1993) *A History of Finnish Shipping,* London: Routledge.

Kelly, J. (1998) *Rethinking Industrial Relations: mobilization, collectivism and long waves,* London, UK: Routledge.

Keohane, R. (1984) *After Hegemony: Cooperation and Discord in the World Political Economy.* Princeton University Press.

Keselj, T. (1999) "Port State Jurisdiction in the Respect of Pollution from Ships: The 1982 United Nations Convention on the Law of the Sea and the Memoranda of Understanding," *Ocean Development & International Law,* 30: 127–160.

Kimeldorf, H. (1988) *Reds or Rackets?: The Making of Radical and Conservative Unions on the Waterfront,* Los Angeles: University of California Press.

Koch-Baumgarten, S. (1998) "Trade Union Regime Formation Under the Condi-
    tions of Globalization in the Transport Sector: Attempts at Transnational
    Trade Union Regulation of Flag-of-Convenience Shipping," *International
    Review of Social History*, 43 pp.369–402.
——. (1999) *Gewerkschaftsinternationalismus und die Herausforderung der
    Globalisierung: Das Beispiel der Internationalen Transportarbeiterfoedera-
    tion (ITF)*, Frankfurt/New York: Campus Verlag.
Krasner, S. (ed.) (1983) *International Regimes*, Ithaca: Cornell University Press,
    1983.
Lavalette, M. and Kennedy, J. (1996) *Solidarity on the Waterfront: The Liverpool
    Lockout of 1995/96*, Merseyside, UK: Liver Press.
Lee, E. (1997) *The Labour Movement and the Internet: the New Internationalism*,
    London: Pluto Press.
Lewis, H. (2003) *The International Transport Workers' Federation (ITF) 1945–
    1965: an Organizational and Political Anatomy*, University of Warwick,
    Department of Sociology, PhD thesis.
Lewis, H. (2004) "The ITF Vigilance Committees," *Historical Studies in Industrial
    Relations*, No. 17, Spring, pp.45–73.
Lloyd's List, various issues.
Lloyd's Register of Shipping (2000) *World Fleet Statistics*.
Lillie, N. (1999) "European Works Councils as Mobilizing Structures: The Case of
    Renault-Vilvoorde," *Conference Proceedings for 16th Annual Graduate Stu-
    dent Conference at Columbia University, School of International and Public
    Affairs*, New York, NY, March, pp. 291–310.
——. (2004) "Global Collective Bargaining on Flag of Convenience Shipping,"
    British Journal of Industrial Relations, 42(1): 47–67.
——. (2005) "Union Networks and Global Unionism in Maritime Shipping,"
    Relations Industrielles/Industrial Relations , 60:1 Winter 2005, pp. 88–111.
Lillie, N. and Lucio, M. M. (2004) "International Trade Union Revitalization: the
    Role of National Union Approaches," in C. Frege and J. Kelly (eds), *Varieties
    of Unionism: Struggles for Union Revitalization in a Globalizing Economy* ,
    Oxford: Oxford University Press, pp. 159–180.
Lindio-McGovern, L. (2004) "Alienation and Labor Export in the Context of Glo-
    balization: Filipino Migrant Domestic Workers in Taiwan and Hong Kong,"
    Critical Asian Studies, 36:2, 217–238.
Logistics Management, various issues.
Lucio, M. M. and Weston, S. (1997) "Trade unions, management and European
    works councils: Opening Pandora's box?" *The International Journal of
    Human Resource Management*, 8, no. 6: 764–779.
Marglin, S. (1974) "What do bosses do? The origins and functions of hierarchy in
    capitalist production," *Review of Radical Political Economics* 6: 33–60.
Marine Log, New York, June 2004.
Markholt, O. (1998) *Maritime Solidarity: Pacific Coast Unionism 1929–1938*,
    Tacoma, WA: Pacific Coast Maritime History Committee.
Marsh, A. and Ryan, V. (1989) *The Seamen: A History of the National Union of
    Seamen*, Oxford: Malthouse Pubishing Ltd.

McKenna, B. and Graham, P. (2000) "Technocratic Discourse: A Primer," *Journal of Technical Writing and Communications*. 30 (3): 219–247.

Metaxas, B. (1985). *Flags of Convenience*, Hants, UK: Gower Publishing Company.

Moody, K. (1997). *"Workers in a Lean World: Unions in the International Economy*, London: Verso.

Müller, T., Platzer H-W, and Rüb, S. (2004) *Globale Arbeitsbeziehungen in globalen Konzernen? Zur Transnationalisierung betrieblicher und gewerkschaflicher Politik*, Wiesbaden: VS Verlag für Sozialwissenschaften.

Munck, R. (2004) "Introduction: Globalisation and Labour Transnationalism," in R. Munck (ed.), *Labour and Globalisation: Results and Prospects*, Liverpool: Liverpool University Press.

Northup, H. and Rowan, R. (1979) *Multi-national collective bargaining attempts*, Philadelphia, PA: University of Pennsylvania, The Wharton School, Industrial Relations Research Unit.

———. (1983) *The International Transport Workers' Federation and Flag of Convenience Shipping*, Philadelphia, PA: University of Pennsylvania, The Wharton School, Industrial Relations Research Unit.

Northup, H. and Scrase, P. (1996) "The International Transport Workers' Federation Flag of Convenience Shipping Campaign: 1983–1995," *Transportation Law Journal*, 23 (Spring): 369.

Norwegian Seamen's Union (NSU), *The Norwegian Seamen's Union*, video, undated

Notteboom, T. (2002) "Consolidation and contestability in the European container handling industry," *Maritime Policy and Management*, 29:3, pp. 257–269.

Obando-Rojas, Welsh, B.I., Bloor, M., Lane, T., Badigannavar, V., and Marguire, M. (2004) "The political economy of fraud in a globalized industry: the case of seafarers' certifications," *The Sociology Review* 52 (3) pp.295–313.

O'Brien, R. (2004) "Globalisation, Imperialism and the Labour Standards Debate," in R. Munck (ed.), *Labour and Globalisation: Results and Prospects*, Liverpool: Liverpool University Press.

O'Brien, R., Goetz, A. M., Scholte, J. A., and Williams, M. (2000) *Contesting Global Governance: Multilateral Economic Institutions and Global Social Movements*, Cambridge: Cambridge University Press.

Organization for Economic Cooperation and Development (OECD) (2001) *The Cost to Users of Substandard Shipping*, Prepared for the OECD Maritime Transport Committee by SSY Consultancy & Research Limited, OECD: Paris.

O'Rourke, D. (2000) *Monitoring the Monitors: A Critique of Price Waterhouse Coopers (PwC) Labor Monitoring*, Independent University Initiative Report.

Öffentliche Dienste, Transport und Verkehr (ÖTV) (1998) *Solidarisch über Grenzen: 50 Jahre Billigflaggen Kampagne*, Stuttgart: ÖTV.

Overdoest, C. (2004) "Codes of Conduct and Standard Setting in the Forest Sector: Constructing Markets for Democracy?" *Relations Industrielles/Industrial Relations*, Winter, Vol 59, Issue 1.

Pacific Business Journal, 18 Sep 2002

Palan, R. (2003) *The Offshore World: Sovereign Markets, Virtual Places and Nomad Millionaires*, Ithaca, NY: Cornell University Press.

Palvelun ammattilaiset, Palvelualojen Ammattiliitto newsletter, 23 April 2004.

Paperiliitto-lehti, Paperiliitto newsletter, 5/2005, http://www.paperiliitto.fi/paperiliitto/suomeksi/paperiliitto_lehti/2005/0505/ruotsi.php. (accessed 23 Sept. 05).

Paris Memorandum of Understanding (MoU) Website, (accessed 23 Sept. 05)

Pedraja, R. (1992) *The Rise and Decline of US Merchant Shipping in the Twentieth Century*, New York: Twayne Publishers.

People's World Weekly, 24 March 2001.

Ramsay, H. (1997) "Solidarity at Last? International Trade Unionism Approaching the Millennium," *Economic and Industrial Democracy*, Vol 18: pp. 503–537.

———. (2000) "Know Thine Enemy: Understanding Multinational Corporations as a Requirement for Strategic International Laborism," in Michael Gordon and Lowell Turner (eds) *Transnational Cooperation among Labor Unions*. Ithaca, NY: ILR Press

Richards, J. (1999) "Toward a Positive Theory of International Institutions: Regulating International Aviation Markets," *International Organization*, 53(1) pp.1–37.

Riisgard, L. (2004) "The IUF/COLSIBA-Chiquita Framework Agreement: A Case Study," Working Paper No. 94, Geneva: ILO.

Robinson, R. (2002) "Ports as elements in value-driven chain systems: the new paradigm," *Maritime Policy and Management*, Vo. 29, No. 3, pp. 241–255.

Rosen, E. (2002) *Making Sweatshops: The Globalization of the U.S Apparel Industry*, Los Angeles: University of California Press.

Rumpel, E. (1998) *Menschen im Hafen: 1945–1998*. Hamburg: ÖTV.

Salvarani, R. (1998) "How to deal with problem flags," presented at *Is there a better way to regulate the shipping industry?* Conference, 23–24 June, Oslo, Norway.

Sampson, H. and Wu, B. (2003) "Compressing Time and Constraining Space: The Contradictory Effects of ICT and Containerization on International Shipping Labour," *International Review of Social History*, 48, Supplement 11, pp.123–152.

Sassen, S. (2001) *The Global City: New York, London and Tokyo*. Second ed., Cambridge, UK: Cambridge University Press.

Schröder, W. and Weiner, R. (2004) "Designing Institutions in European Industrial Relations: A Strong Commission Versus Weak Trade Unions?" *European Journal of Industrial Relations*, 10:2 pp. 199–217.

Schulten, T. (1998) "European Metalworkers' Federation adopts European coordination rule for national bargaining," European Industrial Relations Observatory, 28 Dec. http://www.eiro.eurofound.eu.int/ (accessed 23 Sept 05)

———. (1999a). "Auf dem Weg in die Abwärtsspirale? Tarifpolitik unter den Bedingungen der Europäischen Währungsunion," in Reinhard Bispinck and Thorsten Schulten (eds), *Tarifpolitik under dem Euro: Perspectiven einer europäishen Koordinierung das Beispiel Metallindustrie*. Hamburg: VSA Verlag.

———. (1999b) "Western and eastern European metalworkers' unions establish interregional bargaining policy network" European Industrial Relations Observatory, 28 April http://www.eiro.eurofound.eu.int/ (access 23 Sept 05)

———. (2002) "A European Solidaristic Wage Policy?" *European Journal of Industrial Relations*, 8:2, pp. 173–196.

———. (2003) "Collective bargaining system under pressure," European Industrial Relations Observatory, 24 Dec. http://www.eiro.eurofound.eu.int/ (accessed 23 Sept 05)

Schwartz, S. (1986) *Brotherhood of the Sea: History of the Sailors' Union of the Pacific 1885–1985*, New Brunswick, NJ: Transaction Books.

Silver, B. (2003) *Forces of labor: workers' movements and globalization since 1870*, New York: Cambridge University Press.

Sinclair, T. (1999) "Synchronic Global Governance and the International Political Economy of the Commonplace," in M. Hewson and T. Sinclair, (eds) *Approaches to Global Governance Theory*, Albany, NY: State University of New York Press.

Sisson, K. and Marginson, P. (2002) "Co-ordinated Bargaining: A Process for Our Times?" *British Journal of Industrial Relations* (40)2: 197–220.

Sklair, L. (2001) *The Transnational Capitalist Class*, Oxford: Blackwell.

Slaughter, A.M. (1997) "The Real New World Order," *Foreign Affairs*, Vol. 76, No. 5 (September/October), pp. 183–197.

Snedden, R. (1957) "The International Shipping Federation," *International Associations* December: 2–7.

Stevis, D. (1998) "International Labor Organizations, 1986–1997: The Weight of History and the Challenges of the Present," *Journal of World Systems Research*. http://jwsr.ucr.edu/ 4: 52–75.

Stirling, J. and Tully, B. (2004) "Power, Process and Practice: Communication in European Works Councils," *European Journal of Industrial Relations*. 10:1 pp. 73–89.

Stopford, M. (1997) *Maritime Economics*, 2nd Ed., London: Routledge.

Strange, S. (1996) The retreat of the state: the diffusion of power in the world economy, Cambridge: Cambridge University Press.

Swepston, L. (1998) "Human rights law and freedom of association: Development through ILO supervision," *International Labour Review*, Vol 137, No. 2.

Tarrow, S. (2001) "Transnational Contention: Contention and Institutions in International Politics," *Annual Review of Political Science*, 4:1–2.

Taylor, G. and Mathers, A. (2004) "The European Trade Union Confederation Crossroads of Change? Traversing the Variable Geometry of European Trade Unionism," *European Journal of Industrial Relations*, Vol. 10 No. 3 pp. 267–285.

Thanopoulou, H. (2000) "From Internationalism to globalisation," *Journal for Maritime Research*, February.

Tilly, C. (1995) "Globalization Threatens Labor's Rights." *International and Working Class History*, No. 47, Spring 1995: 1–23.

Tørres, L. and Gunnes, S. (2003) *Global Framework Agreements: a new tool for international labour*, Norway: FAFO.

Trinca, H. and Davies, A. (2000) *Waterfront: The Battle That Changed Australia*, Milsons Point, Australia: Random House.

Trubeck, D., Mosher, J., and Rothstein, J. (2000) "Transnationalism in the Regulation of Labor Relations: International Regimes and Transnational Advocacy Networks," *Law and Social Inquiry*, Fall.

Tuckman, A. and Whittall, M. (2002) "Affirmation, games and insecurity: cultivating consent within a new workplace regime," *Capital and Class*, 76: 65–94.

Turnbull, P. (2000) "Contesting Globalization on the Waterfront," *Politics & Society*, 28(3): 367–391.

Turnbull, P., Morris, J. and Sapsford, D. (1996) "Persistent Militants and Quiescent Comrades: Intra-industry Strike Activity on the Docks, 1947–89," *Sociological Review* 44 (4):710–45.

Turnbull, P., Woolfson, C. and Kelly, J. (1992) *Dock Strike: Conflict and Restructuring in Britain's Ports*, Hants, UK: Avebury.

Turner, L. (1996) "The Europeanization of Labor: Structure Before Action," *European Journal of Industrial Relations*, Fall.

Ulman, L. (1955) *The Rise of the National Trade Union: the Development and Significance of its Structure, Governing Institutions, and Economic Policies*, Cambridge, MA: Harvard University Press.

United Nations Commission on Trade and Development (UNCTAD) (various years), *Annual Shipping Statistics*

Van der Pijl, K. (1998) *Transnational Classes and International Relations*, London: Routledge.

Van Roozendaal, G. (2002) *Trade Unions and Global Governance: the Debate on a Social Clause*, New York: Continuum.

Ver.di *Schwarzmarkt* newsletter, 1/2005

Voss, K. and Shermann, R. (2000) "Breaking the Iron Law of Oligarchy: Union Revitalization in the American Labor Movement," *American Journal of Sociology*, vol. 106:2 (Sept.), pp. 303–349.

Walsh, D. (1994) *On Different Planes: An Organizational Analysis of Cooperation and Conflict among Airline Unions*, Ithaca, NY: ILR Press.

Waterman, P. (1998) *Globalisation, Solidarity and the New Social Movements*, London: Mansell.

Waterman, P. (1999) "The New Social Unionism: A New Union Model for a New World Order," in R. Munck and P. Waterman (eds), *Labour Worldwide in the Era of Globalization: Alternative Union Models in the New World Order*, New York, NY: St. Martin's Press.

Wellman, D. (1995) *The Union Makes Us Strong: Radical Unionism on the San Francisco Waterfront*, Cambridge: Cambridge University Press.

Wennerlind, C. (2002) "The Labour Theory of Value and the strategic role of alienation," *Capital & Class* #77, pp. 1–21.

Weisband, E. (2001) "Discursive Multilateralism: Global Benchmarks, Shame, and Learning in the ILO Labor Standards Monitoring Regime," *International Studies Quarterly*, Vol 44, No. 4 pp. 643–666.

Wills, J. (2001) "Uneven Geographies of Capital and Labour: Lessons of the European Workers Councils," in P. Waterman and J. Wills (eds) *Place, Space and the New Labour Internationalisms*, Oxford, UK: Blackwell Publishers.

Wills, J. (2002) "Bargaining for the space to organize in the global economy: a review of the Accor-IUF trade union rights agreement," *Review of International Political Economy,* 9 (4) November.

Wills, Jane (2004) "Re-scaling Trade Union Organisation: Lessons from the European Front Line," in R. Munck (ed.) *Labour and Globalisation: Results and Prospects,* Liverpool: Liverpool University Press.

Windmuller, J. (2000) "The International Trade Secretariats," in M. Gordon and L. Turner (eds) *Transnational Cooperation among Labor Unions,* Ithaca, NY: ILR Press.

Zhao, M., Belcher, P., Sampson, H., Thomas, M., and Veiga, J.(2003) *Women Seafarers: Global Employment Policies and Practices,* Geneva: ILO.

GUF WEBSITES (ALL LINKS ACCESSED ON 23 SEPT 05):

EI:	Education International: www.ei-ie.org
ICEM:	International Chemical, Energy, Mine and General Workers' Union, www.icem.org
IMF:	International Metalworkers' Federation: www.imfmetall.org
IFBWW:	International Federation of Building and Wood Workers: www.ifbww. org
IFJ:	International Federation of Journalists: www.ifj.org
ILO:	International Labour Organisation: www.ilo.org
ITF:	International Transport Workers Federation, www.itf.org.uk
ITGLWF:	International Textile, Garment, and Leather Workers' Federation: www.itglwf.org
IUF:	International Union of Food, Agricultural, Hotel, Restaurants, Catering, and Allied Workers' Associations: www.iuf.org.uk
PSI:	Public Services International: www.world-psi.org
UNI:	Union Network International: www.union-network.org
UNI-Europa:	Union Network International, Europe: www.union-network.org/UNIsite/Regions/Europa/Europa.html

Index

Lightning Source UK Ltd.
Milton Keynes UK
UKOW03f1019210114

224943UK00004B/378/P